WATERCOLOR
ARTIST'S INDEX

Urban
Landscape

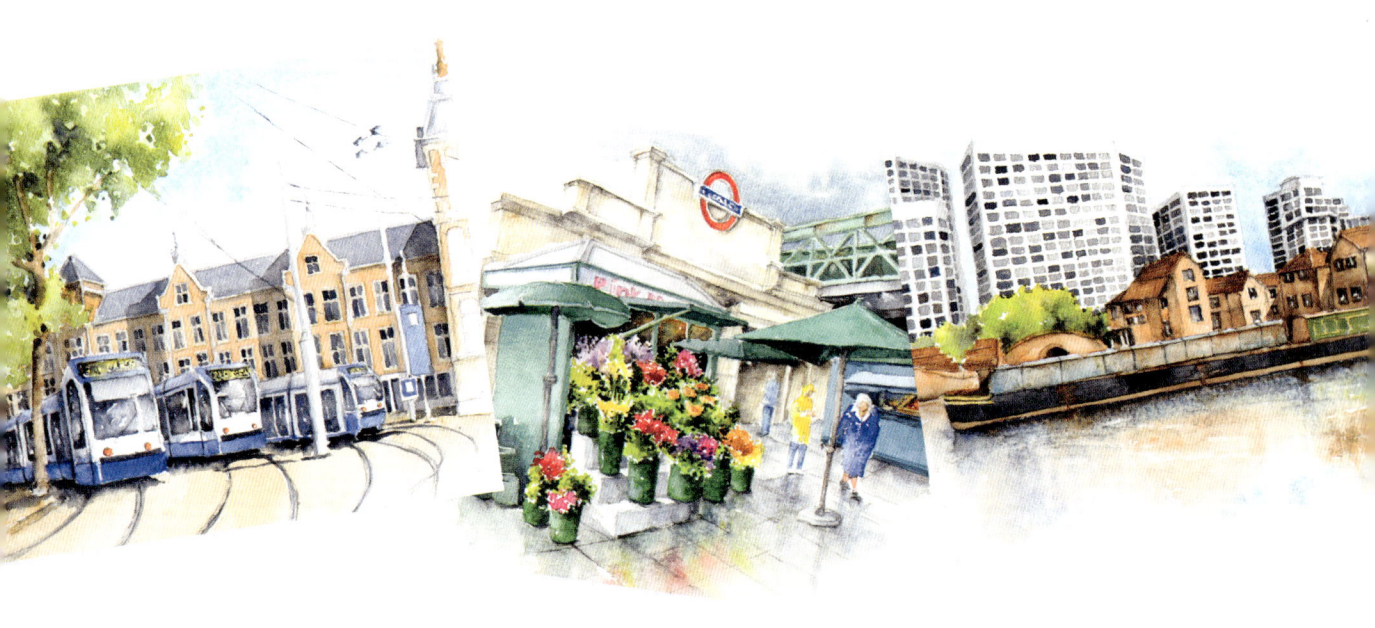

WATERCOLOR ARTIST'S INDEX

Urban
Landscape

A Field Trip of Features and How to Paint Them

RICHARD TAYLOR

DAVID & CHARLES
—PUBLISHING—

www.davidandcharles.com

Contents

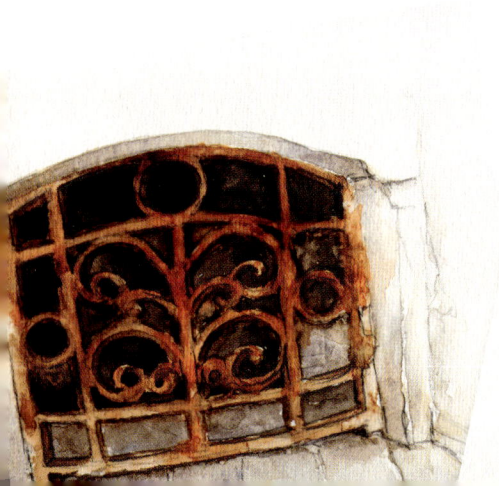
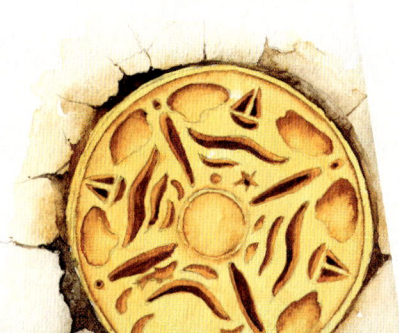
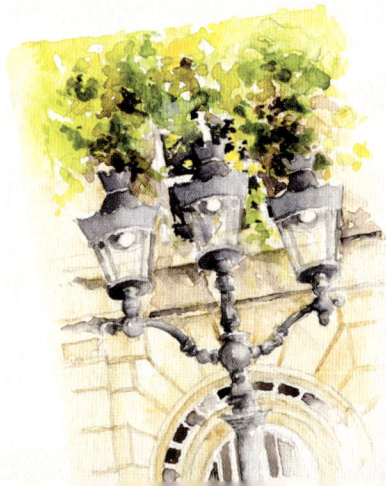

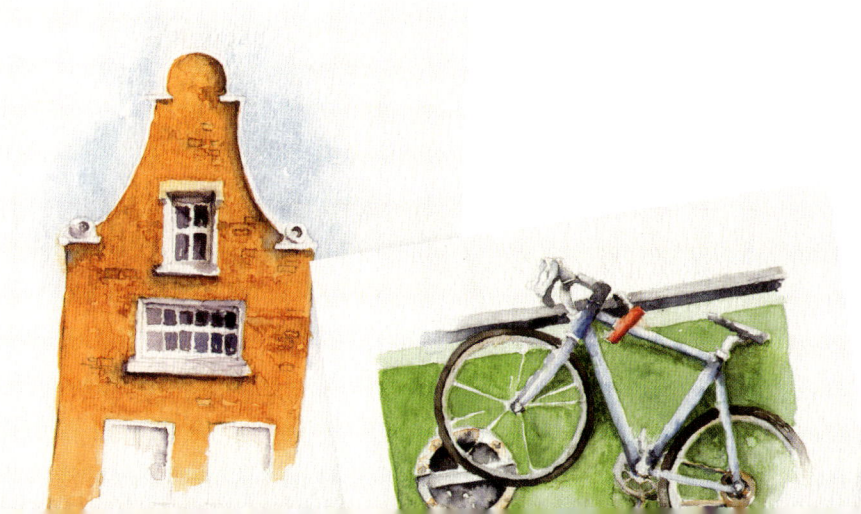

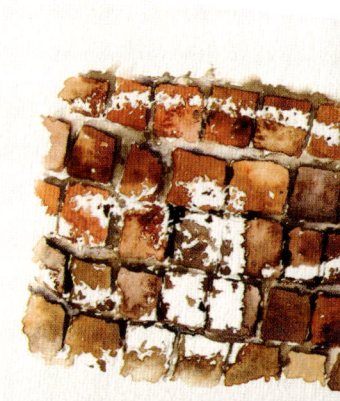

Introduction

I was born and grew up in the suburbs of North London, England. My formative years were spent among Georgian-fronted homes, modern high-rise appartment blocks, brick terraces, and a wealth of other building types. These, of course, fronted busy main streets and side roads. All of the trappings of the urban environment were part of my everyday life. And, of course, a short bus ride took me into the city itself, where the streets came to life by day and night. As my interest in drawing and painting grew, I became increasingly attracted to the bustle of urban living and the proliferation of the many new types of transport on the roads. But it was always the decaying, derelict buildings, the rusting iron gates, the cracked sidewalks, and the crooked, faded road signs that caught my attention the most. The sights, colors, sounds, and smells of the urban environment were truly in my blood.

The aim of this book is to invite you to join me in my passion for recording the urban environment in watercolor. As you journey through the pages you will see a pattern—on the right-hand page will be a painting on a very specific theme. On the left-hand page will be a set of studies explaining elements found in the main painting. These will not always be evident in the main painting, but they will include the key elements that you will need to observe carefully. To take you through the stages of painting one picture would enable you to paint just that one picture. My aim is to encourage you to stand on your own artistic feet and to tackle any type of scene that you may encounter on your urban wanderings. You will also, from time to time, find step-by-step images. These take you through the three stages of my working practice in "visual real time," allowing you to observe the buildup of washes and how the addition of the darkest paint can make the middle tones come alive. You might even opt to practice these mini-projects yourself.

A few words about painting techniques. I often refer to "environmental" colors in my notes and annotations. By this I mean the colors of all the surrounding objects that will reflect light and cast shadowing onto the subject being studied. "Local" color might sound more appropriate, but this means something entirely different in art training (that is, the color of any one object without the influences of shade or reflections from other objects). On bright or dull days, these environmental colors will influence the way you see your subject.

The urban environment often lacks much real color, but requires a lot of subtle variations of grays and neutral tones. My standard mixture for these tones is a combination of burnt umber and ultramarine blue. This can be tempered by introducing many levels of dilution. It can be watered down so as to appear almost translucent, or bolstered by using tube paints to act as the darkest of shadows. Sometimes the tone will vary, again, according to the environmental colors that surround you. These tones can also be achieved by creating "palette mud." This is created by washing together the remnants of all of the colors you have mixed in your palette to create a muddy yet tinted wash.

Finally, you will soon see that I don't always take my painting out to the four corners or border lines of a precise rectangle. Sometimes a free flow of paint can give a sense of energy to a composition, drawing your eye in to, or out from, the central point. I don't like any painting to be restricted—especially by four pencil lines!

So, it's over to you now to dip into the city-themed subjects in the following pages. Copy the studies, or go out and find your own. The fact that you are painting the urban environment is all that matters. Good luck and enjoy it!

Richard Taylor

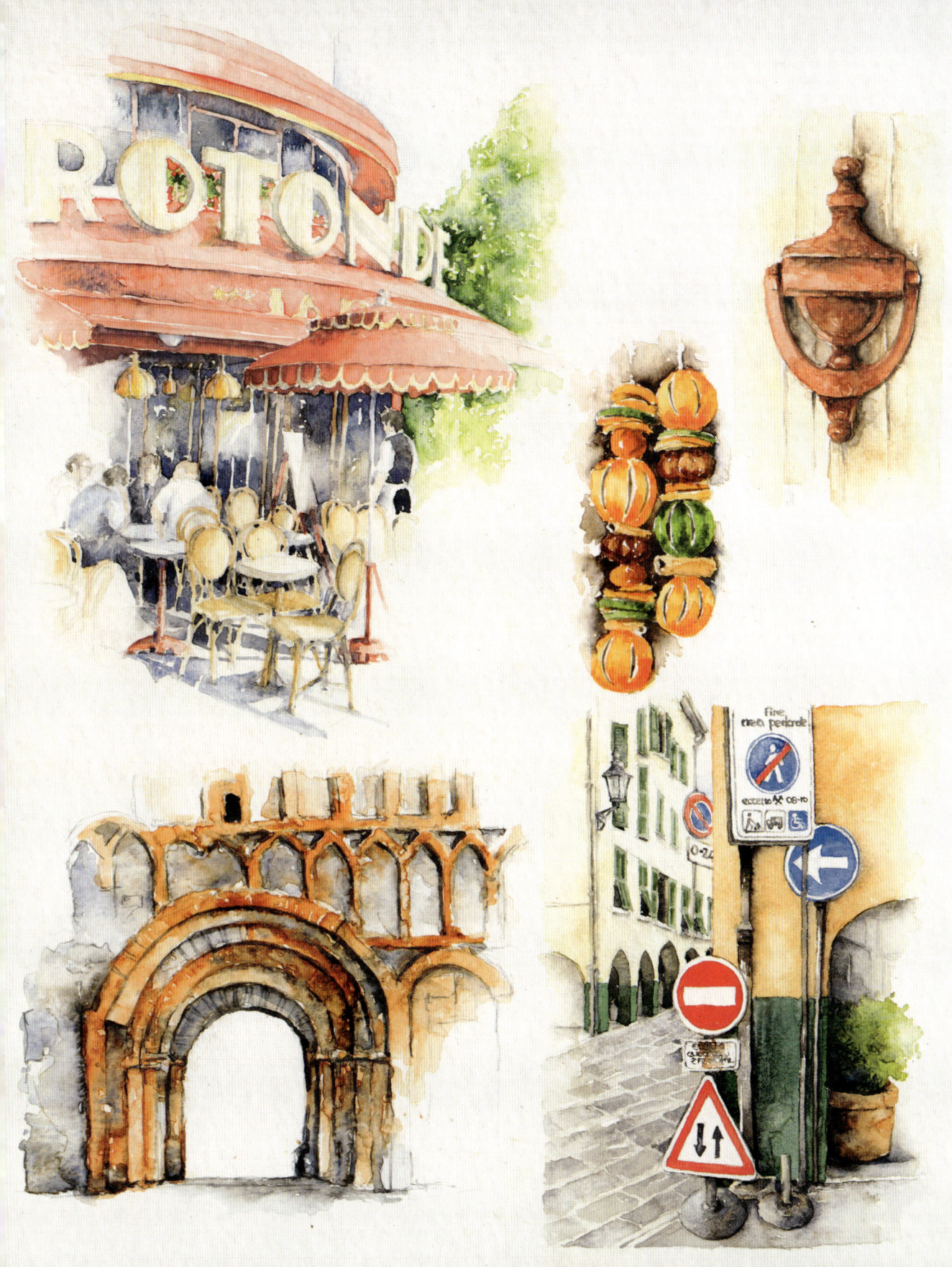

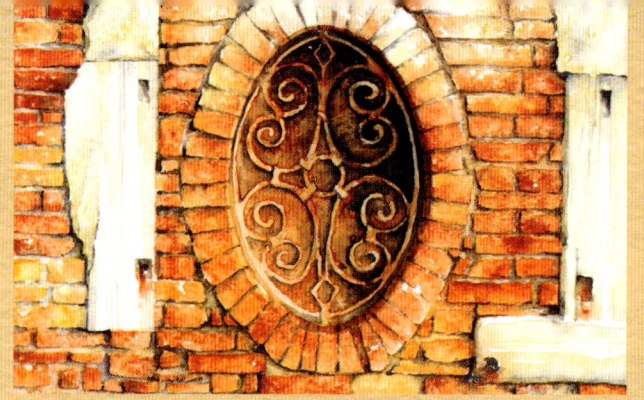

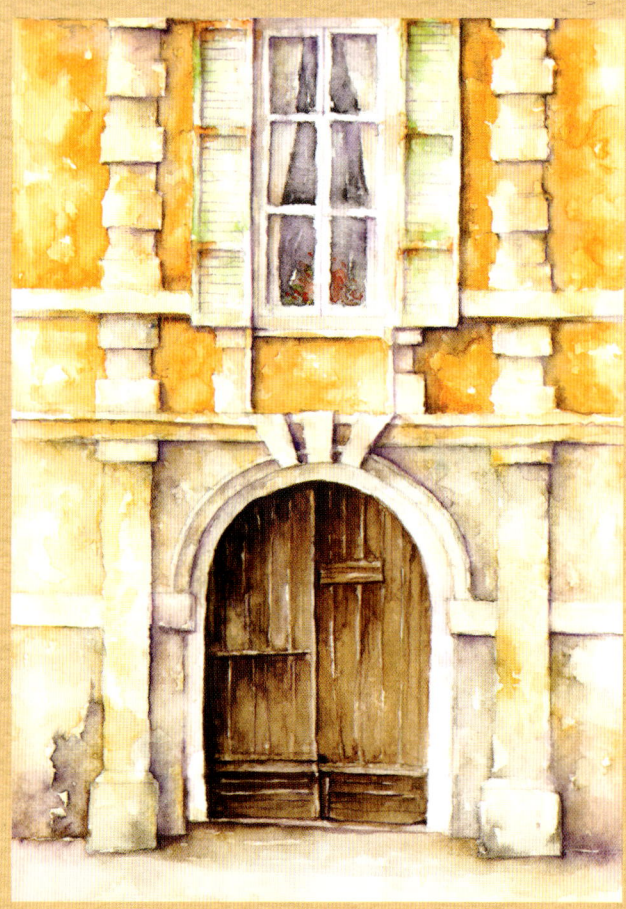

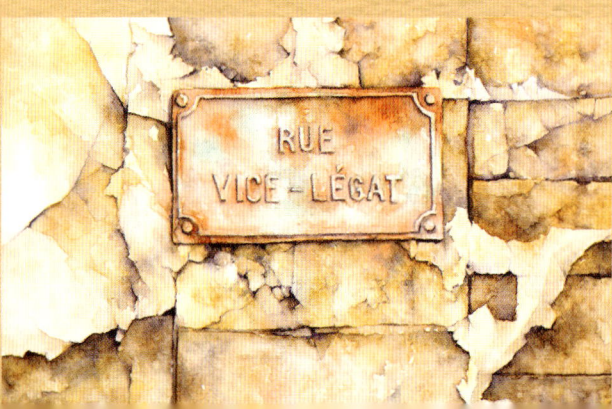

CHAPTER ONE:
Basics

In this chapter I have explored the materials, paints, and techniques that I consider "basic" for watercolor painting in the urban environment. I have two sets of paper and paints—a sketch pad for studies, and loose sheets for compositions. I tend to use pan paints for sketches and tube paints for other paintings, although these can be interchangeable—I don't work by rigid rules.

This chapter also looks at both painting techniques and perspective. While my painting techniques invariably involve using a lot of water—I enjoy applying washes to damp or wet paper and allowing the paint to do most of the work for me—perspective can't quite work in the same way. You will need to work with a structure to ensure that a line of buildings recedes into the distance in an orderly manner and that you don't have too many leaning structures in your compositions. Painting in the urban environment requires both skills—working with the freedom of washes to build up a selection of textures, and establishing a linear structure within which to do this.

Materials

The equipment needed for watercolor painting is, on the surface, very simple—paper, paints, and brushes. But careful selection of these can make a real difference to your painting.

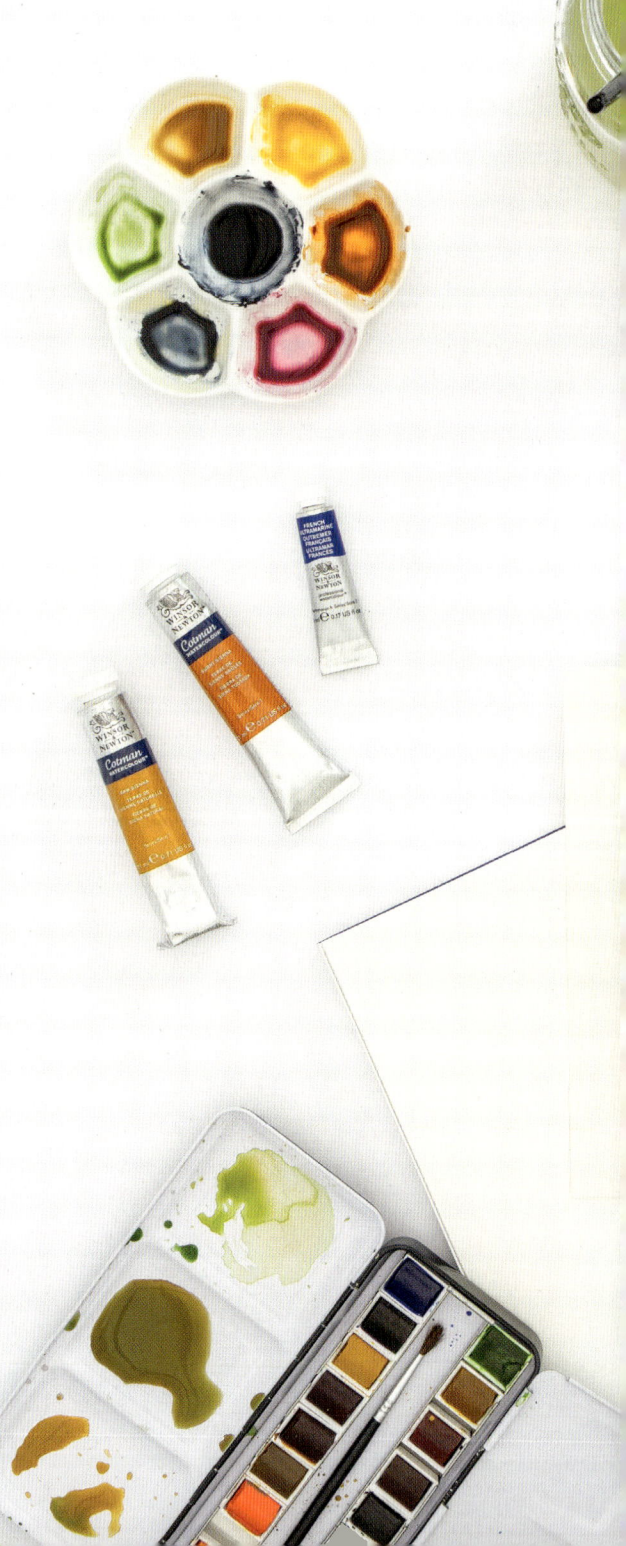

PAPER

The most basic equipment required for watercolor painting is paper. This comes in many forms—cold pressed for texture, hot pressed for smooth, rough for expressive—and then there are the different brands, each of which adds a little extra something to its papers. It is as well to experiment and find a paper that suits your needs. It took me a good few years to settle with two types.

I have used two types of watercolor paper throughout this book. The sketches and studies have been painted onto a sketchpad of 300gsm cold pressed paper.

The main paintings are all on 535gsm cold pressed paper, which is a much stronger paper that allows a longer drying time—good for creating textures.

PAINTS

I use two types of paints, although these are completely interchangeable. The sketches and studies are, largely, made from pan paints which sit nicely in a tin. The main paintings have more input from tube paints, which can be used to achieve stronger colors.

BRUSHES

I use three brushes only—very small, small, and medium. Different manufacturers use different sizing systems so it is difficult to reference the precise size of brushes. Sable brushes hold water very well and allow free-flowing washes to be achieved, but synthetic brushes also do a very good job.

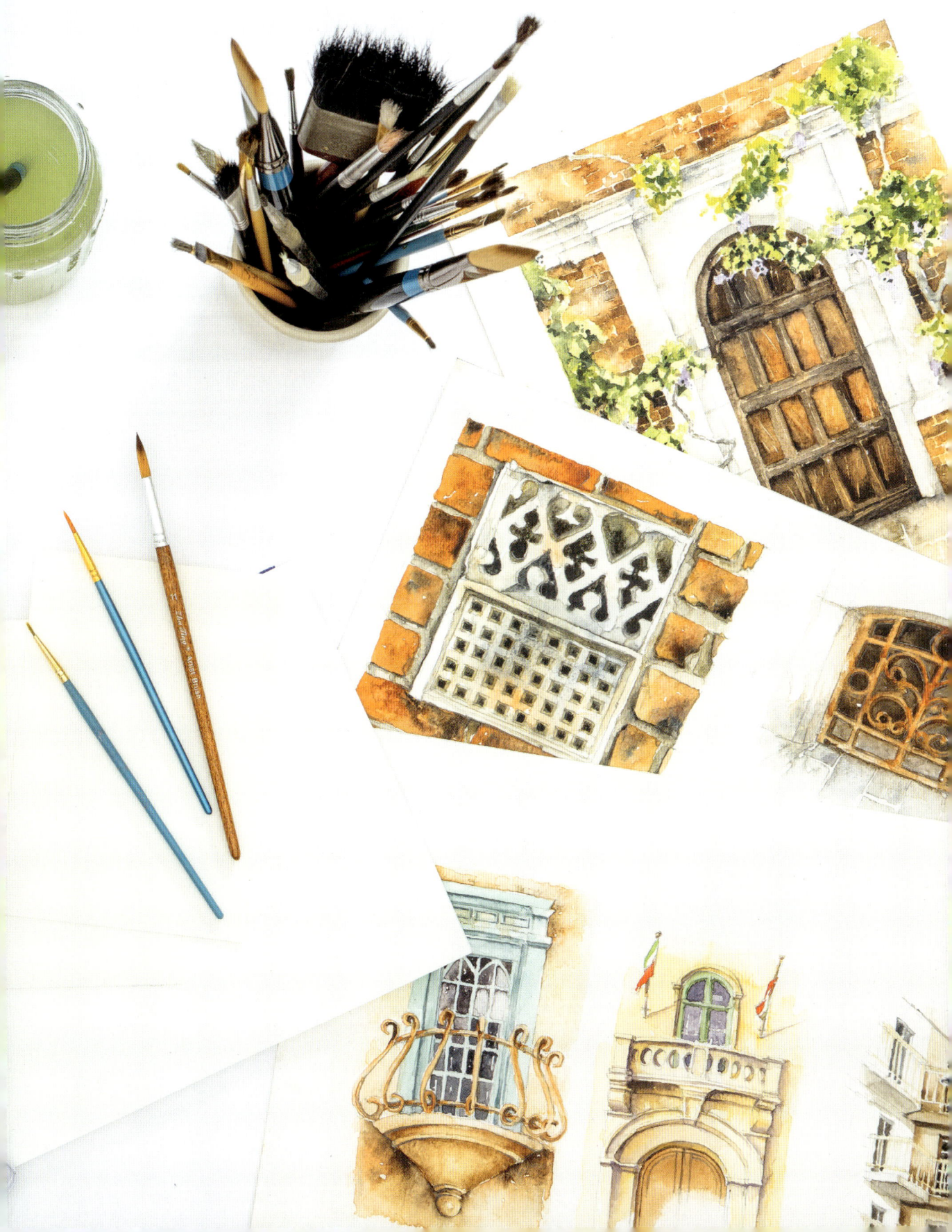

Paints and Colors

Second to paper, in terms of watercolor essentials, are paints. The economy end of the market is probably best avoided, especially if you have paid a lot for your paper. I do not endorse any specific brand but you will doubtless be familiar with the market leaders—their pigments are pure and they use less filler, giving overall better results.

FOUNDATION COLORS

These are the "basic" colors that I use in the fabric of most buildings. The combination of these colors affords the painter a wealth of tonal outcomes.

SUPPLEMENTARY COLORS

The urban environment holds a wealth of colors that supplement the basic building tones. These are the colors that I have found most useful.

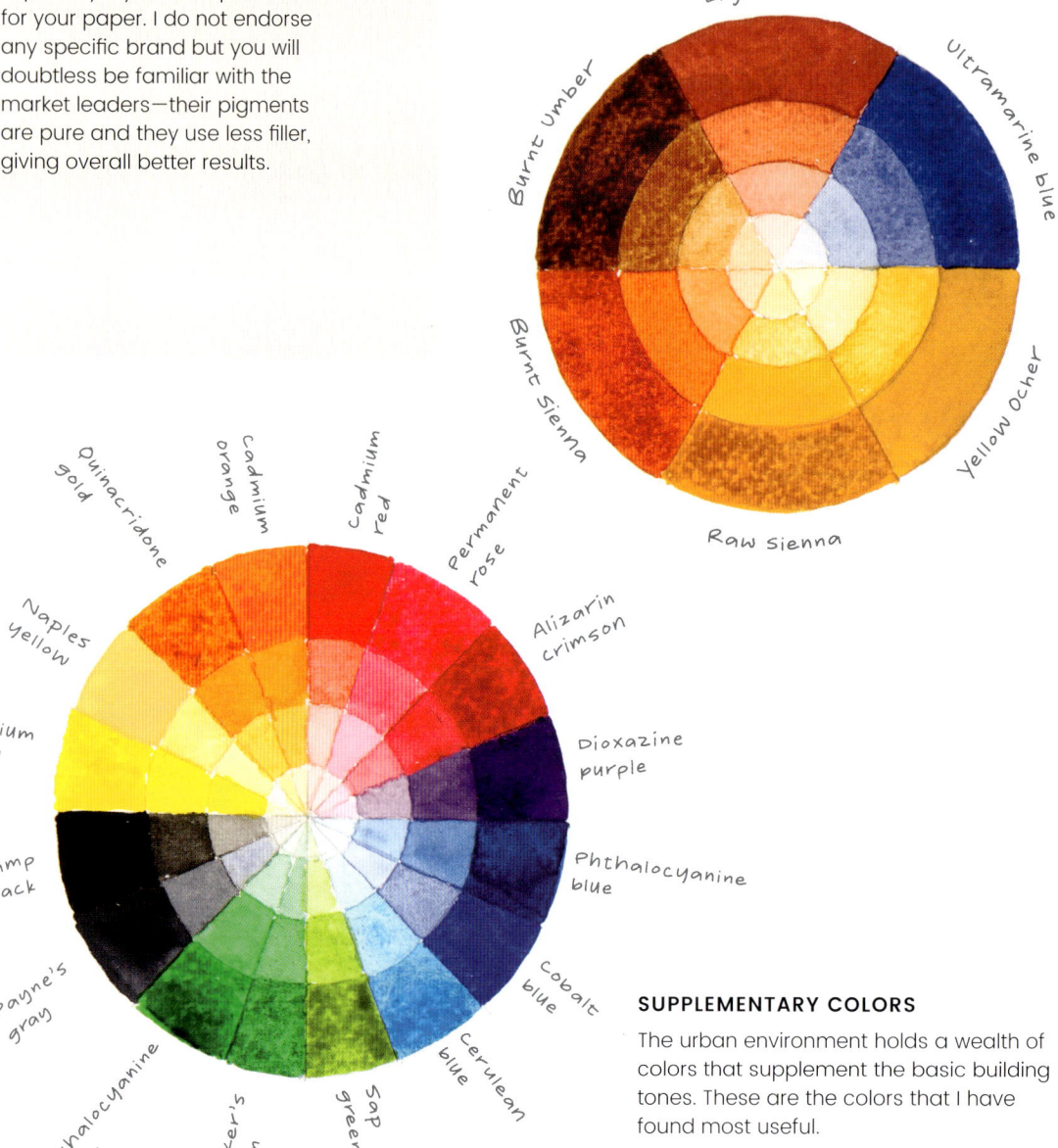

Ochers benefit from the addition of a premixed orange to add warmth to painted walls.

Applied "raw," burnt sienna is an invaluable color for creating rust bleeds.

Yellow ocher and raw sienna are similar, but can be used "in tandem" to create the subtle differences in plaster.

A diluted wash of sap green was used to create the sun-bleached shutter.

Dioxazine purple is a valuable color for creating shade and shadows in warmer climates.

A combination of ultramarine blue and burnt umber helps to create a more "grimy" type of staining.

Burnt umber and burnt sienna are useful colors for creating a wood effect. The sienna adds a little warmth.

Light and Shade

Once you have sketched the basic shape of a building or scene, you will need to quickly observe where the light is coming from as this will determine the position and length of your shadows. Even in poor lighting, shadows still exist. Although they may sometimes seem dull and insignificant, all shadows serve to anchor a picture onto solid ground.

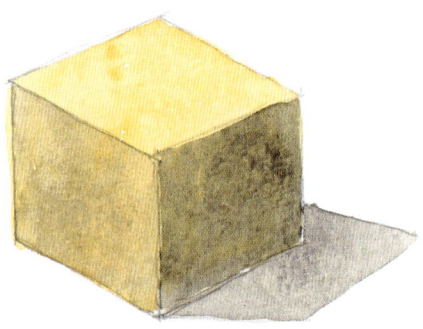

NEUTRAL SHADOW

Burnt sienna and ultramarine blue have been mixed to give a "neutral" gray shadow tone.

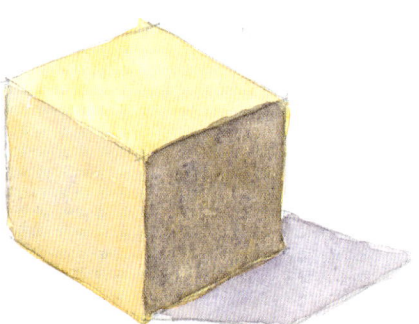

ADDING WARMTH AND DEPTH

Adding dioxazine purple to the burnt sienna and ultramarine blue mix gives a slight "warmth" and a little substance to the shadow tone.

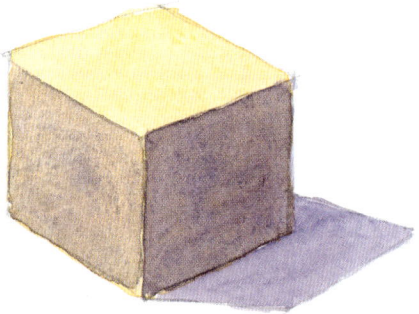

INCREASING WARMTH AND DEPTH

A mix of ultramarine blue and dioxazine purple, but without burnt sienna added, holds greater warmth and depth.

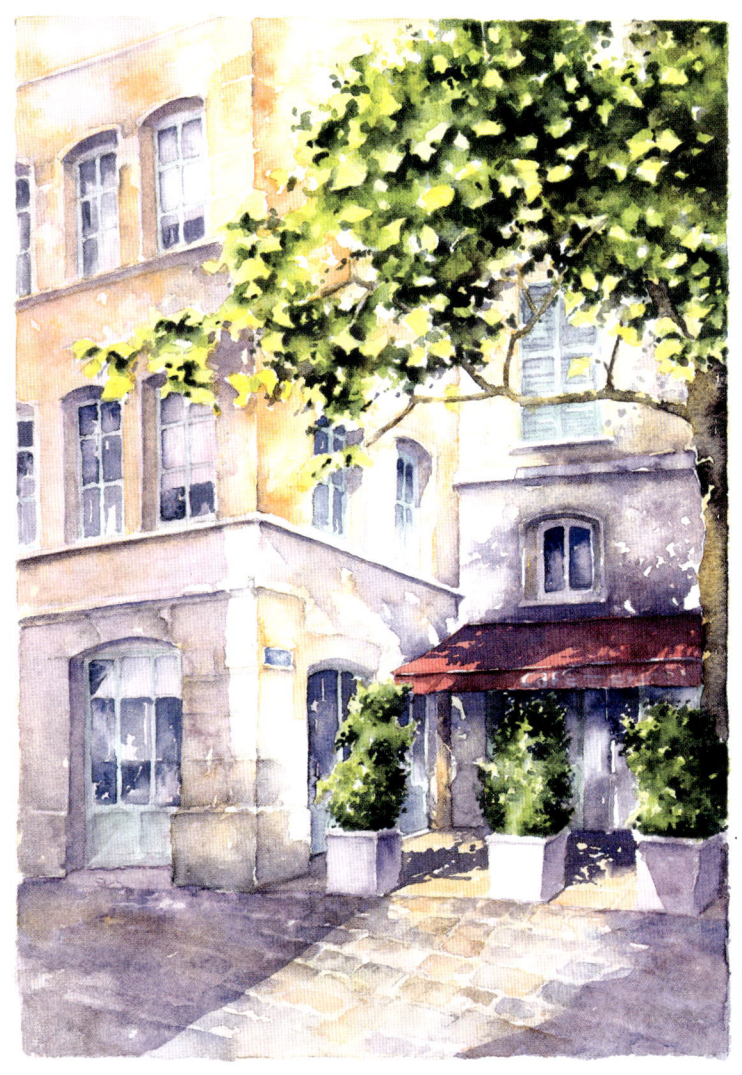

This painting captures early morning light. The shadows are loaded with dioxazine purple, softened by the addition of a little ultramarine blue.

The shadows fell across the paved street and on to the buildings opposite, giving shape and a sense of form to the scene. There was also the advantage of few people out and about, allowing for a less "cluttered" scene.

One-Point Perspective

Perspective is a system of representation that evolved from the early 1500s. Developed by artists, it allowed them to create the illusion of a three-dimensional image on a flat sheet of paper or canvas. One-point perspective is the first step on the perspective adventure. It allows you to create a sense of depth on architectural facets such as door surrounds.

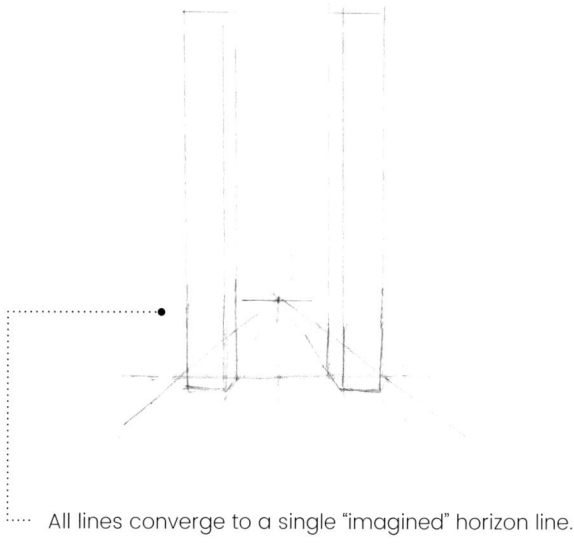

All lines converge to a single "imagined" horizon line.

This allows the angles of the top and bottom of the subject to become established.

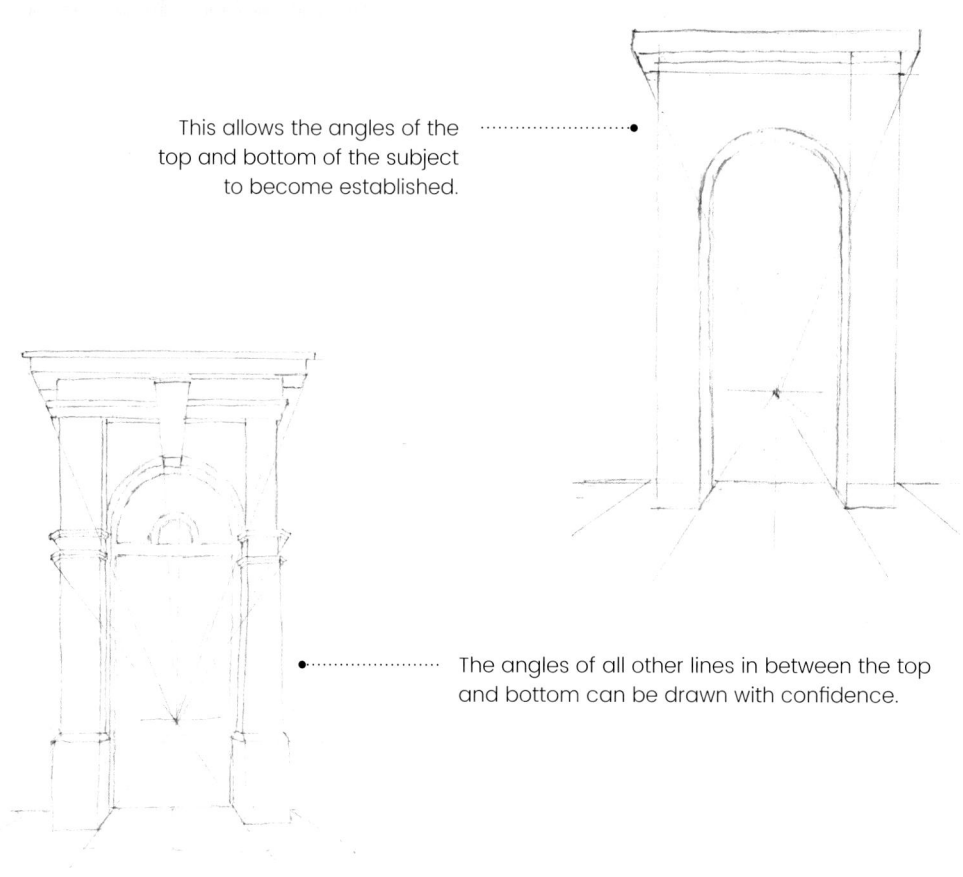

The angles of all other lines in between the top and bottom can be drawn with confidence.

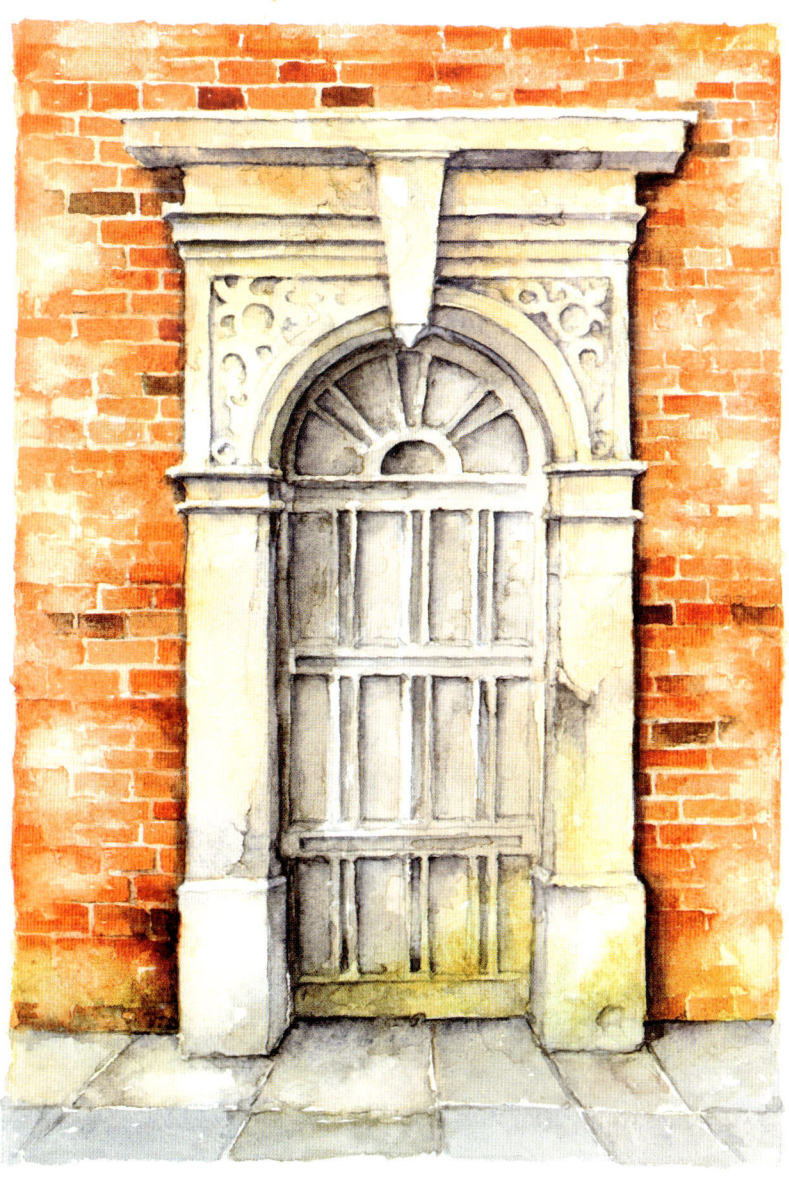

Even the columns and moldings of a doorway set into a brick wall are subject to the "rules" of perspective. Following these will allow you to establish the "relief" effect and, along with the painted shadows, allows you to create a three-dimensional illusion on a flat surface.

Two-Point Perspective

Traditionally, when constructing an image using two-point perspective, the corner of the building or chimney stack, for example, will be lined up along the vertical third of your paper so that one side appears to go off into the distance for one third of the space, while the other side takes up two thirds, converging in the opposite direction.

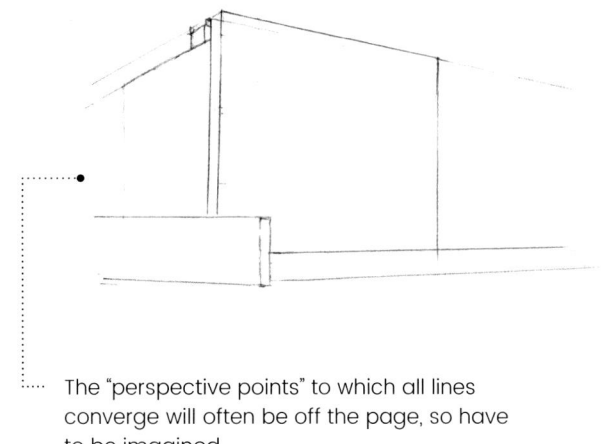

The "perspective points" to which all lines converge will often be off the page, so have to be imagined.

It is important as you start to establish detail that vertical lines are upright, avoiding "building slip."

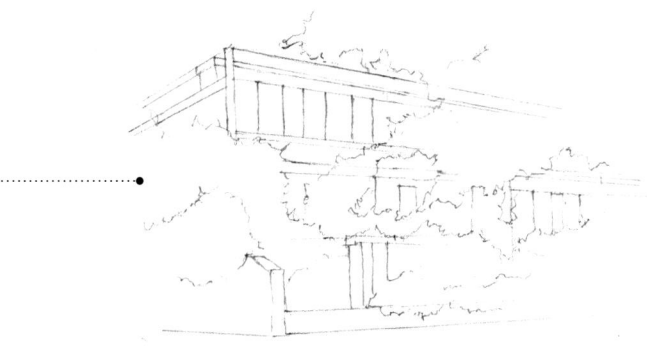

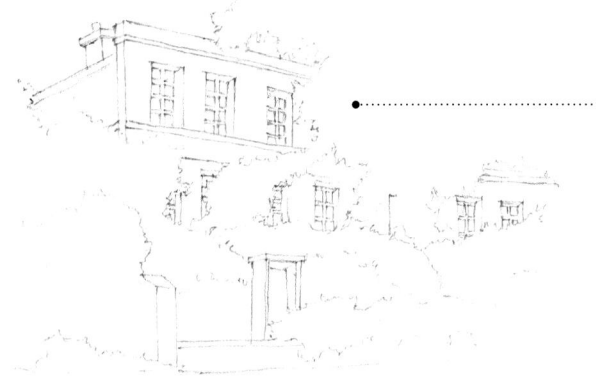

The perspective "guidelines" give way to the pictorial detail as the structure of your picture develops.

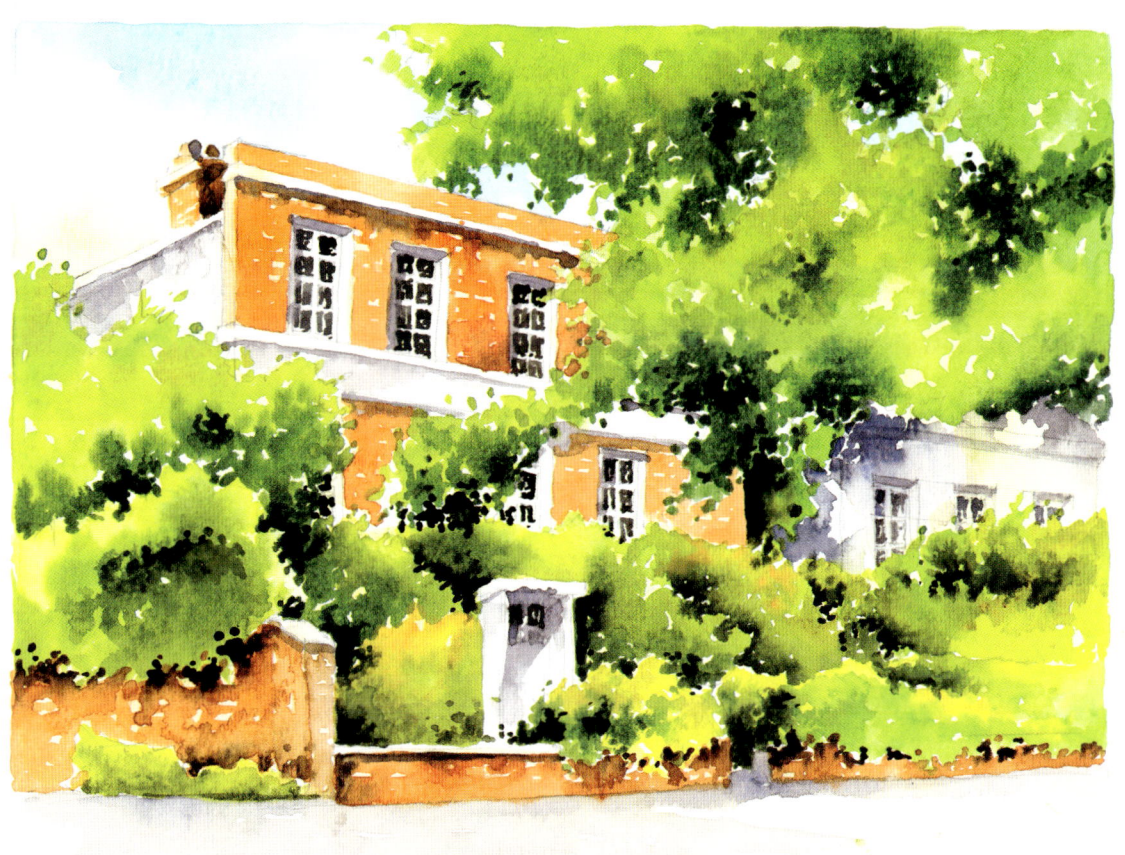

In this painting of a wide, leafy avenue, all "perspective lines" converge to points that can't actually be seen within the composition, and all features appear to diminish in scale as your eye moves to the right. Architectural perspective requires mathematical accuracy—but watercolor painting should be much more fun

TIP

Keep your perspective lines simple and don't create too many. Once you have a few in place you can start freehand drawing before you begin the painting.

Brickwork

Bricks are, possibly, the most common building materials to be found in the urban environment. New bricks may still glow a bright reddish-orange. Bricks burned in a kiln will hold a bluish-brown metallic sheen. Others will be coated with the grime that comes from the air pollution of several centuries.

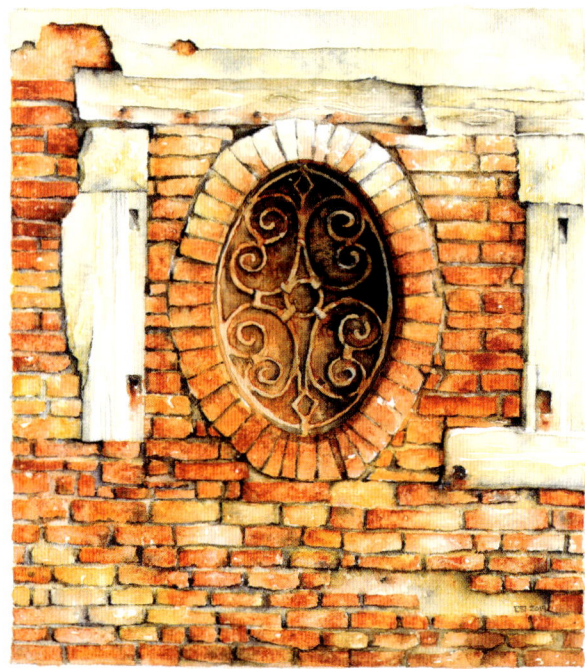

The colors in this wall and window surround are prime "granulators." That is, the aging effect relies on the reactions of burnt sienna and light red with water—the granules separate and dry unevenly. It is a look that many artists try to avoid, but it is desirable for painting the urban environment.

Note that some of the gaps between bricks are light, and some are dark. This is the nature of urban decay and the sort of detail worth studying.

TIP

Don't be afraid to leave white paper showing. This is the best form of white that you can find.

STEP 1

Apply raw sienna to damp paper.

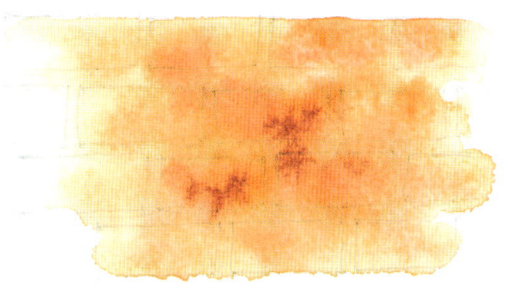

STEP 2

Before the paper has time to dry, apply burnt sienna and light red and allow the paint to bleed freely.

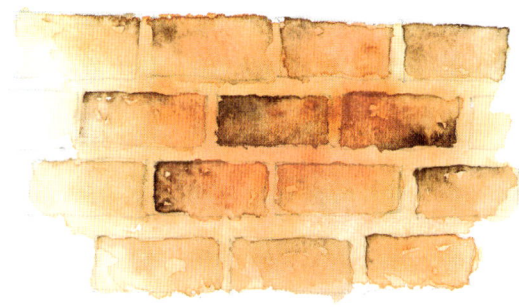

STEP 3

Once dry, add burnt umber to the mix, to give a sense of form to the bricks.

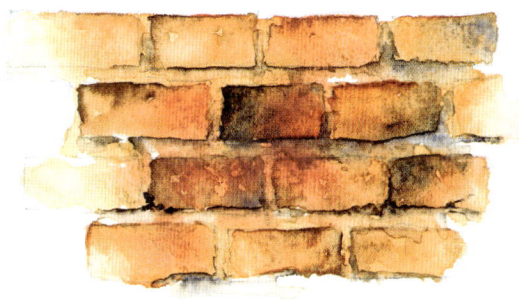

STEP 4

Mix ultramarine blue and burnt umber to give the final definition to each brick.

Stone

One of the attractions of stone buildings is that they can defy the rigid symmetry of brick structures. Stone walls are often full of cracks, fissures, and, occasionally, gaps. The contrast between the light and dark created by these features makes them a rewarding challenge to record.

Exposed and aging stone rarely follows any clearly discernible pattern. It is particularly interesting to paint the cracks and fissures that occur, though. This painting uses the technique of applying paint along the edge of a crack and pulling the paint away from the line using pure water. This has the effect of diluting the tone gradually. Once dried, the crack itself can be clearly defined by almost drawing along the edge with a fine line of paint.

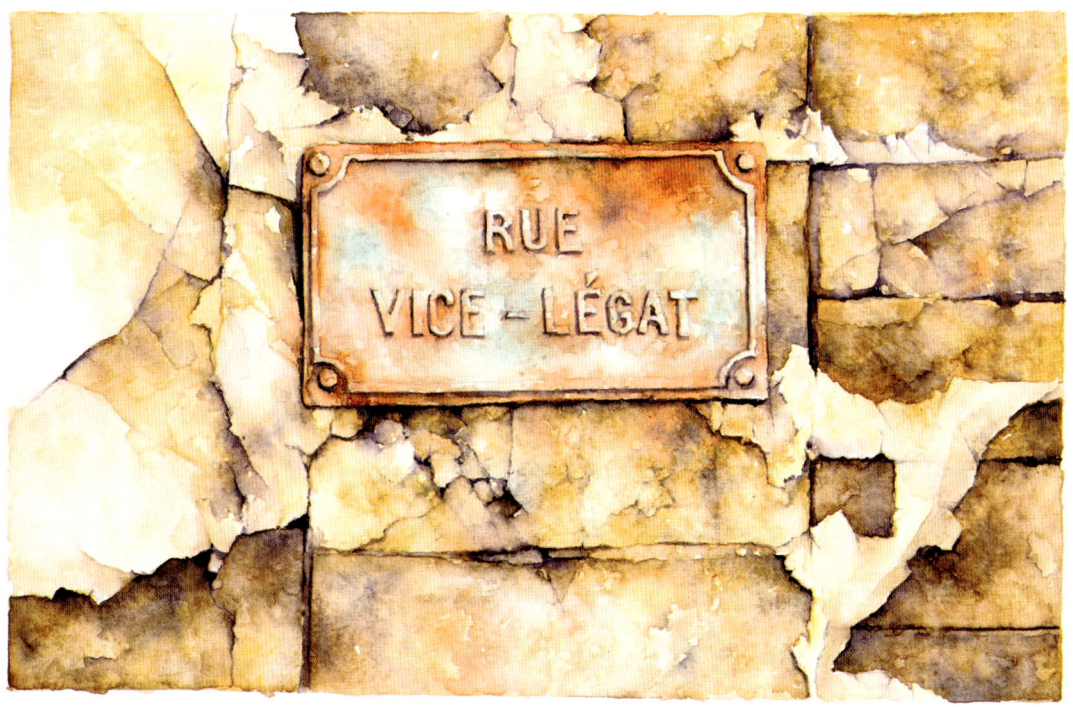

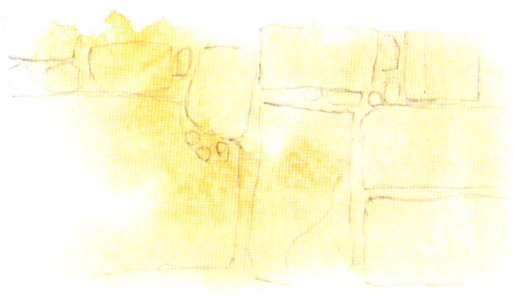

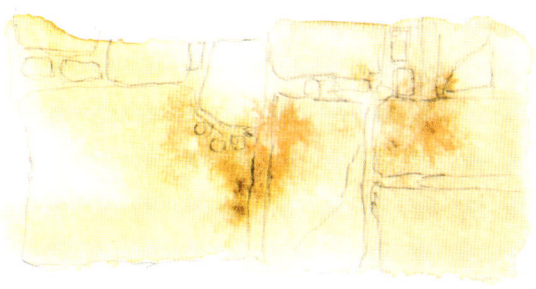

STEP 1

Apply yellow ocher and raw sienna to damp paper individually and allow the two colors to mix freely.

STEP 2

Before the paper dries, drop a watery mix of burnt umber onto the paper and allow it to bleed.

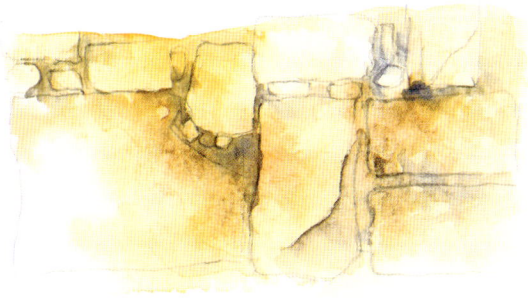

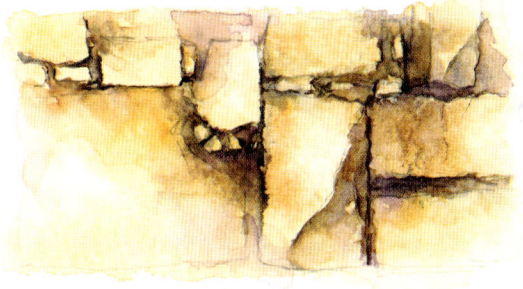

STEP 3

Add ultramarine to burnt umber and paint onto the dry paper.

STEP 4

Once fully dry, add dioxazine purple to the Step 3 mix to sharpen the shadows and to introduce an element of warmth.

Plaster

Plaster walls can, sometimes, be neutral in color—neither white nor any other discernible tone that might be found on a color chart. There again, they may have been painted a pink, yellow, or even green tint. Plaster holds the effects of weathering more than most other surfaces and requires a more subtle approach to painting.

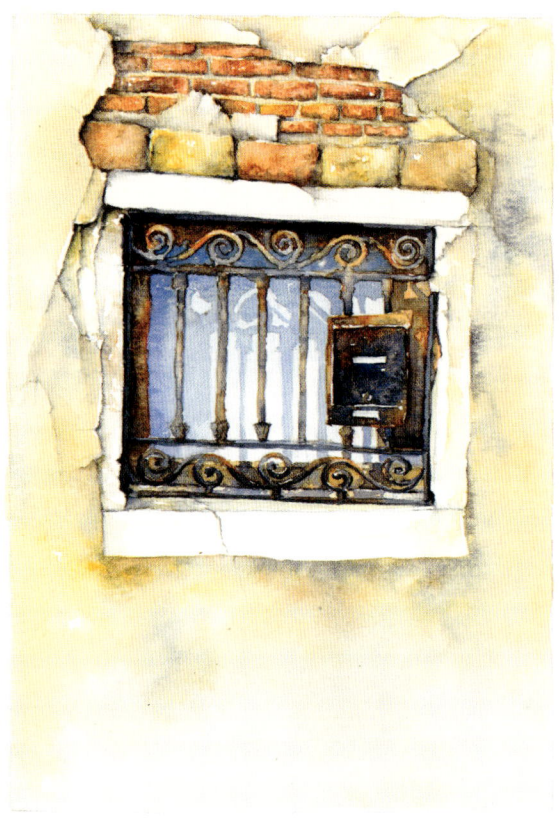

The technique required for painting cracks in plaster is similar to that of stone, but requires more delicate handling. My personal success marker is "Could I fit a fingernail behind the plaster and lift it off my painting?". I often achieve this by finishing a painted crack with a fine pencil line. The staining is best achieved by dropping ultramarine blue and burnt umber onto damp paper and allowing them to bleed into one another.

TIP

The cold early morning shadow was created using ultramarine blue, cerulean blue, and the smallest touch of burnt umber.

STEP 1

Apply raw sienna to damp paper, working around the gaps in the plaster.

STEP 2

Before the paper dries, apply burnt umber and allow it to bleed.

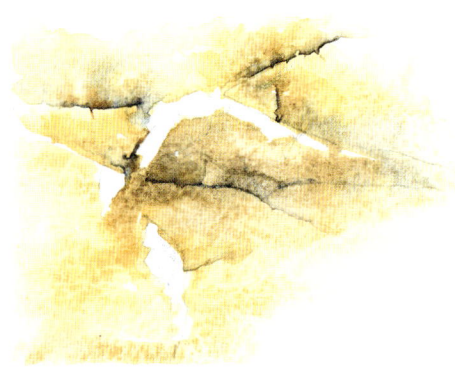

STEP 3

Once dry, use ultramarine blue alongside burnt umber to establish the shapes of the cracked plaster.

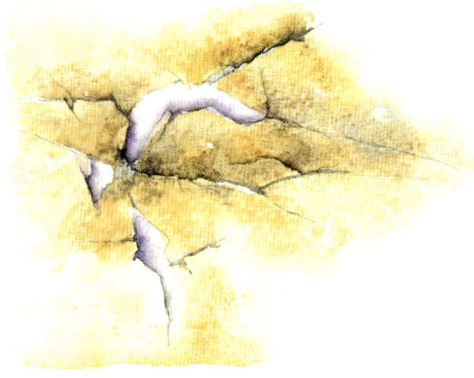

STEP 4

Using a small brush, apply dioxazine purple along the "insides" of the plaster cracks to sharpen the lines.

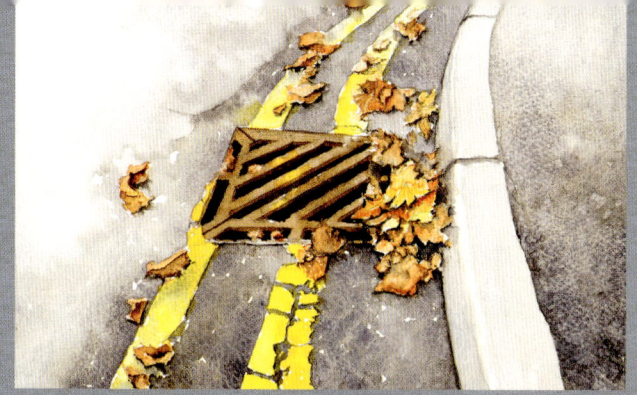

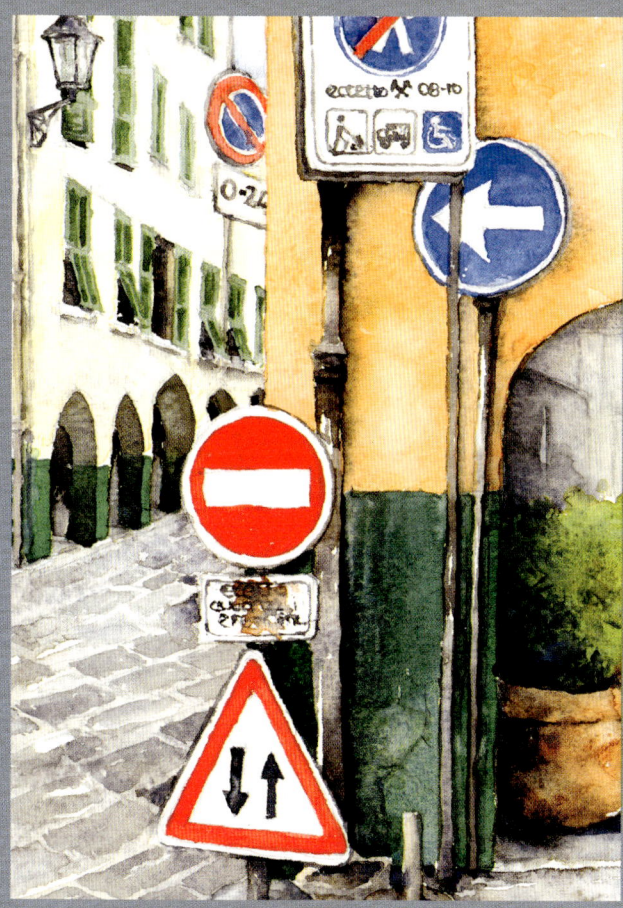

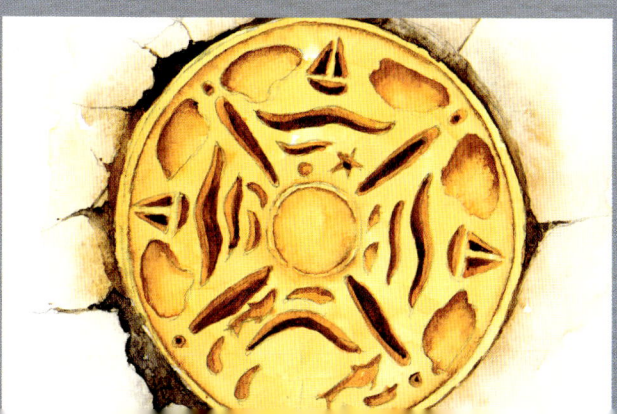

CHAPTER TWO

Streets

Roads, curbs, and sidewalks—we walk and drive on them daily without giving the fabric much thought. But slow up and take some time to look down. There you will find patterned metal grids, fractured concrete, drain covers under a layer of wind-blown russet leaves, along with cast shadows and fire hydrants. Then look ahead and you will find a wealth of colored road signs and, inevitably in the urban environment, parked vehicles.

A collection of shiny, brand-new colored road signs can be very appealing, as can weather-beaten, rusting signs. Decay in towns and cities is a feature I personally seek out frequently. This allows a full range of potential to be unleashed with a few watercolor paints and a jar of water. Many artists work hard for years to practice a technique that avoids watermarks occurring as watercolor paint dries. I have spent about the same amount of time encouraging them—they allow me to record the textures that I enjoy so much.

Road and Tarmac

Across the globe, roads and tarmac are invariably gray in nature. To make these look appealing you might look for shadows cast across the scene. My grays are usually a mixture of burnt umber and ultramarine blue, plus any other colors washing around in the palette. I often use the same colors for shadows, but with a little dioxazine purple added.

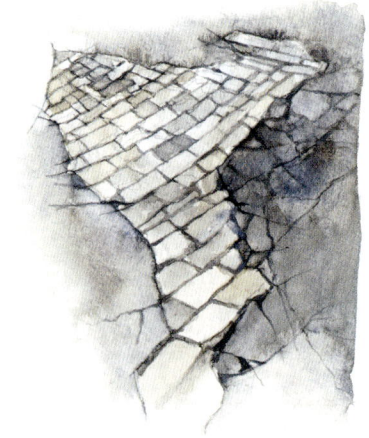

Cracked and broken sections of tarmac can produce a fascinating selection of shapes and tones. In this tonal study, three colors were mixed freely to create "palette mud," which was altered either by adding more water or increasing any one of the colors.

This small sketch captures the way some local residents dealt with a cracked sidewalk—they came out and painted it.

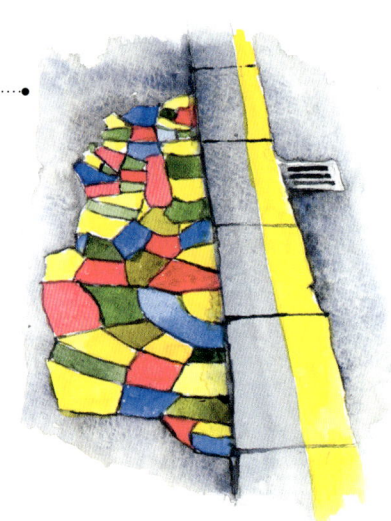

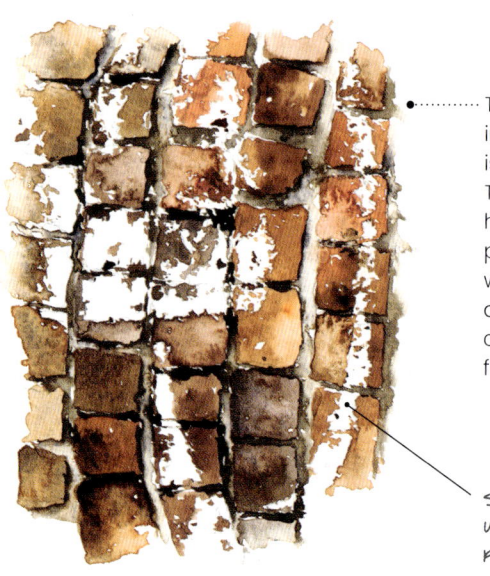

The chipped white paint in this cycle lane sign is actually bare paper. These "negative" shapes have been created by painting around them with a small brush, using a stippling technique to create the impression of flaking paint.

Stippling technique used to paint around plain white paper.

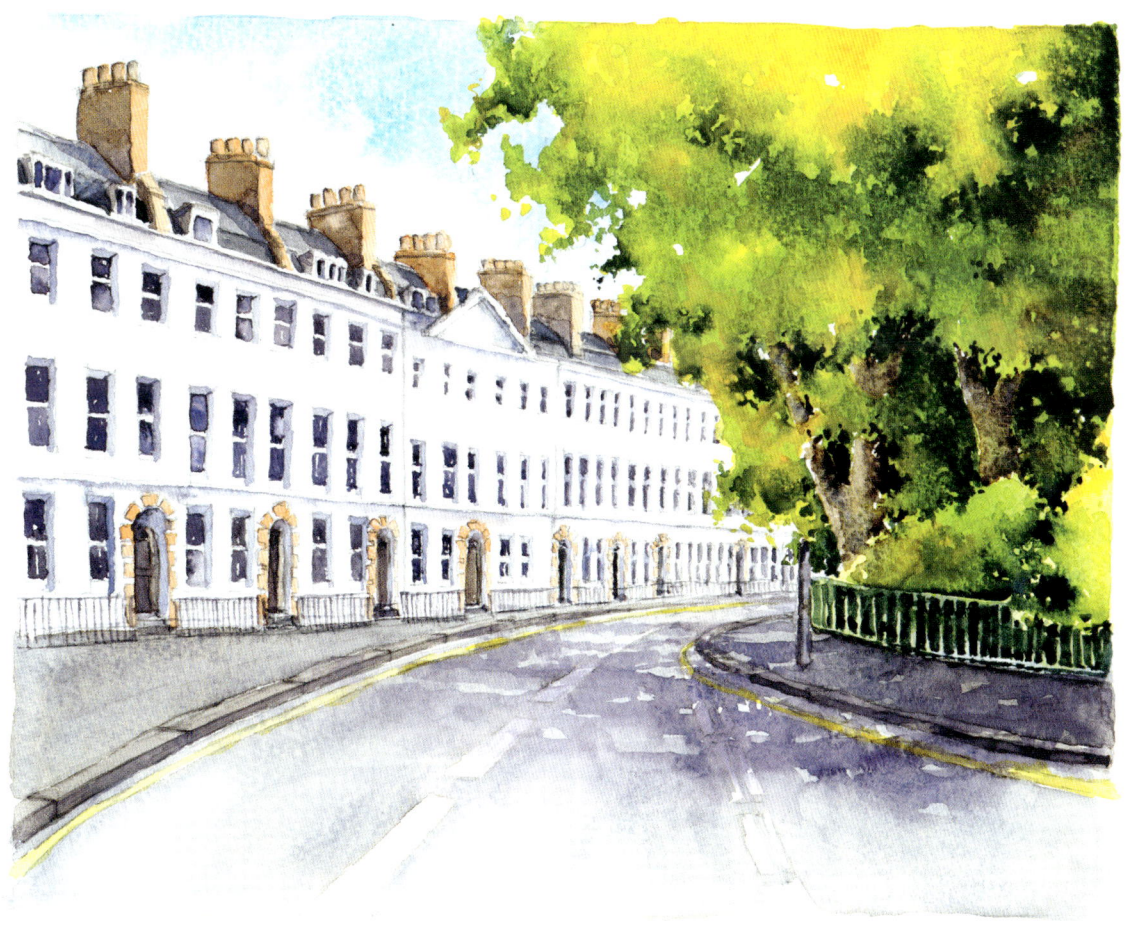

For this morning scene, I was drawn to the way in which the shadows from the trees and the flashes of light fell across the sidewalk, then dipped slightly to cross the road. Both sets of perspective lines—chimneys, windows, and doors—and the road markings and curbs recede in tandem around the bend in the road, allowing the large, urban trees to act as a visual punctuation mark as a major part of the composition.

Gutters and Drains

Due to the functional and usually dirty nature of gutters and drains, they are often overlooked by artists. We tend to look up toward the skyline and straight ahead at the buildings, posters, and colors of the urban environment, but rarely do we look down at our feet for sources of inspiration. Gutters and drains may not hold much color of their own, but always have solid, discernible shapes and, occasionally, patterns.

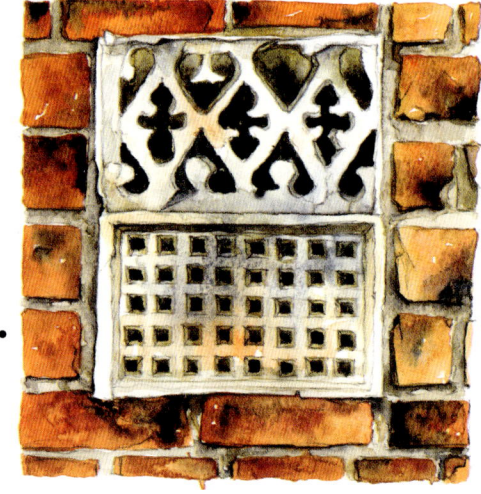

The staining on this grille was created by using a lot of water. Cobalt blue was dropped onto very wet paper, along with a touch of raw sienna, and allowed to bleed freely. Once dry, it needed little more to suggest years of neglect and accumulated urban grime.

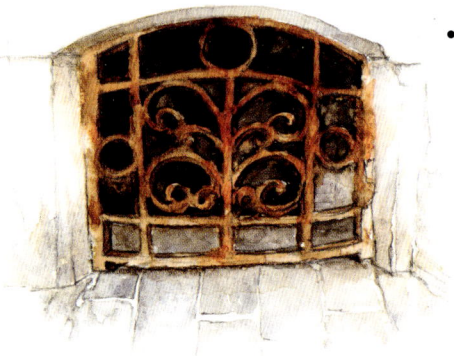

The rust colors on this symmetrical grille were achieved with a lot of water and frequent applications of raw sienna and burnt sienna before the paper dried fully.

In this scene, the strong yellow in the painted lines breaks up the dull grays found in the sidewalk and road. The rust colors of the fallen leaves complement the yellow particularly well, creating a harmonious balance.

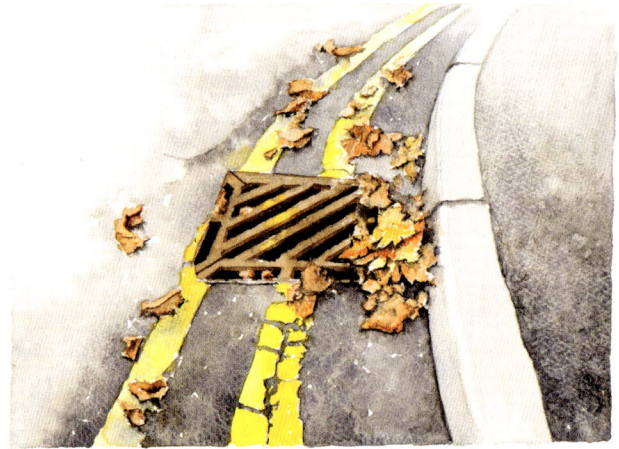

EXAMPLE: DRAIN GRID

STEP ONE

Wash a thin gray tone onto the pencil line drawing.

STEP TWO

Establish the color of the drain.

STEP THREE

Use a dark mixture of burnt umber and
ultramarine blue to "push" the drain grid forward.

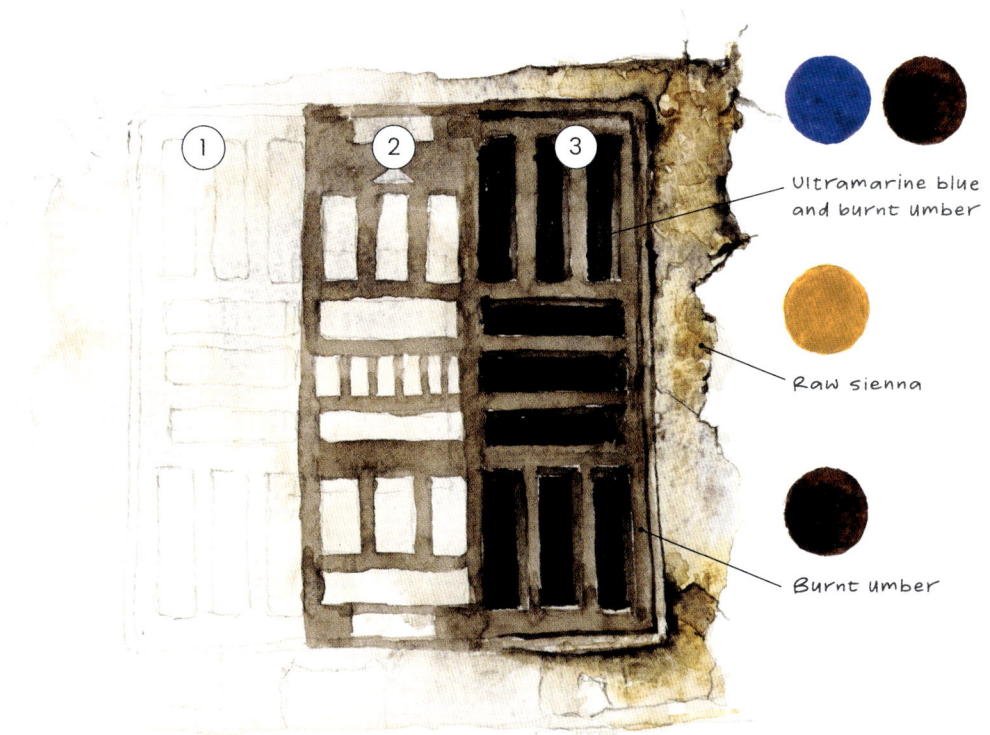

Ultramarine blue
and burnt umber

Raw sienna

Burnt umber

Road Signs

Most road signs give instructions to the road user so need to be clear, concise, and uncluttered by unnecessary information. Individually they can be very effective, but not always interesting. Collectively, however, they can be chaotic, colorful, and give a sense of local identity to a scene.

The red in this study was tempered with the slightest touch of burnt sienna. The blue is pure, simple ultramarine blue.

Road signs often have white lettering on a colored background. To record these successfully, mix more of the color than you think you may need—a free flow of paint will really help you to work around the words or characters.

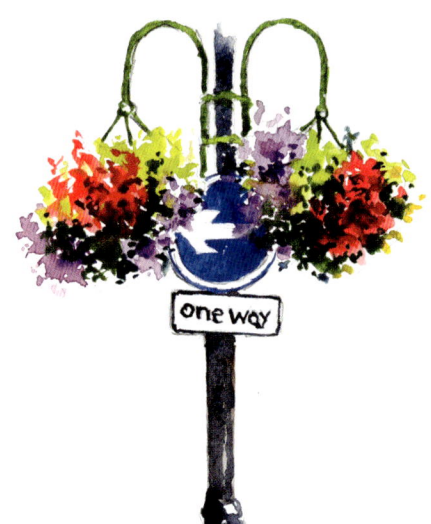

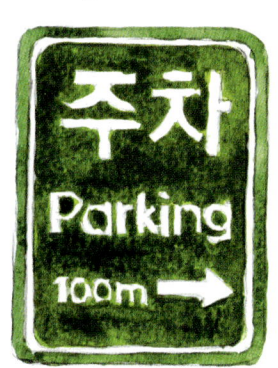

Some signs can be a little more decorative than truly functional—they are, however, excellent sketchbook subjects.

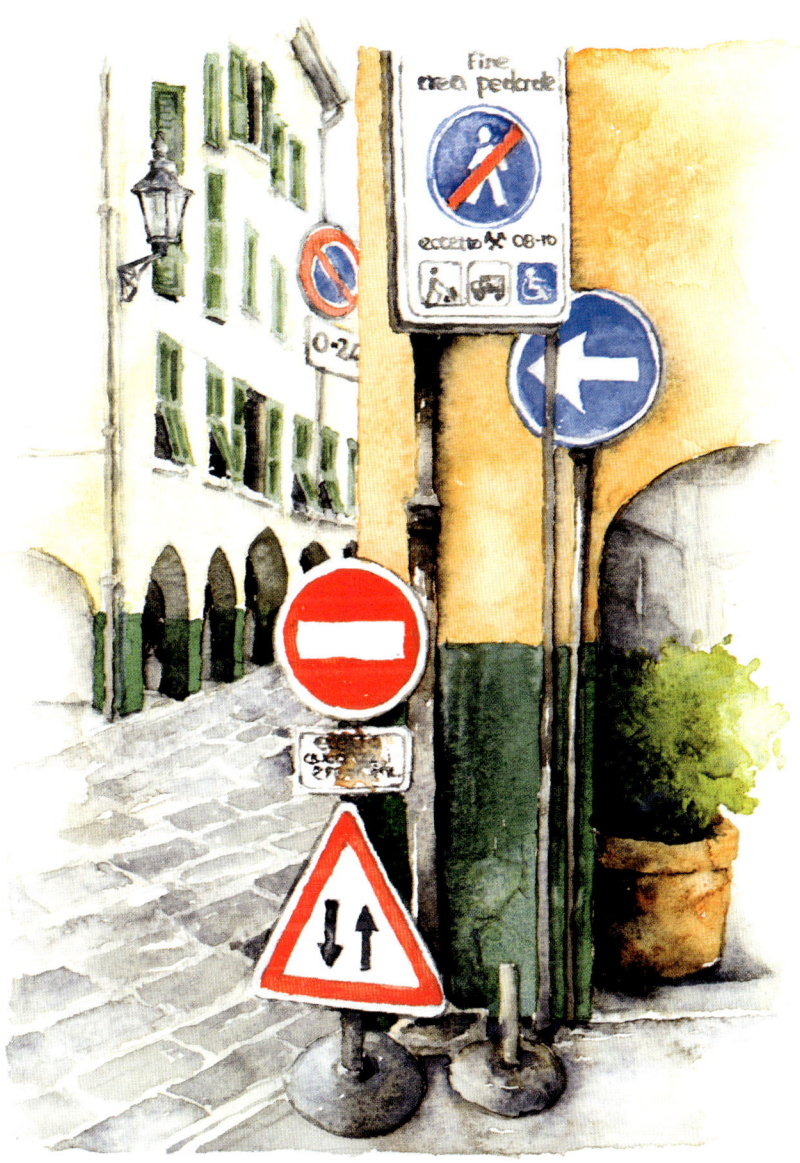

This profusion of road signs may be confusing for the motorist but the colors and the visual clutter created by these signs suggest ideal painting material. The spaces between the posts and the differently shaped signs are important to the composition. The irregularity of these helps to build a visual tension that adds even more interest to the chaotic scene.

Urban Decay

I always advise a visit to the more run-down side of any town or city as the scenery can be really rewarding. Textures can be created using the textural qualities of watercolor paper and a free flow of wet paint onto wet paper. You will only need a few basic colors to create a wealth of tones using these techniques.

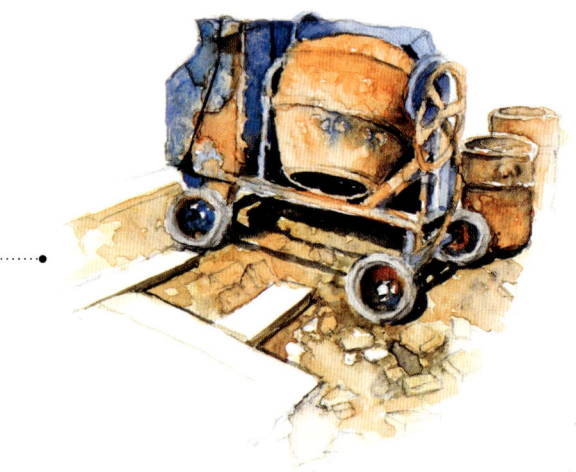

This scene contains a variety of textures in the rust, chipped paint, and rubble. Bricks on the ground are created by suggestion—negative shapes, achieved by painting palette mud around them.

The gray tone of this old trash can was achieved by mixing ultramarine blue with cobalt blue to soften the tone. A touch of burnt umber was used to add the patina.

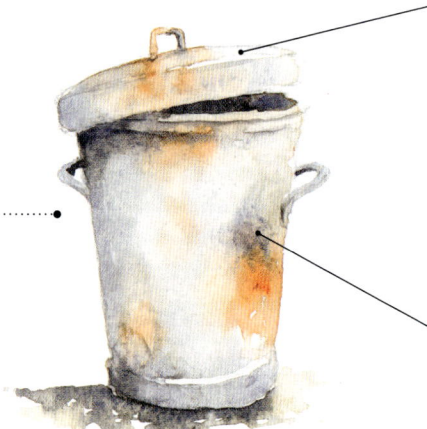

Highlight emphasizes curve of lid.

Dents created by dropping dark paint onto damp paper.

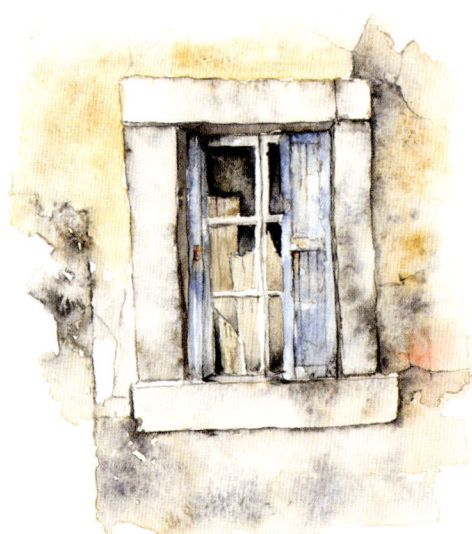

The mold covering this decaying facade was created by using a lot of water and many applications of wet paint. Layers of texture build as the paper dries.

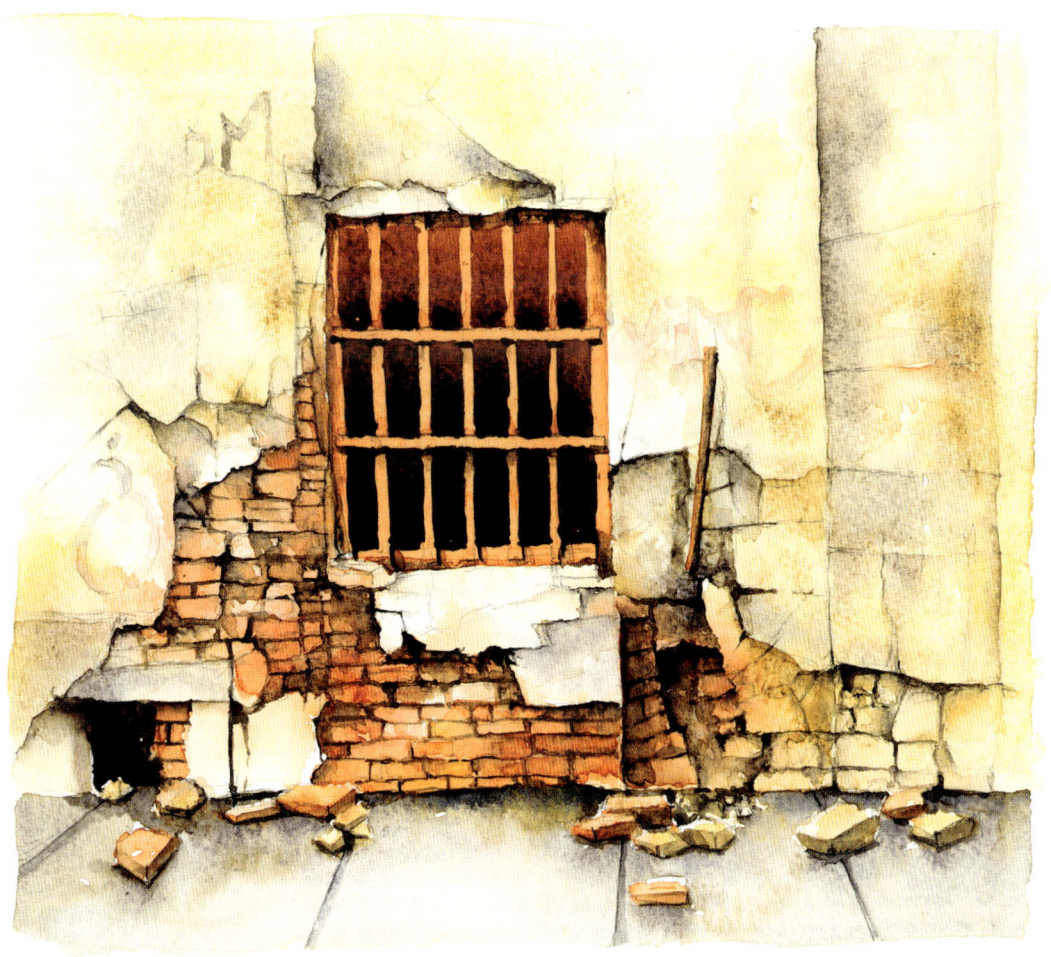

In this scence, the visual chaos of the cracked rendering, the unusual lines of the bricks, and the muted tones of the grubby walls epitomize elements found in the more run-down corners of towns and cities. I only used a handful of the foundation colors—chiefly raw sienna, burnt sienna, burnt umber, and ultramarine blue.

The way in which this crumbling facade spilled out onto the sidewalk also appealed to me. No practical attempt has been made to control the disorder.

Fire Hydrants

Being made of metal, fire hydrants will rot, chip, and even sometimes bend over the years. They are also usually red. This can create some issues as most red paints, when initially applied, will look strong and vibrant, but as they absorb into the paper will often soften to a strong pink tone. Apply another wash before the paint fully dries to obtain the vibrancy required, or even a small amount of alizarin crimson.

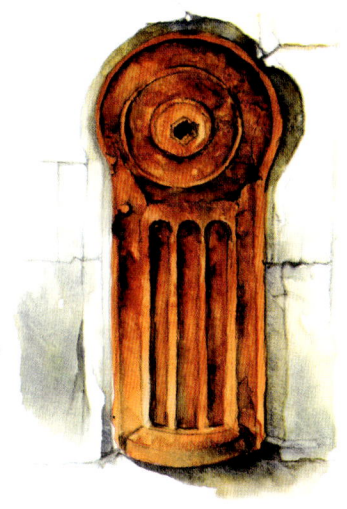

Burnt sienna is the dominant color of this rusty piece, enhanced by combinations of burnt umber and ultramarine blue, used to give shape and form to the decorative ridges.

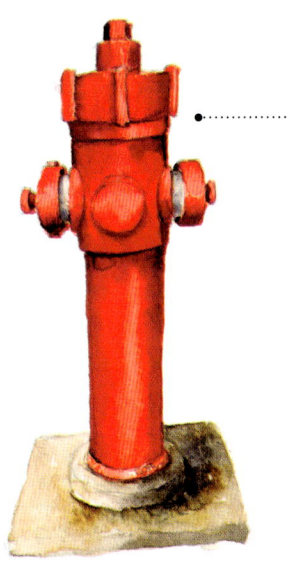

Making red darker while maintaining the integrity of color is difficult. Here, a touch of alizarin crimson was added to cadmium red for the darker tones, with a touch of dioxazine purple for the shadows.

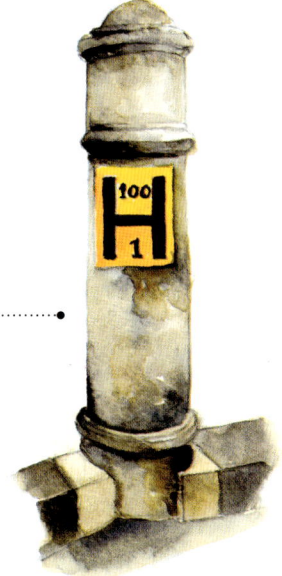

The lettering on this fire sign may appear black, but is actually an intense mixture of burnt umber and a dominant ultramarine blue.

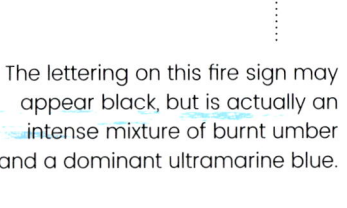

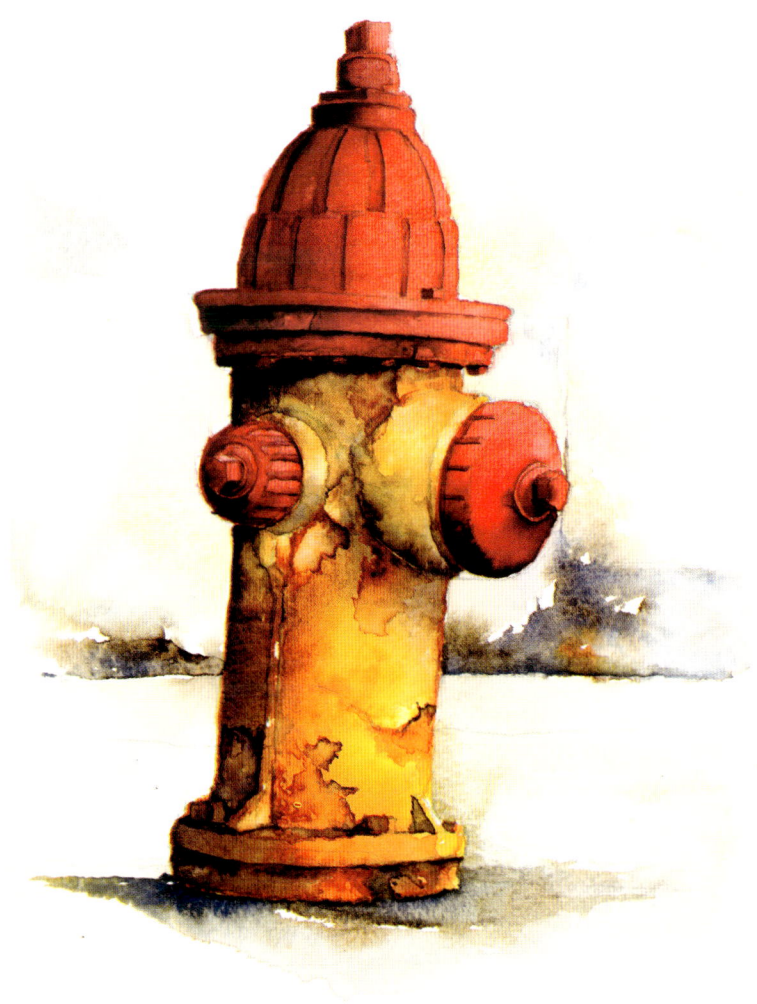

For the peeling paint on this old, rust-stained hydrant, I applied wet paint—cadmium yellow with a touch of burnt sienna—and allowed it to dry unevenly with the resulting watermark. I then used a darker mix, created by adding just the slightest touch of ultramarine blue, to draw around the lines of the watermark using a very small brush. I carefully pulled this line of paint away from the watermark using clear water, to diffuse the soft shadow.

Covers, Grids, and Grilles

It is strange that such functional items of street furniture can be so attractive to artists, yet largely so unnoticed by passersby every day. It must be the symmetry of the patterns, or the corporate identities that the designs hold, that make them so appealing.

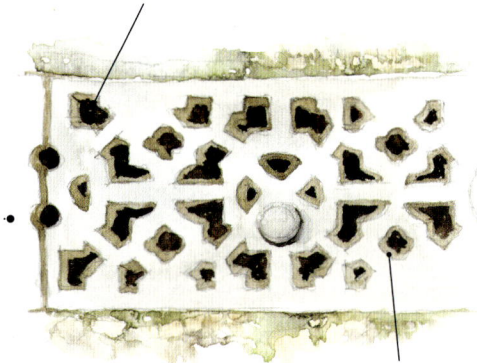

Darker colors push lighter colors forward.

Middle tones help to suggest depth to the grid.

In this three-tone study, the light tone for the metal grille is supplemented by a mid-tone for the inset shapes, adding depth. The darkest tone, painted in the gaps, visually pushes the grille forward.

This grille also requires a three-tone approach. The brassy tone is created by adding quinacridone gold to yellow ocher. Burnt umber is used for the darkest gaps.

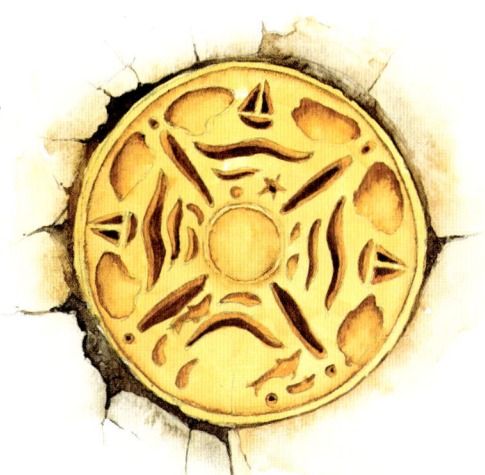

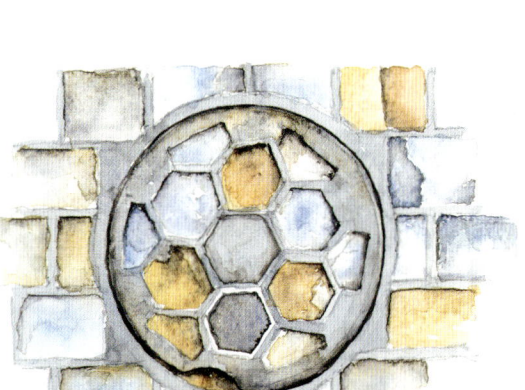

These vault lights, made from reinforced glass, need to be painted with light tones, created with a lot of water. Blues and ochers are the key colors.

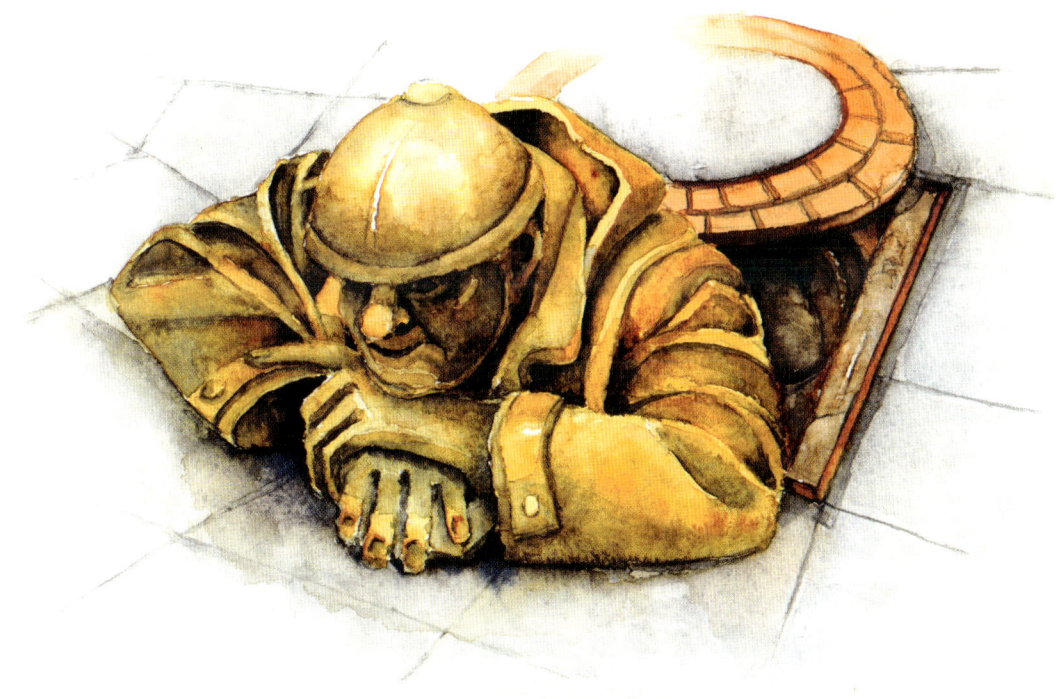

It is difficult to ignore these bronze figures found in some European cities. They are unique, cleverly situated, and simply eccentric. Often their hats or helmets are polished from frequent rubbing—this gives a brass-type effect.

To recreate the coloring, I used a mixture of raw sienna and quinacridone gold, darkened where necessary with burnt umber and ultramarine blue. I created the sharp highlight on the old soldier's helmet by painting around the ridge, leaving it showing pure white paper.

TIP

If it is not glaringly obvious where to "end" your composition, use water to wash the ground tone out toward the edge of your paper.

Stationary Vehicles

Parked and stationary vehicles allow you some time to observe and paint them. While the shapes, colors, and tones may well capture your attention, don't neglect the shadows as these help to anchor your vehicles to the ground, connecting them to the environment in which you first spotted them.

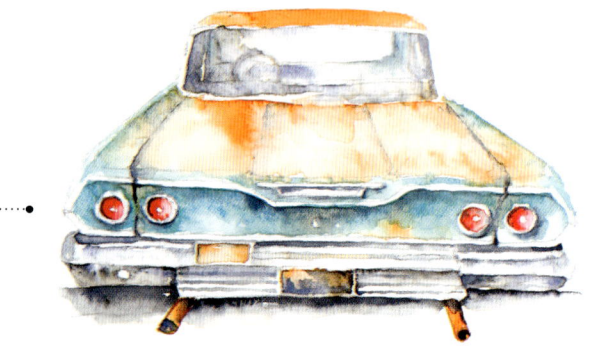

The peppermint color of this old car is a mix of strong and vibrant phthalocyanine green with cerulean blue, heavily diluted. The rust color was mixed using burnt sienna.

The transparent plastic is painted by pulling thin paint across dry paper.

The light colors of this scooter would be lost against a white paper background without a darker color to push them forward. The shadow, created by adding a touch of burnt umber to the blues of the paintwork, anchors the bike to the ground, visually "pushing" the light colors forward.

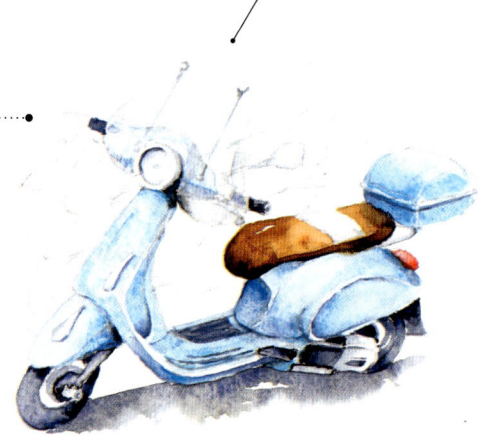

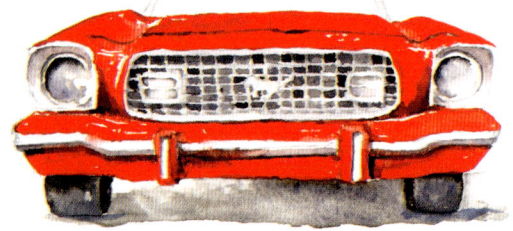

The strong, bright red of this car was achieved using a mixture of cadmium red with a little water and a similar mixture of alizarin crimson.

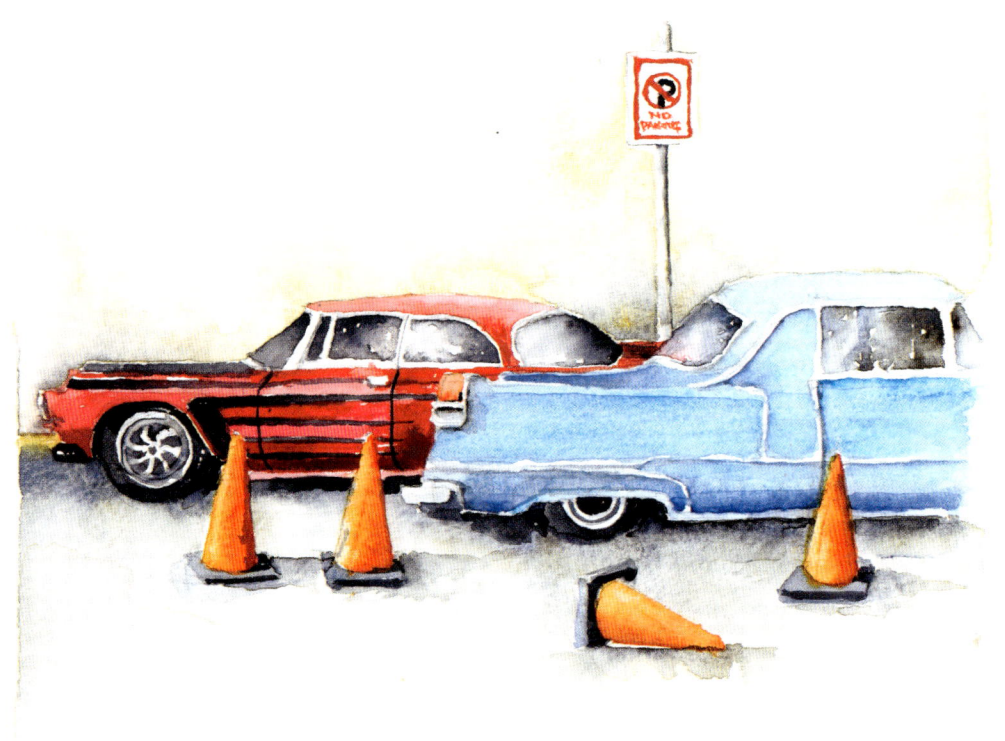

This painting is based not so much on color, tone, or texture, but on the dynamics of the composition. The visual tension created by the two cars facing in opposite directions, and the blue car being in front of the red car, aided this. There is no symmetry—just an imbalance and visual "pull" created with both cars facing different directions.

TIP

Look underneath the vehicles to gauge the shapes and strength of the shadows, and always add some of the car color to your shadow mix.

Street Lighting

Street lights form a large part of the array of street furniture. While the visually interesting bits will often be at the top, meaning that you will be looking upward to record them, the base of a lamppost may hold some detail worth recording as well.

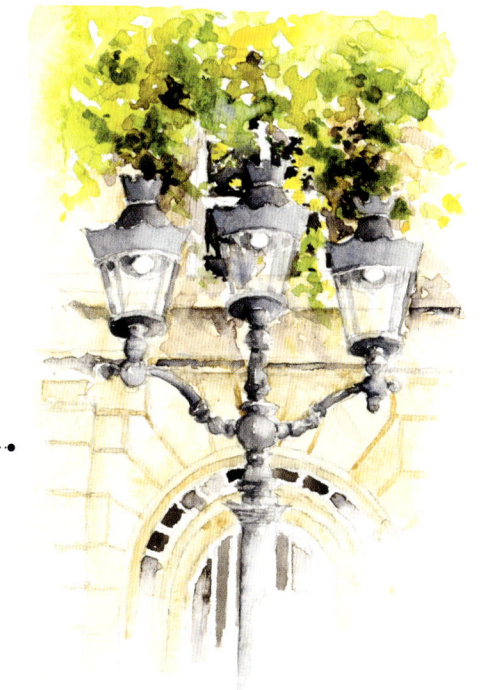

Sometimes architectural and functional objects can become visually absorbed into the urban landscape and don't appear simply as stand-alone features.

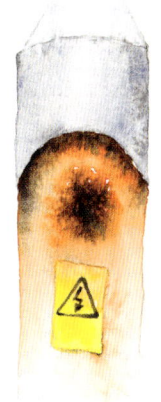

Two key blue paints were used in this study—ultramarine blue for the darker side, supplemented by a touch of diluted cobalt blue for the side catching the light.

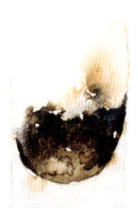

Sometimes it is the "business end" of an object that can be most interesting for the artist. Granulating siennas and umber were key to creating the rust effect here.

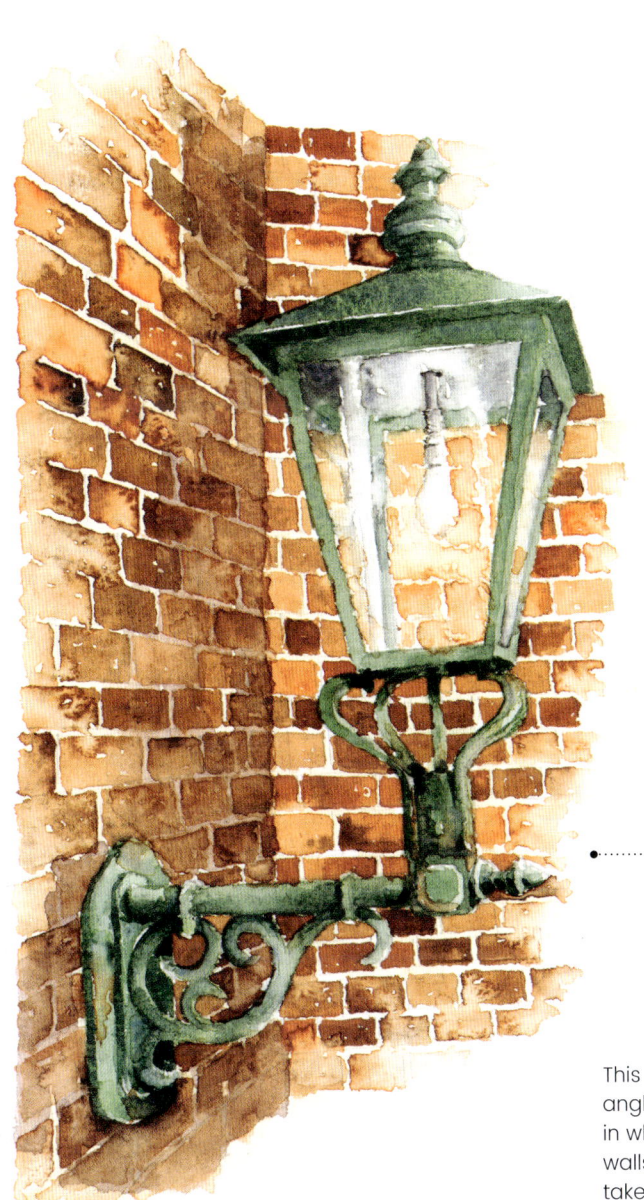

This painting is based largely on angles. The angles of the walls are irregular and the way in which the top of the lamp cuts across both walls is a consideration. A composition like this takes careful observation. While the bricks are important, I faded out the right-hand side in order to avoid too much solidity in the painting.

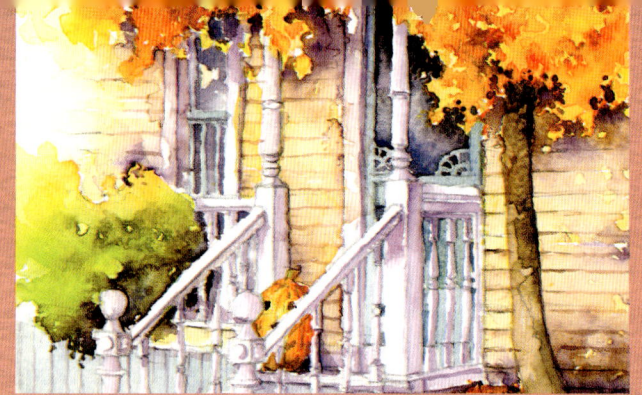

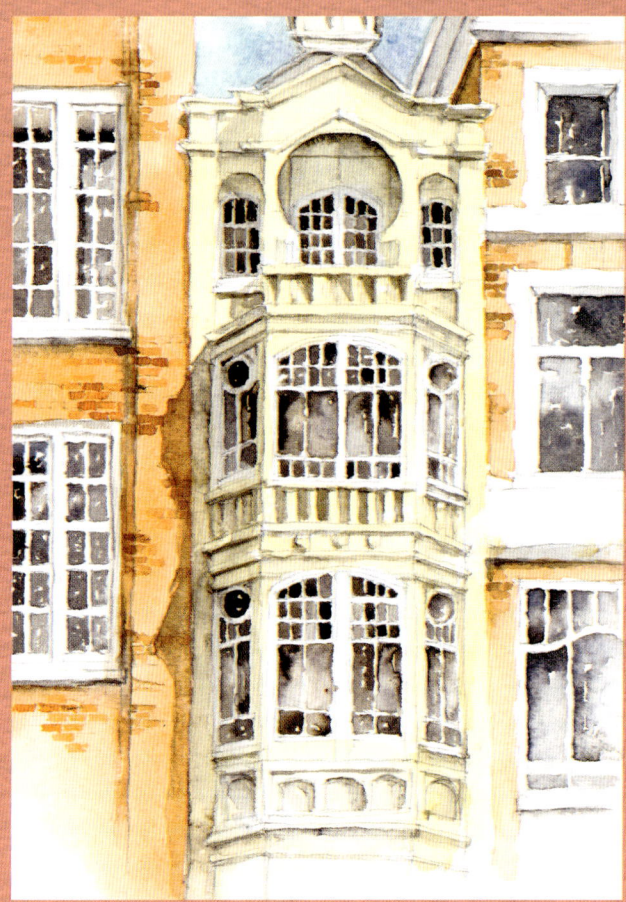

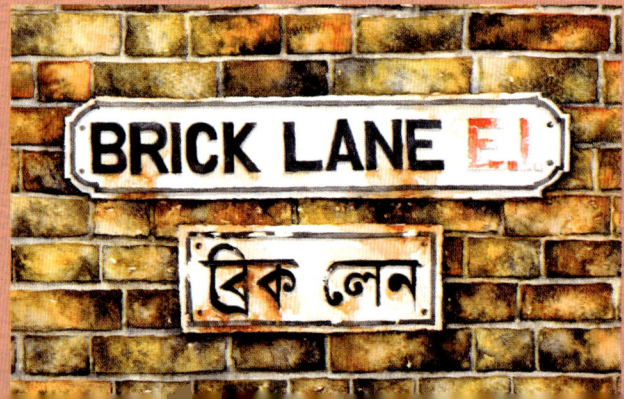

CHAPTER THREE:
Buildings

Buildings have many facets—the most common being doors and windows. But, as artists, we often seek out the least common. Rusting locks and key holes, angled shadows cast across stone, and wooden stairs are the types of details worth seeking out to study—either for the sake of sketching itself or to gain the knowledge that will help you to fill in gaps in compositions at home. Then, as you look up you will find balconies, windows, shutters, and, often, potted flowers, hanging through balcony railings.

Buildings come in many shapes and sizes and have a wealth of purposes. This is what makes them exciting as subjects, and watercolor is a medium well suited to recording these. A wash applied freely can color a wall, while cracked plaster or new brickwork can be added during the drying process, creating an authentic painting with minimal equipment in a relatively short period of time.

Windows and Glass

Glass is often transparent. It usually holds no color of its own, making it quite a challenge to record with colored paint. Look for the color of the sky for the initial tint, then look for what lies behind the glass to help you even more. I tend to paint windows on dry paper so I can leave some white streaks, painting around them to suggest reflections.

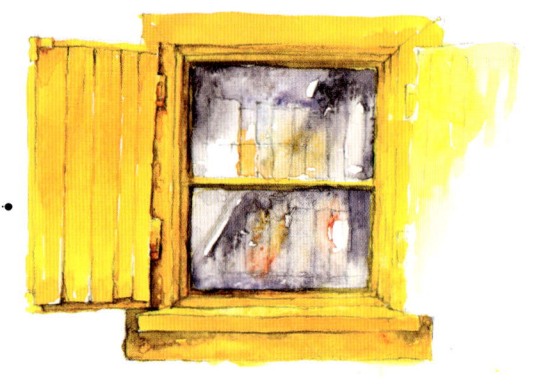

This grimy window involved using a strong mix of burnt umber and ultramarine blue around the book shapes. Water was then dropped onto the paint and pulled diagonally, following the lines of the reflections. As it began to dry, dioxazine purple was added for warmth.

To recreate the derelict feel of this window, burnt umber and ultramarine blue were used for the dirt.

Fine lines of dark tones are used for cracks.

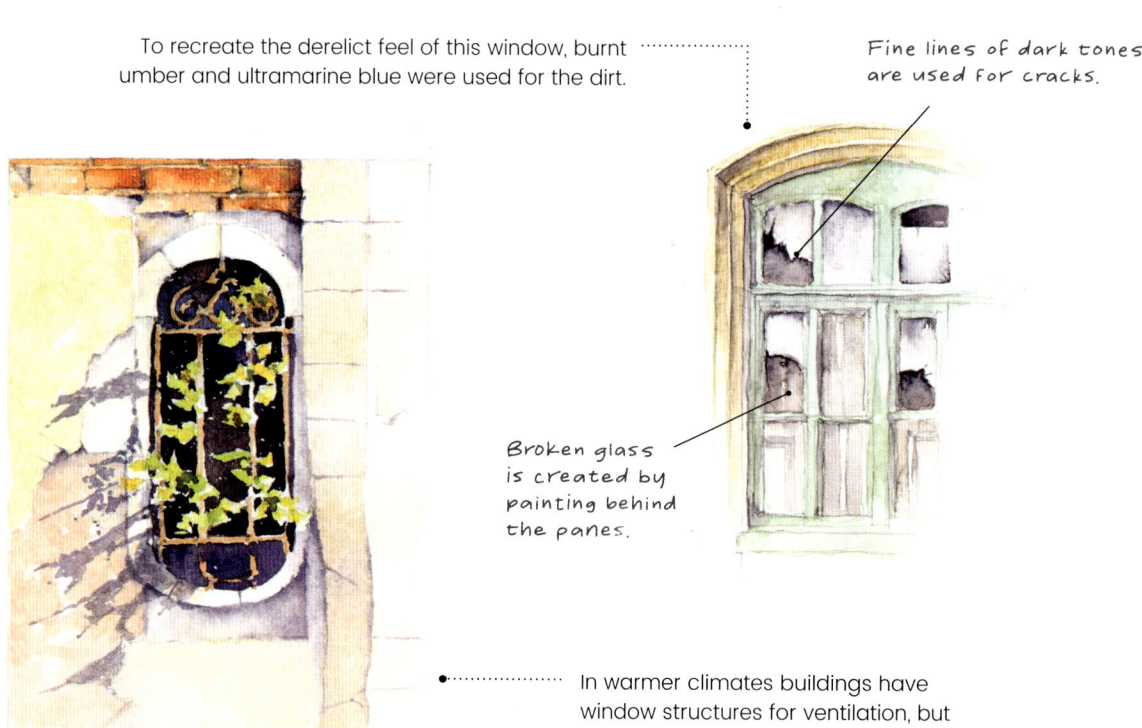

Broken glass is created by painting behind the panes.

In warmer climates buildings have window structures for ventilation, but with no glass to impede the flow of air.

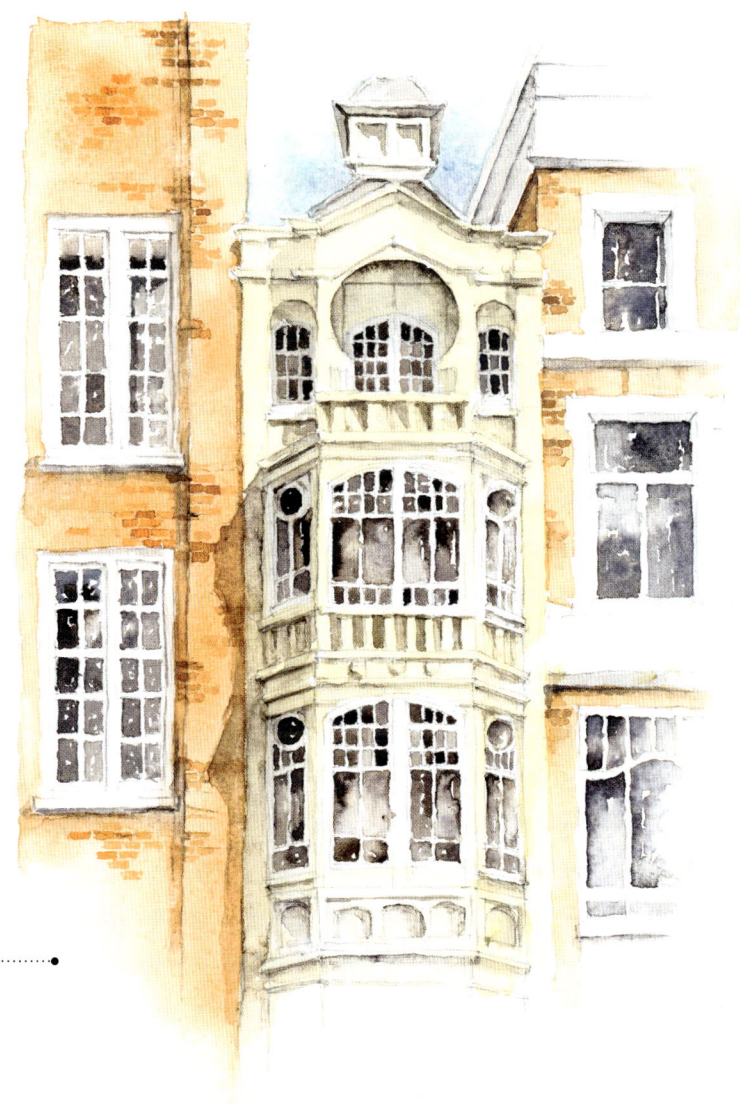

This city center building is awash with glass and full of shadows, shapes, and reflections. My key colors for glass reflections are usually the blue of the sky (often ultramarine blue and sometimes cerulean blue) mixed with a touch of burnt umber. I always apply this mixture in a watery form, which dries lighter than it looks at first. This creates different tones in windows and prevents "black holes" in buildings.

Steps and Stairs

Steps and stairs need shadows and shading to make them stand out and to prevent them from looking flat. Observe where the light is coming from—usually hitting the top of the step—then look again for the shadows cast onto the vertical drop. This will help you to achieve a three-dimensional effect.

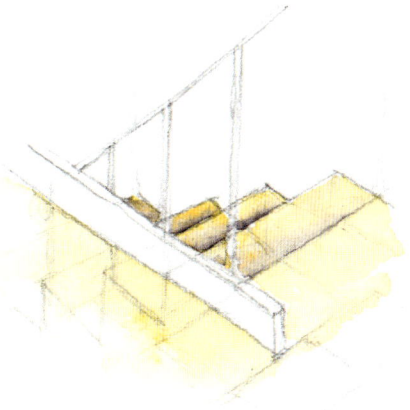

This small study was made from the top of the steps, looking downward. Shadows help to separate the individual steps from each other.

To define steps by the use of shadows, make sure you mix a really good quantity of paint—dioxazine purple and ultramarine blue here—to prevent broken and fragmented brushstrokes.

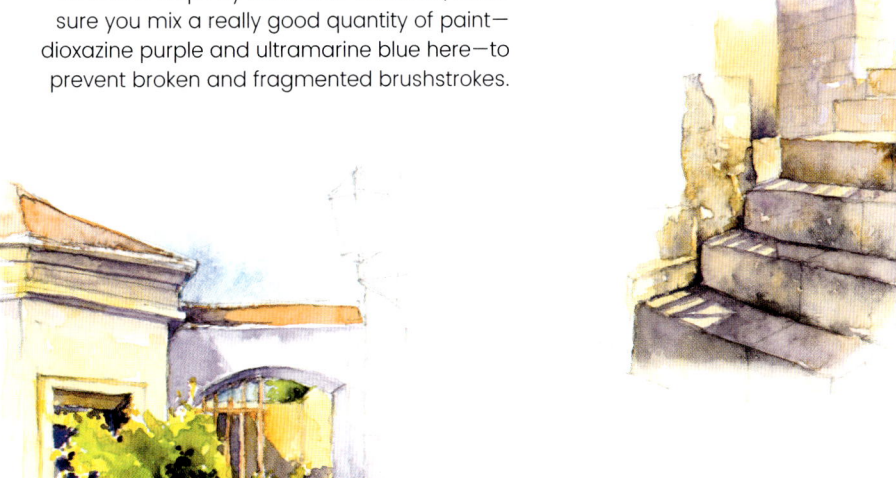

In this sketch, the vertical drop of each step was painted a little darker than the flat top to add the three-dimensional effect.

Top of step in shadow, but still kept light.

Vertical drop of step painted in a darker tone.

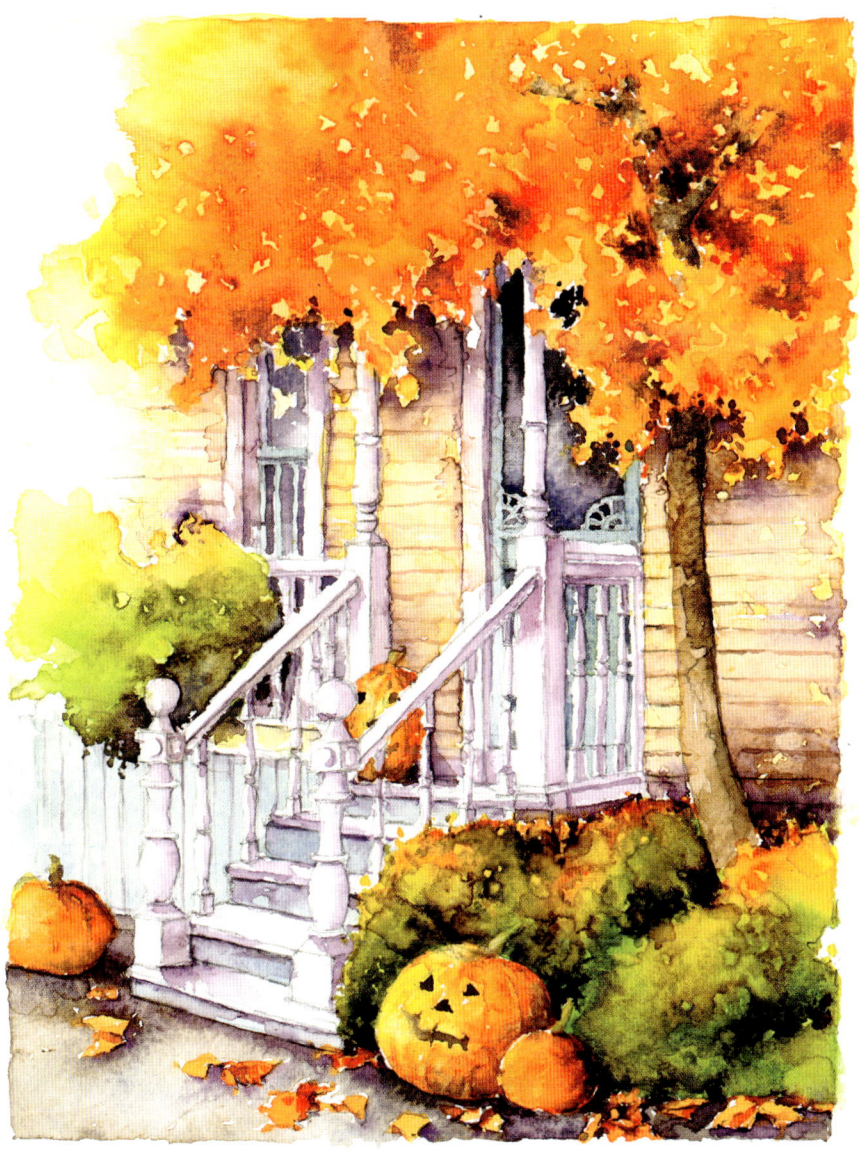

This seasonal painting is dominated by oranges, yellows, siennas, and ochers. Even the shadows are a mixture of cadmium orange and dioxazine purple. It is important that color is allowed to spread. The overall tone is warm and based upon cadmium yellow and cadmium orange. These colors are infused into the trees, woodwork, and the sidewalk. Even the steps have a touch of these colors in the all-important shadows. This can be helped by not changing the water in your jar. The water takes on a hint of the colors washed from your brushes and influences all further color mixes.

Rust and Metal

Rust and metal are best recorded by using the basic earth colors — raw sienna, burnt sienna, and burnt umber—and copious amounts of water. These paints are granular; left to dry without interference, the granules will separate, helping to create the textures found in your rusting subjects.

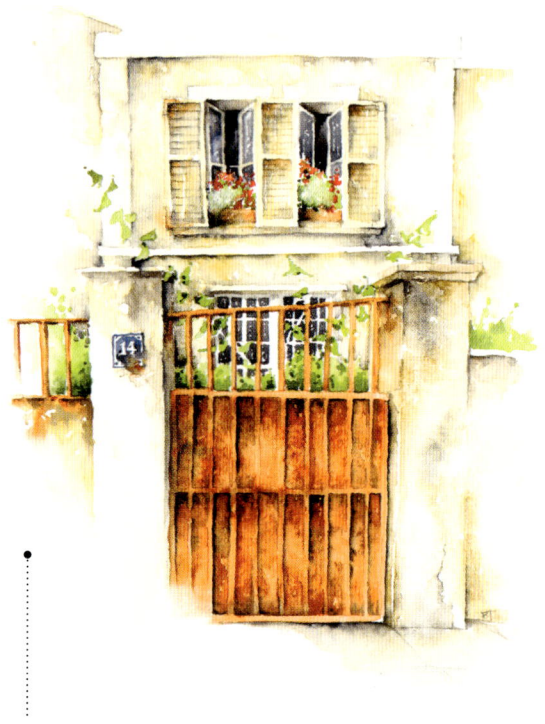

This rusting gate was created using liberal washes of burnt sienna and burnt umber on very damp paper, allowing both to bleed freely—they are natural granulators so helped to develop texture. The shadows were created by adding burnt umber with a little ultramarine blue—but only once the paper had fully dried, otherwise the sharp definition required would have been lost.

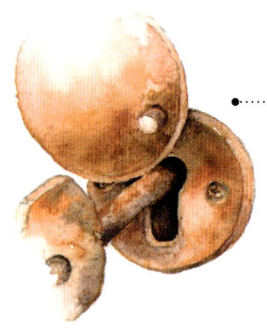

The deepest, darkest recesses of this old lock were painted using a very strong mixture of ultramarine blue and burnt umber, starting with the blue paint and adding the umber.

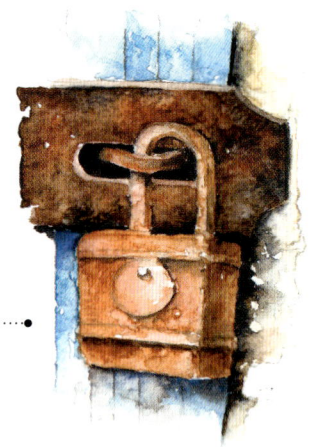

The texture on this rusty padlock was created by dropping a little light red onto a very watery mixture of burnt sienna and allowing the paint to dry. The watermarks enhance the appearance of aging.

EXAMPLE: RUSTY BOLT

STEP ONE

Apply raw sienna to damp paper and allow it to bleed freely.

STEP TWO

Add burnt sienna while the paper is still damp. This helps the paint to granulate, adding texture.

STEP THREE

Apply burnt umber to darker areas to create the internal shapes. You can enhance this with a touch of ultramarine blue for the darkest sections.

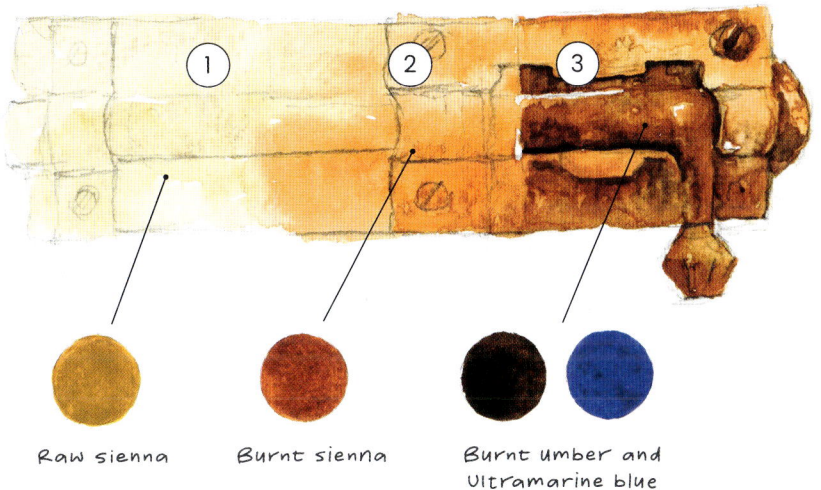

Raw sienna

Burnt sienna

Burnt umber and Ultramarine blue

Door Surrounds

While doors themselves tell us much about the character of a building, they will always be set into a wall with some form of surrounding structure, be it simple or highly decorative. Perspective lines are important when recording these surrounds as they will help to give a sense of depth to the surrounding woodwork or stone.

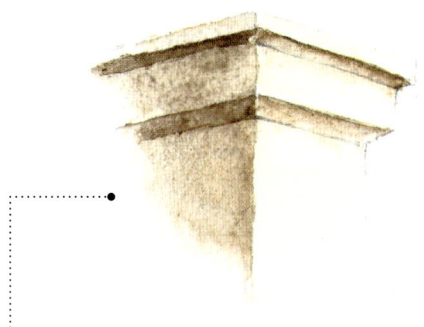

This molding is viewed from an angle, so one side is cast into shadow. Raw sienna, burnt umber, and ultramarine blue were used to create the shadow tones.

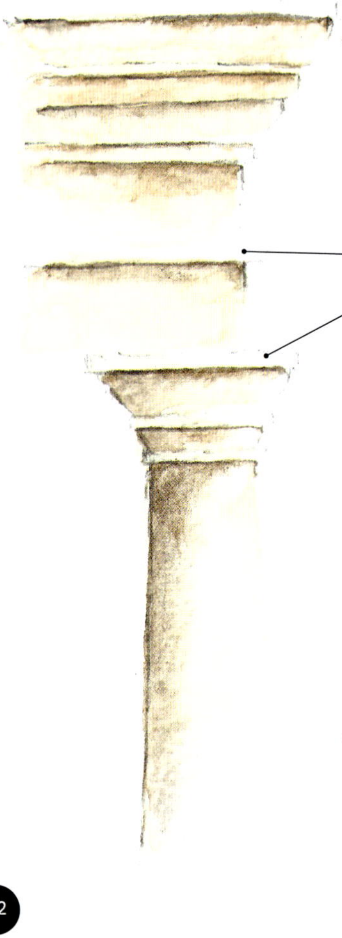

It is fine to leave some of the molding unpainted. The white of the paper makes these sections stand out against the painted stone or plaster.

Unpainted sections enhance the effect.

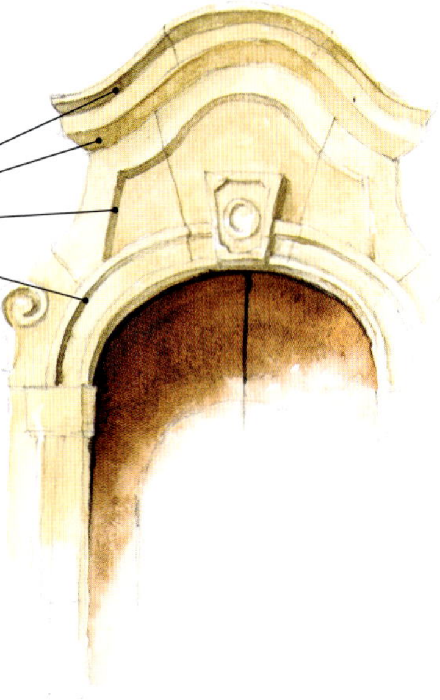

Shadow tone applied to dry paper is pulled around the curves to dilute its strength.

The curves of this door molding required a graduated change in tone. A base of raw sienna was left to dry, then a mix of burnt umber and ultramarine blue was added to the darkest section and pulled around the curve using a wet brush to dilute the tone.

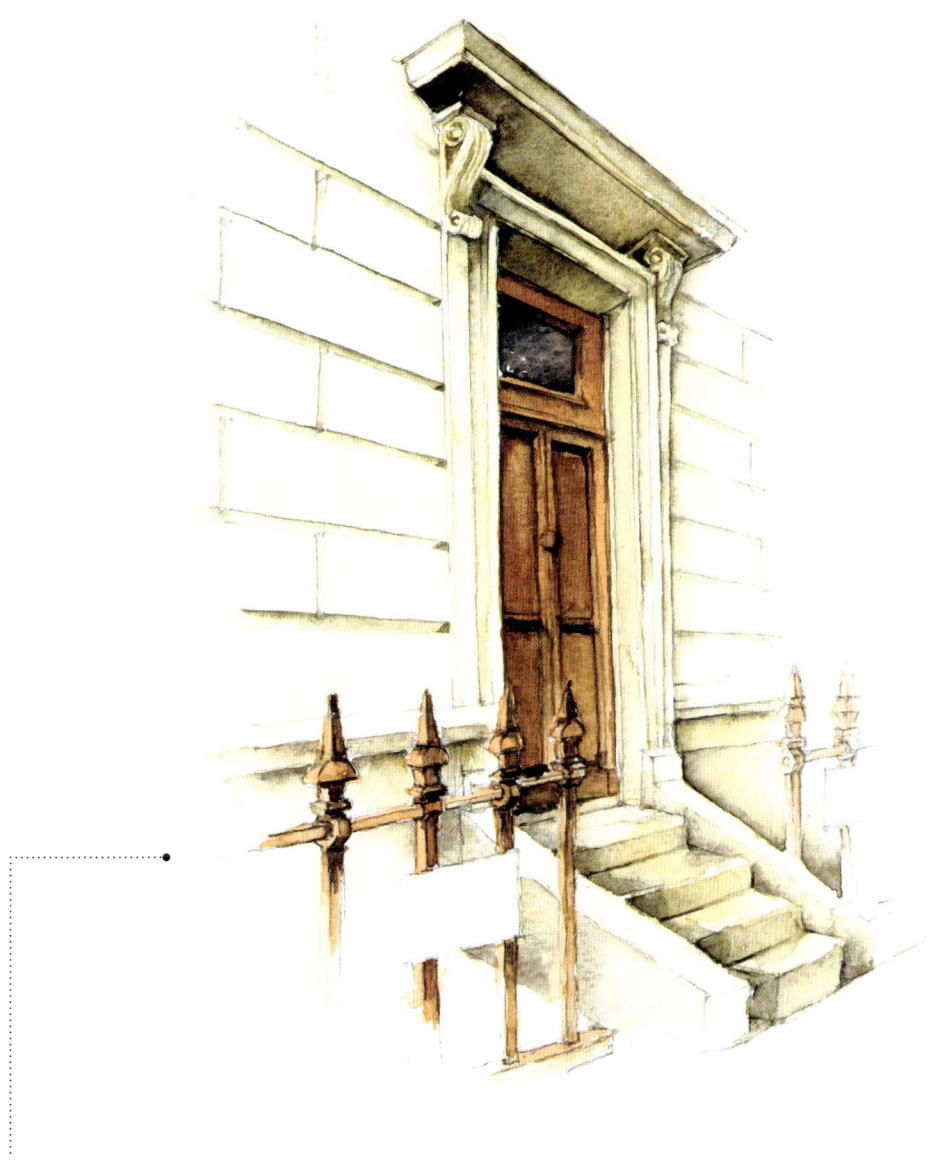

This composition employs one-point perspective (see Chapter One: Basics). The vanishing point cannot be plotted here so must be imagined.

From the sidewalk, you will usually be looking up at door surrounds, and need to observe tones accordingly. Tone is important here as the painting is not far away from being monochrome. The base color is diluted yellow ocher and the shading and shadows mixed by adding ultramarine blue and burnt umber to the wash.

Doors

Doors are frequently wooden—some untreated, some painted—but a degree of texture will often be visible. I usually establish the color wash on the door, allow this to dry, and then almost "draw" on top of this with a small brush to create the wood grain and texture.

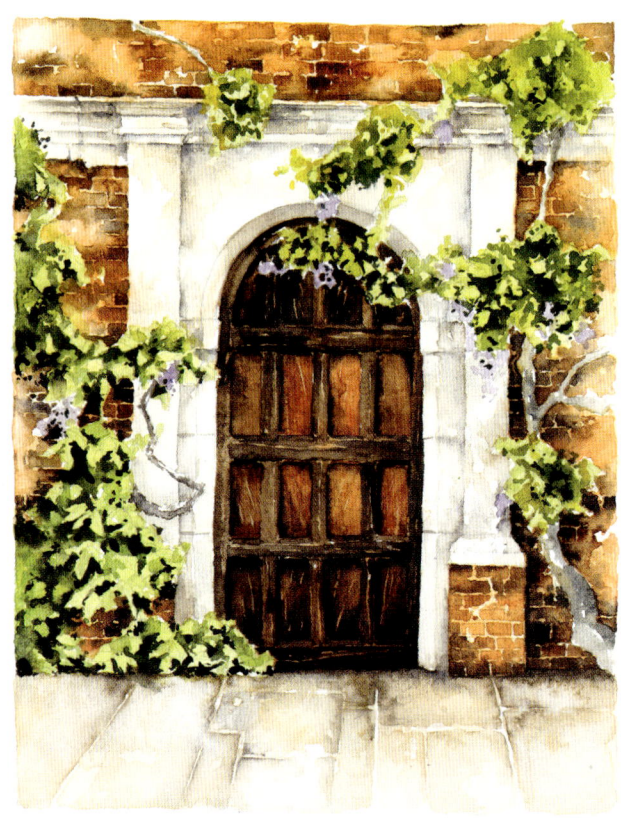

This door has a wealth of natural wood tones as well as grain texture. The whole door was painted with a watery wash of raw sienna. Once dry, the wood panels were painted with varying intensities of raw sienna and burnt umber using a small brush and leaving flashes of the underwash showing through to represent the wood grain.

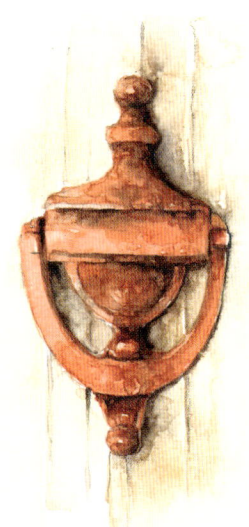

This study of a rusty old door knocker relies on the two natural allies, sienna (for the rust) and burnt umber (for the shadows).

The screw holes on the numbers of this brass plate help to give the study authenticity, as do the slight shadows cast by the numbers.

EXAMPLE: MAILBOX

STEP ONE
Wash raw sienna onto dry paper to create the basic undertone.

STEP TWO
Mix quinacridone gold with raw sienna to create the warm brass color of the mailbox, and paint on top of the dry undertone.

STEP THREE
Use burnt umber to paint the shadows cast by the relief details.

STEP FOUR
Touch a little sap green and cobalt blue in to create the verdigris effect.

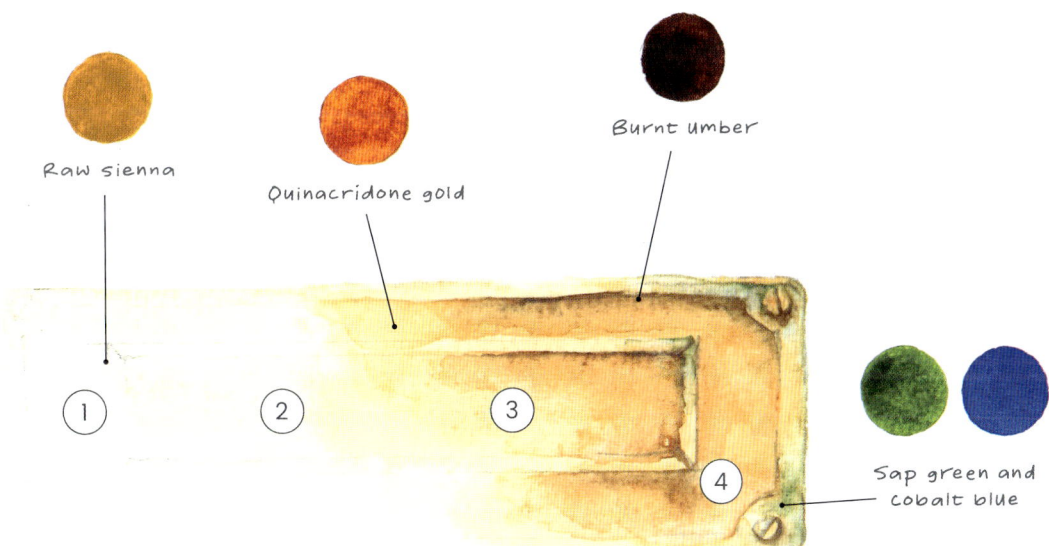

Raw sienna

Quinacridone gold

Burnt umber

Sap green and cobalt blue

Shutters

The shutters that cover windows in the hotter parts of the globe can hold some wonderful textures—especially those that have been well weathered over many years. There can be a wealth of colors. They can sometimes be inside window surrounds, but often sit on the outside, too, so look closely at how and where to paint shadows.

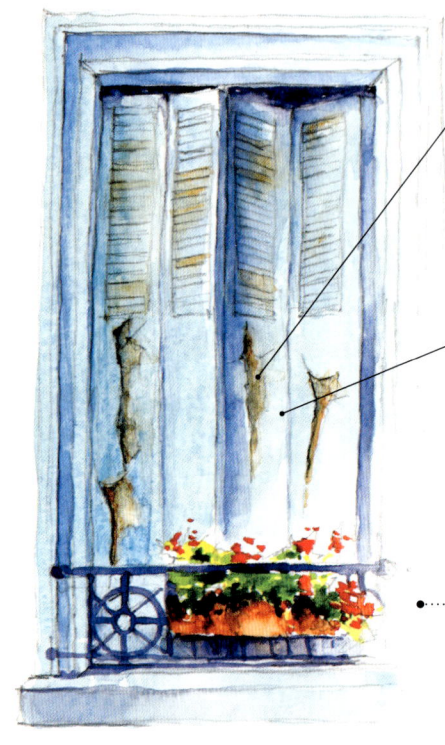

Burnt sienna and burnt umber applied along the "inside" of the crack.

Paint "pulled" outward with a damp brush to create a graduated tone.

Here, the cracks in the paint were achieved by running a line of burnt sienna and burnt umber along one side of the crack. This was then carefully pulled outward using a damp brush.

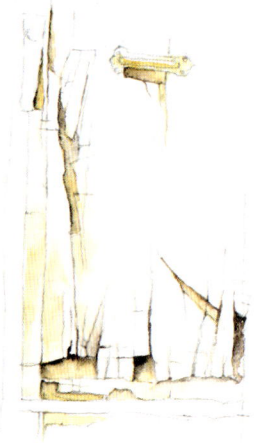

Years of exposure to the sun has left this wooden shutter cracked and split. This was recorded in pencil, adding raw sienna and burnt umber to create the shadows. A touch of ultramarine blue was added to darken some shaded areas.

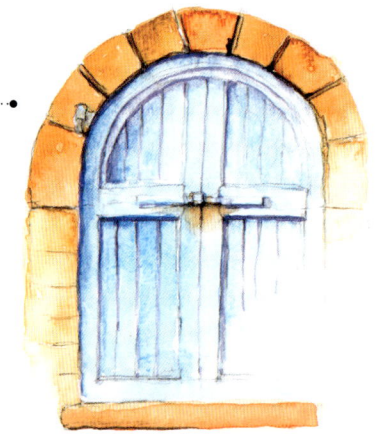

The soft shadows seen in these shutters were painted with an ultramarine blue/dioxazine purple mix.

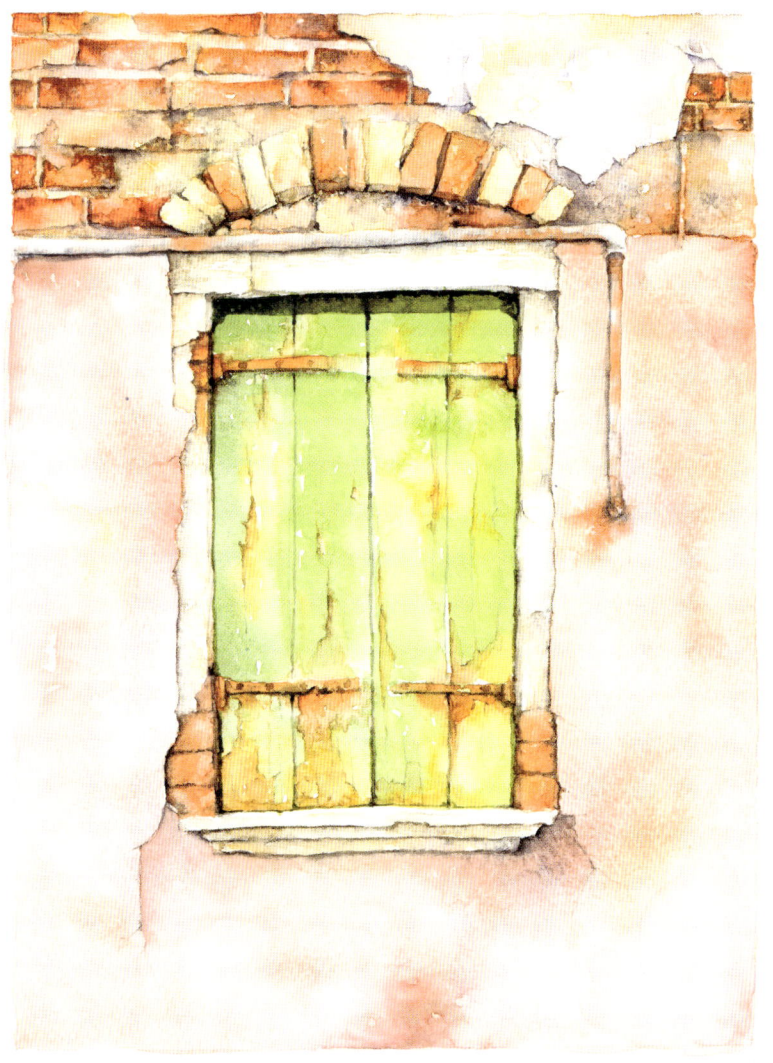

I created the peeled and cracked paint on these
shutters by running a thin line of paint along
the inside line of the peel and quickly pulling it
outward with a thin wash of water. This can be
enhanced by dropping a small amount of darker
paint and allowing it to bleed. This creates the
tones of the exposed wood.

Balconies

Balconies are functional parts of buildings, but can also be highly decorative. If you are recording these from ground level you will invariably be looking upward with a good view of the underneath. If it is possible to record them from a facing window or platform, this will allow you not just a good sight of the decorations, but also some view inside the room.

Look for darkest shadows under balconies.

Balconies will usually be above eye level. As we will nearly always be looking up at them, it is the underneath that we will need to concentrate on.

Negative shapes created by painting behind wooden supports.

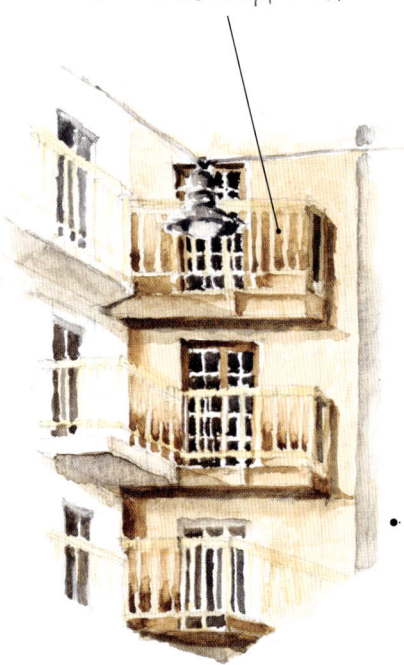

By standing back, it is easier to see a balcony as part of the whole building and, therefore, part of its character.

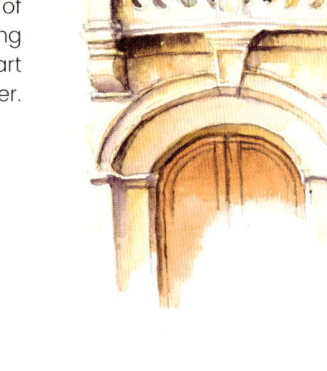

These balconies are a web of positive and negative shapes, with the darker tones visually pushing the lighter tones forward.

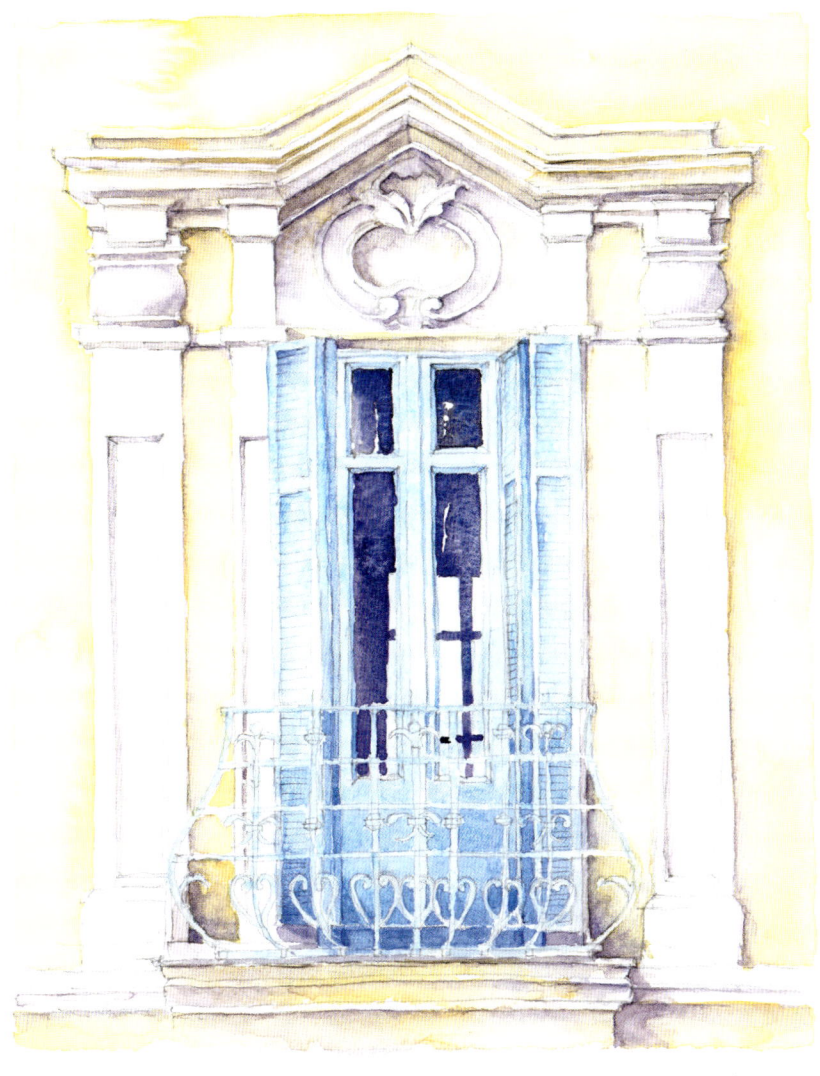

This composition is based on a series of positive and negative shapes. The plasterwork on the colonial-style balcony surround, the railings, and the view into the room all rely on a little visual push and pull. The walls were painted using Naples yellow, the shutters and railings cobalt blue, and the interior shadows dioxazine purple.

Wall Signs

As with road signs, wall signs are designed to give you information. The key difference is that they can be highly decorative and of any color. They may be street names, or they may be signage for cafés, bars, or industrial sites. Whatever, they serve to give some identity to the area you are in.

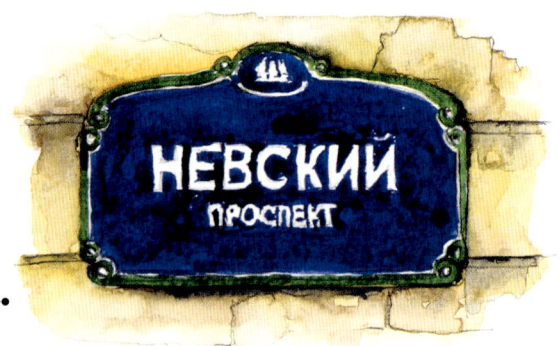

Enamel road signs are to be found on walls around the globe—often blue. My preference for recording these is a very strong mixture of pure ultramarine blue.

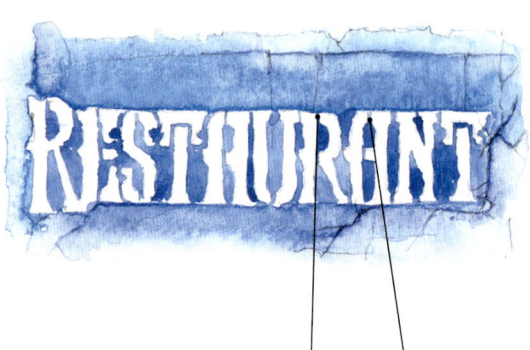

Stenciled lettering can produce some highly decorative effects. Painting between the gaps in individual letters is best done using the tip of a very fine brush.

Stencil effect created by using the tip of a fine brush to paint the gaps.

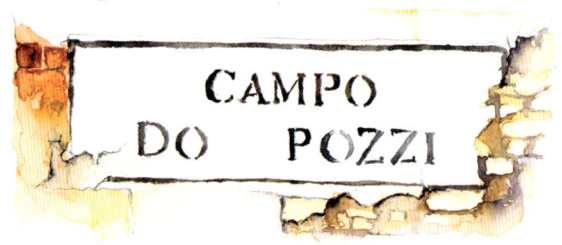

Here, the letters are not painted as negative shapes. Instead, I used a strong mix of ultramarine blue and burnt umber and painted them with the tip of a small brush and not too much water.

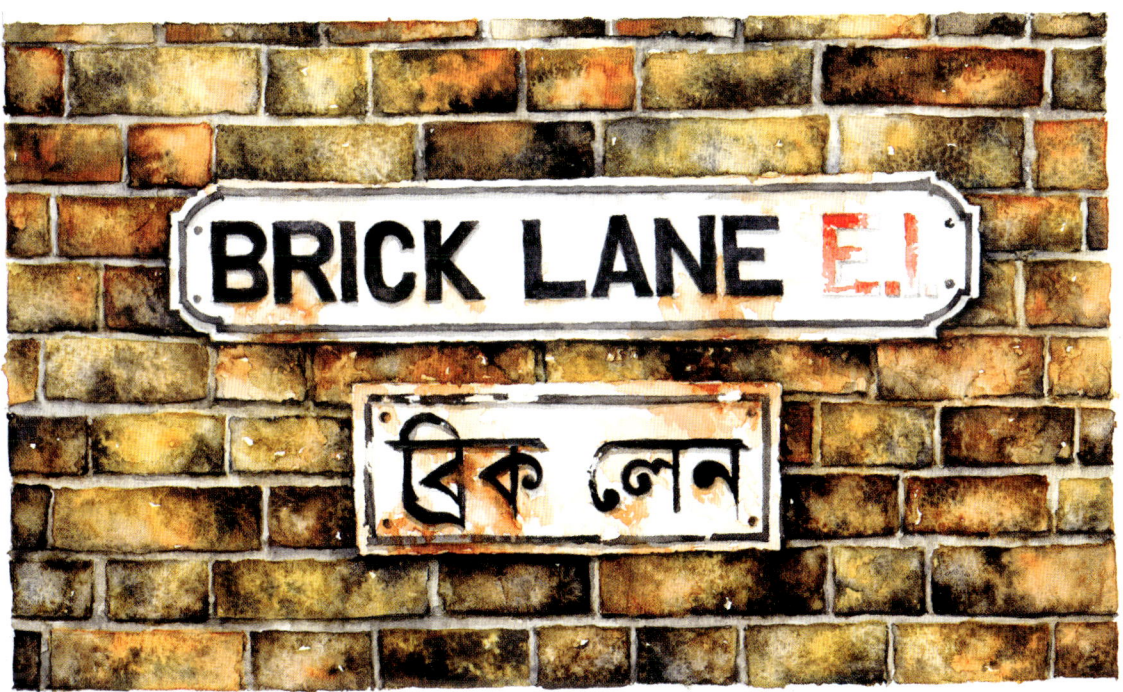

This dark, smog-stained city brickwork required a full mix of siennas, umbers, and ochers, with ultramarine added to enhance the shading. The lettering is an intense mix of ultramarine blue and burnt umber. The rust bleeds were created by wetting the paper and dabbing on burnt sienna. This then bled into the wet paper, creating a soft effect as it dried.

TIP

Almost always, opt to use burnt umber and ultramarine to represent black. Pure black paint can often "flatten" a painting.

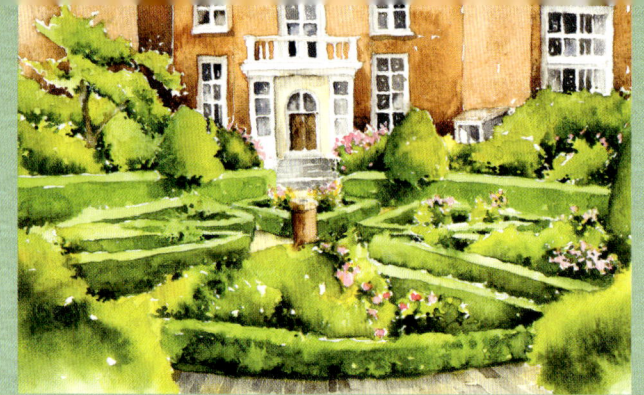

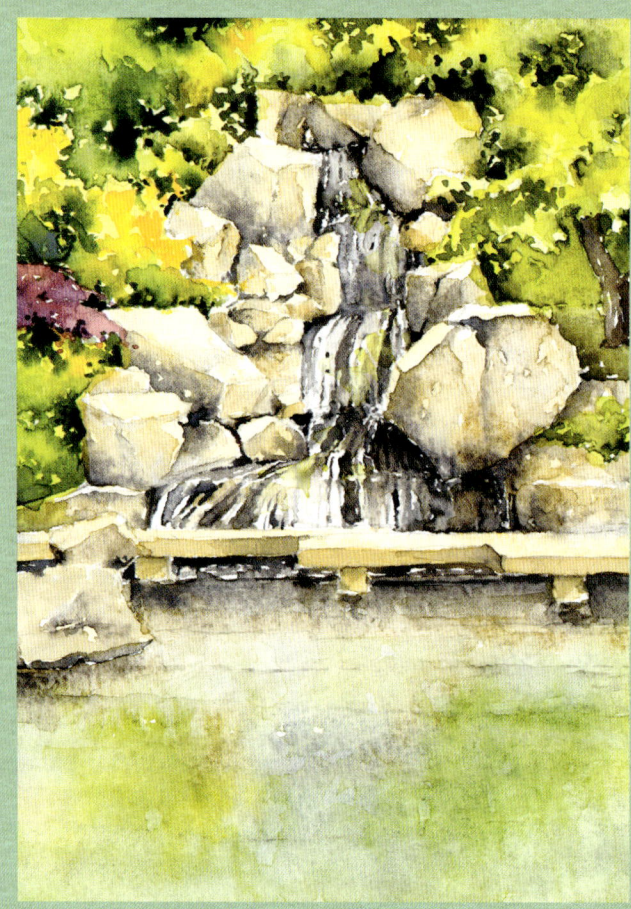

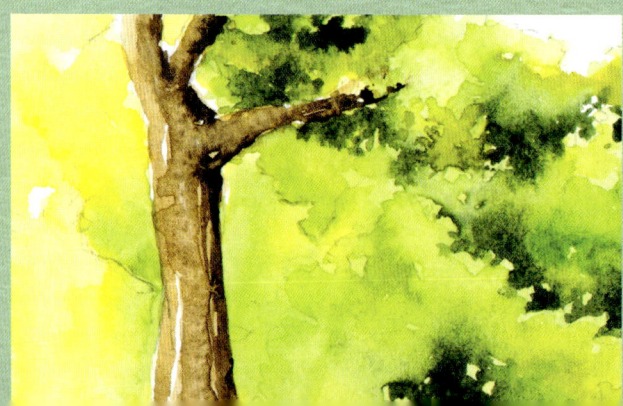

CHAPTER FOUR:
Parks

As towns and cities developed, city elders and philanthropists understood the need for clean air and green spaces where the inhabitants could stroll, play, and generally relax. As a result, most urban environments have some form of public gardens where a wealth of subjects can be found.

Fountains, water features, statues, and stone proliferate in most parks and gardens, and can often be recorded using exactly the same techniques as those used for painting buildings on the high street. Then you will find an abundance of foliage in the form of trees and bushes, as well as ponds, lakes, and ornamental water features.

Other elements of park life that I find of particular interest are bins and benches. I find myself attracted to the shapes and shadows cast by these in a way that many passersby might find strange. Frequently, it is the less common that we, as artists, find the most appealing.

Trees and Bushes

Trees, shrubs, and plants hold such a wide variety of tones (not always green) that it is hard to advise with any level of precision exactly what mixtures to use. I always apply the lightest tones to any foliage first, then look for the middle tones. When these are really dry I apply the darkest tone to establish a sense of depth.

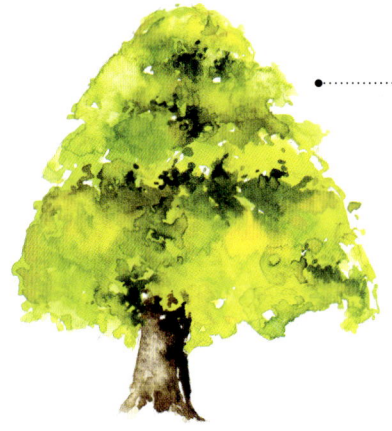

Initial washes of yellows and greens should be applied to damp paper. This allows the paint to bleed and soften the blends. Once these washes have fully dried, a mix of burnt umber, sap green, and ultramarine blue can be applied to emphasize the three-dimensional feel.

This Japanese maple was painted using cadmium red and alizarin crimson, with ultramarine blue added for the shadows.

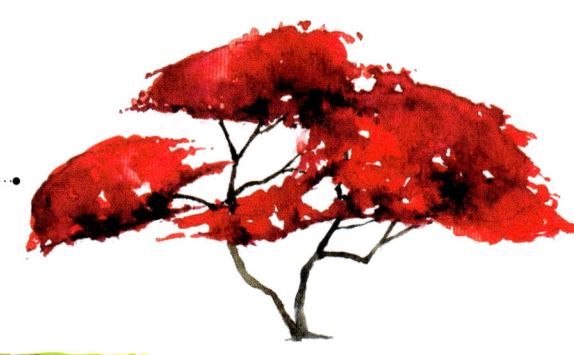

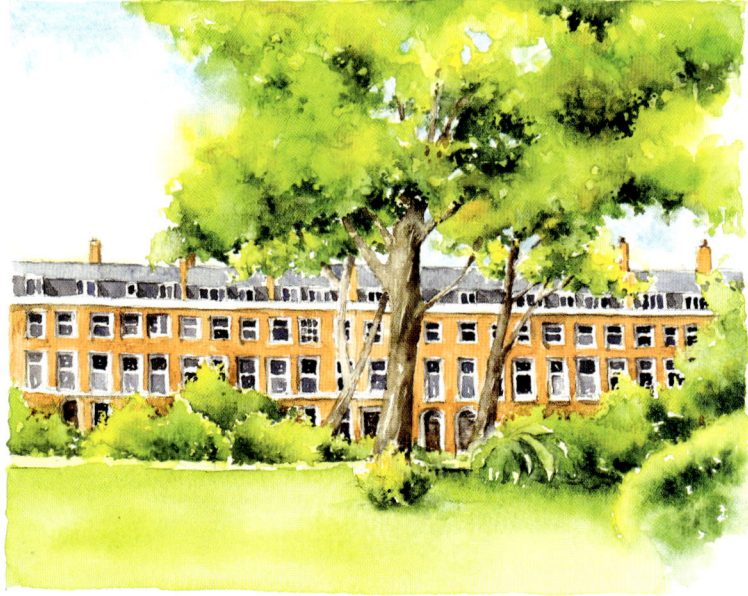

My basic technique for painting summer foliage is to start with a wash of cadmium yellow. As this begins to dry, I apply a wash of sap green. The two paints bleed unevenly, drying to a wealth of tones. Once they are fully dry, I draw around the larger leaves and under the tree canopies with a mixture of sap green, burnt umber, and ultramarine blue, to create light and shade.

EXAMPLE: GREENERY

STEP ONE

Apply a watery wash of cadmium yellow to the foliage and bushes to act as a base color.

STEP TWO

Apply a thin wash of sap green unevenly to the greenery, allowing some of the yellow to show through as highlights.

STEP THREE

Before the sap green is dry, apply a mix of burnt umber and ultramarine blue in the shaded areas, separating the bushes and adding a sense of form. This will bleed a little, preventing the bushes from looking two-dimensional. Repeat once the paper has dried to sharpen some shadows.

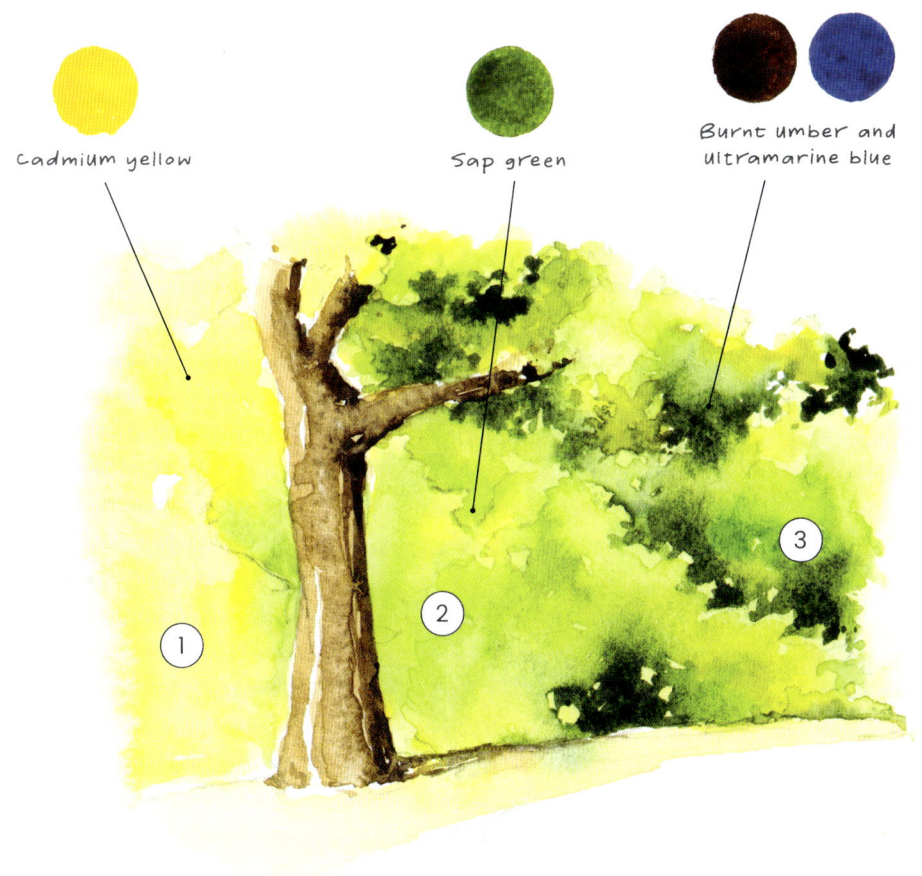

Cadmium yellow

Sap green

Burnt umber and ultramarine blue

Statues and Stone

Painting stone requires a limited set of colors—yellow ocher, raw sienna, and burnt umber—but unlimited quantities of water. The key to recording old, weatherworn stone is not to let the paper dry fully until you have finished. Keeping it damp allows you to build up a wide variety of tones within a limited color range.

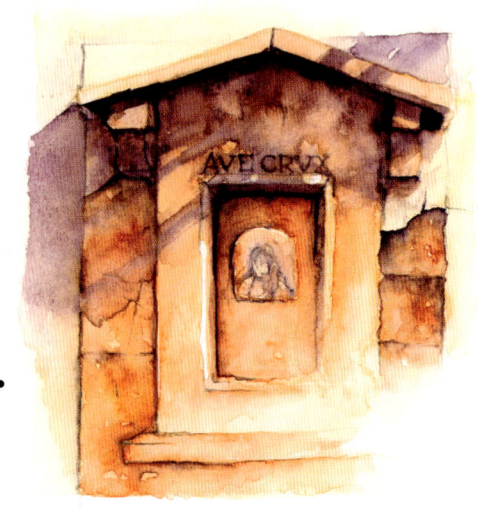

This relief feature has a base of burnt sienna, enhanced by a touch of light red. The warm climate demanded a shadow wash of dioxazine purple, tempered with a touch of ultramarine blue.

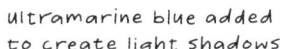
ultramarine blue added to create light shadows.

This ornamental plinth has a base application of yellow ocher, allowing the stone to hold a little warmth.

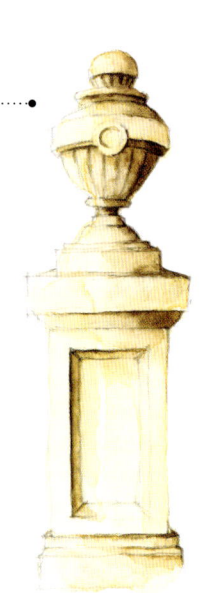

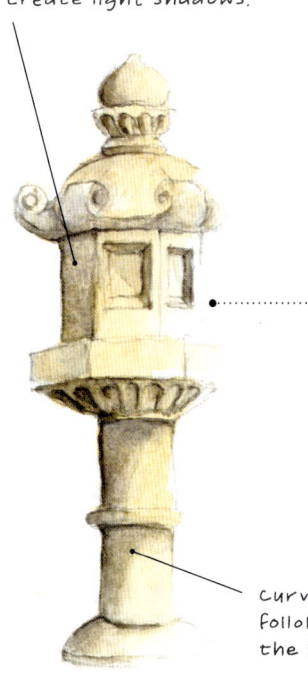

The accumulated grime and weathering led to this stone structure having a raw sienna underwash.

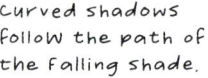
Curved shadows follow the path of the falling shade.

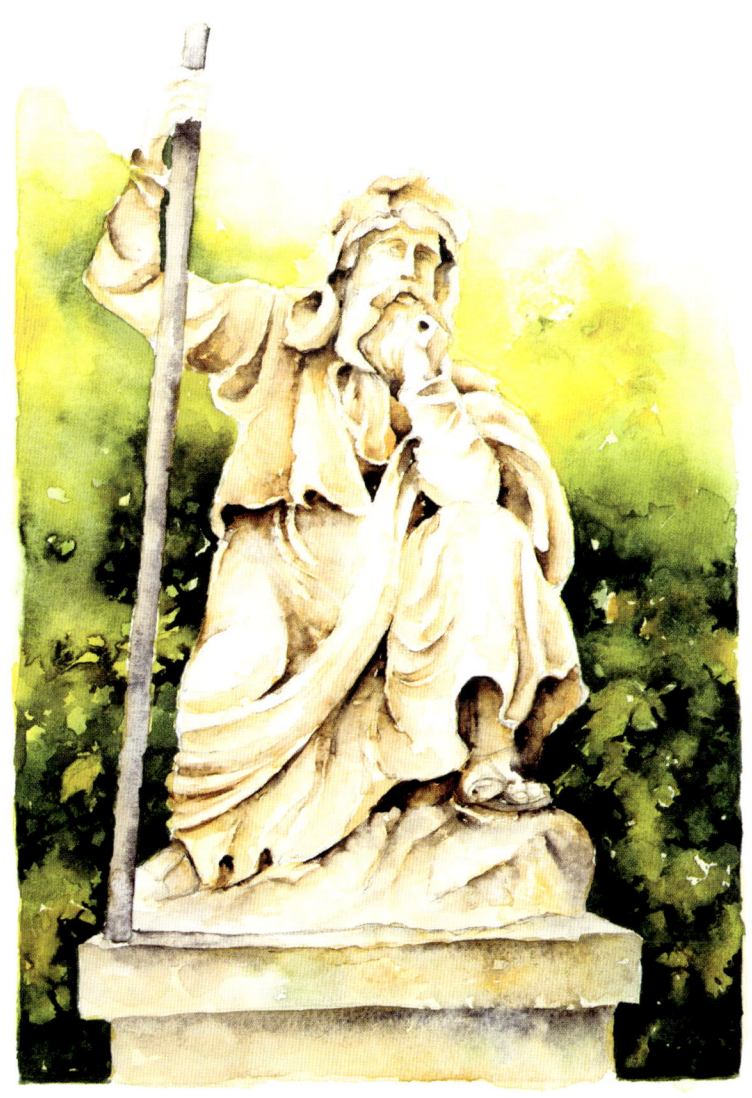

Statues feature in many city parks. I started with a light wash of yellow ocher for warmth and to create an undertone. I then began to develop the folds and creases by adding raw sienna. I created the deepest shadows inside the folds using a mixture of ultramarine blue and burnt umber, applied to dry paper and then washed outward using a wet brush to diffuse the edge of the shadow. This is a good technique to use when painting curved surfaces.

Water Features

Water features may, or may not, contain water. Where they do, it is best treated as glass—use the environmental colors (see Introduction) to establish the basic tone, and then use this color to work around some pure white paper to suggest the way in which light catches any moving water.

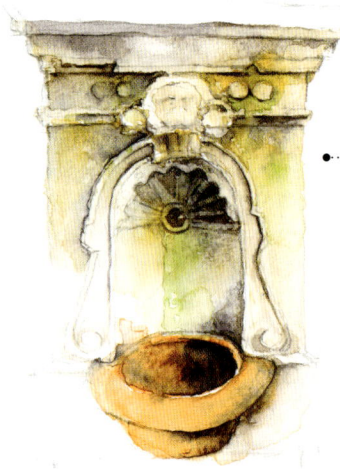

Fountains show signs of staining and damp. The softness of this is best recorded with a mix of sap green and cobalt blue. This mix is applied to wet paper to gain the most effective result.

The gentle trickle of water from this fountain was created as a negative shape, painting around the vertical shape, leaving pure white paper showing.

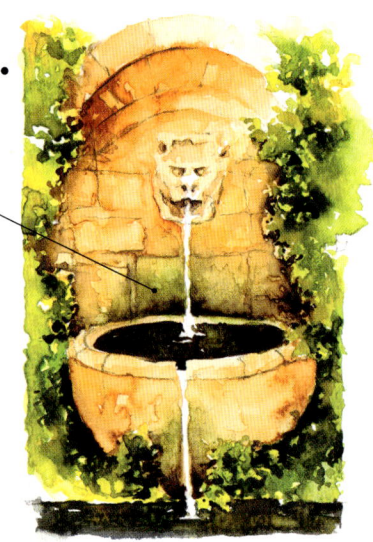

Sap green added to damp paper to create mold effect.

Dark greens make the light stone feature stand forward.

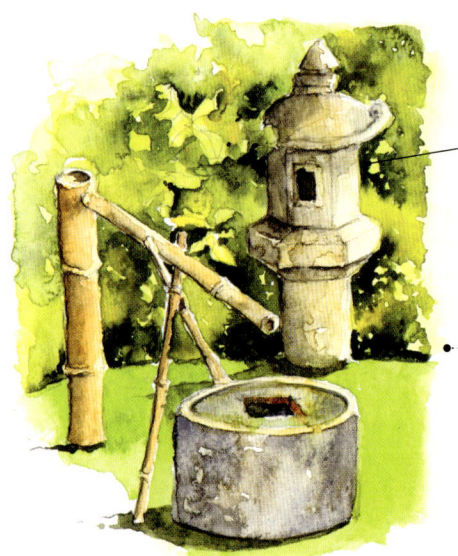

These bamboo poles were painted using yellow ocher for the warmth, and burnt umber for the shadow. The shadows that emphasize the hollow nature of the bamboo require a light touch of paint.

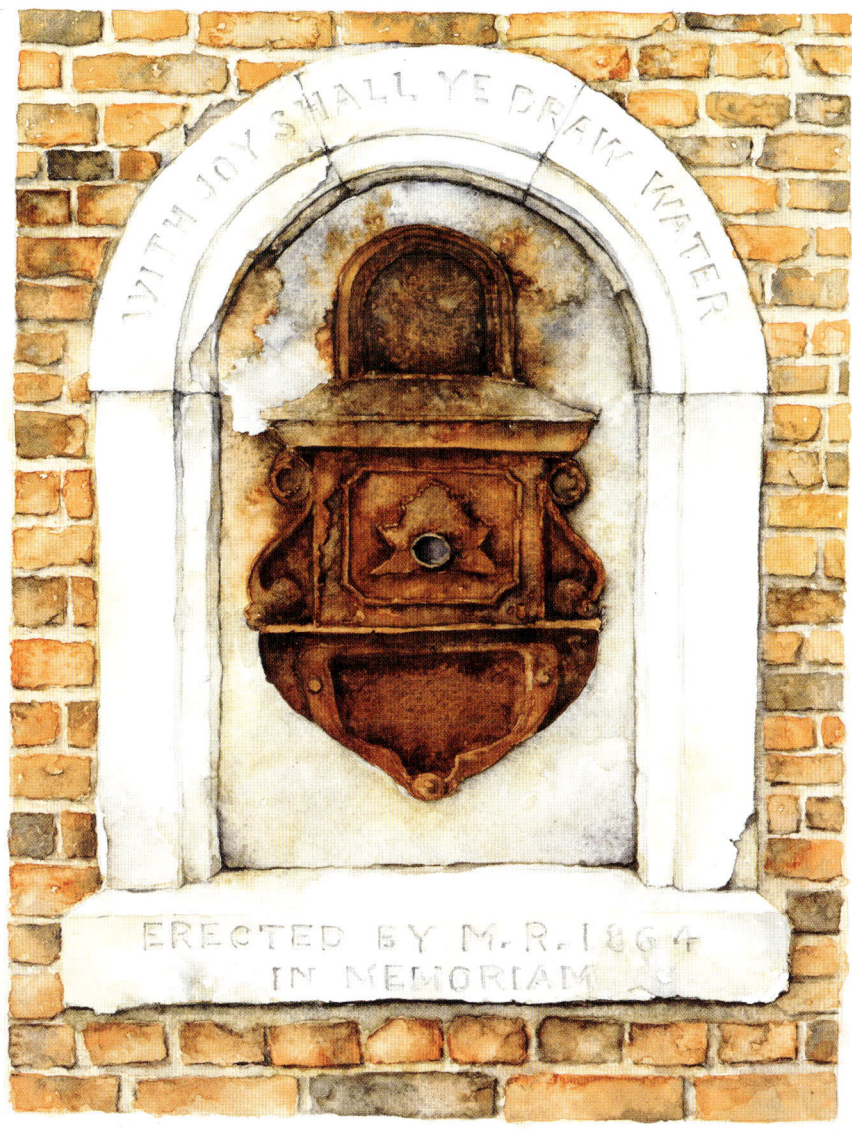

The carved wording was created by running a fine line of burnt umber and ultramarine blue along the "inside" of each letter—at the top and one side only—using a small brush with a fine tip. This was then pulled downward with the same brush, but this time holding just a little water to dilute and soften the slight shadows.

Ponds and Lakes

Ponds and lakes don't often contain moving water, except when fed by streams or waterfalls. This means that the still water will reflect the surroundings. Painting these scenes requires a judicious application of paint. If you apply the reflections to the lake when the paper is wet it will run uncontrollably. So, wait until your paper is damp, then add the colors and let them bleed softly.

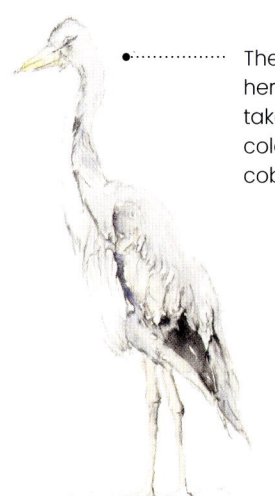

The monochrome nature of this heron means that shape and tone take precedence over color. The colors used were ultramarine blue, cobalt blue, and burnt umber.

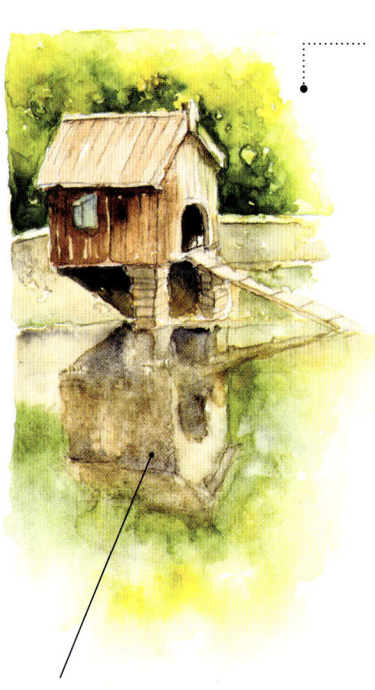

Reflections are often not exact mirror images—it is sometimes the underneath of an object that is reflected. Always look carefully when painting bridges, for example.

Paint onto damp paper to create light reflections.

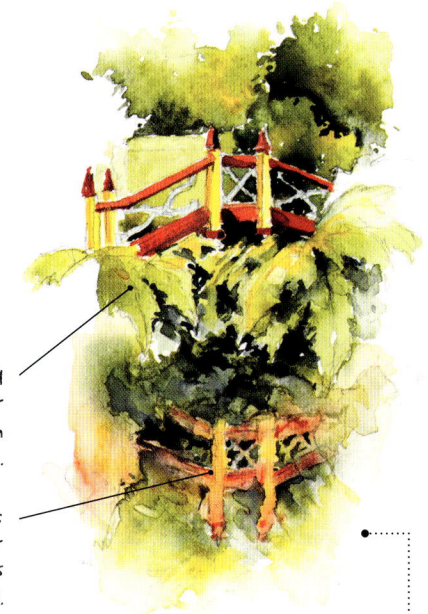

Light leaves stand out against darker leaves, creating a sense of height.

Reflected colors are usually lighter than the objects being reflected.

Paint reflections in still water onto damp paper, once a soft sheen appears. This will keep the paint roughly where you place it, and the edges will soften as the paper dries. Keep your paints for the land wet and active as you work.

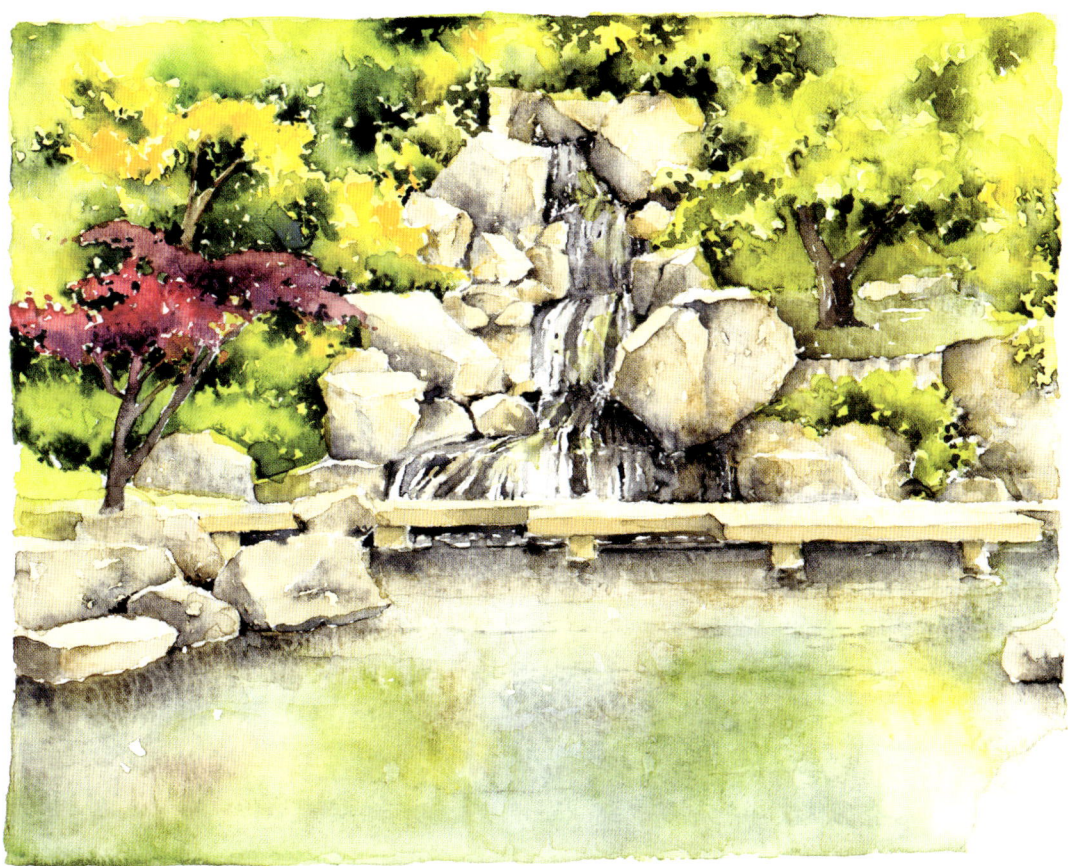

The still water in the foreground of this pond sits in marked contrast to the tumbling waterfall behind it. Both elements require different techniques. The foreground of the pond was painted by soaking the paper and, as it dried, applying a very watery mixture of all the background colors. The paper was then tilted, allowing the wet paint to bleed downward onto the damp paper. The falling water was painted onto dry paper, working around lines of white paper to represent the sense of movement.

Benches and Bins

Park benches and bins may not be the most inspirational subjects in themselves, but look for the shadows they cast. Slotted bins and seats allow the light to filter through them, creating a whole series of positive and negative shapes that can be very satisfying to record.

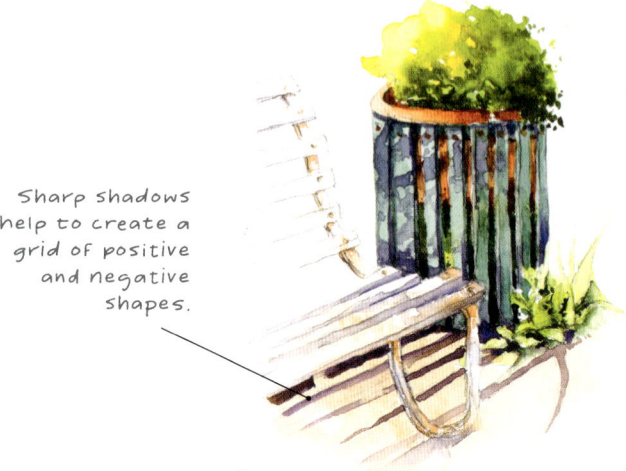

Sharp shadows help to create a grid of positive and negative shapes.

The "raked" light creates the subject here—the shadows. Always look around and underneath slatted seats and bins as a wealth of shapes and patterns can often be found in the form of shadows.

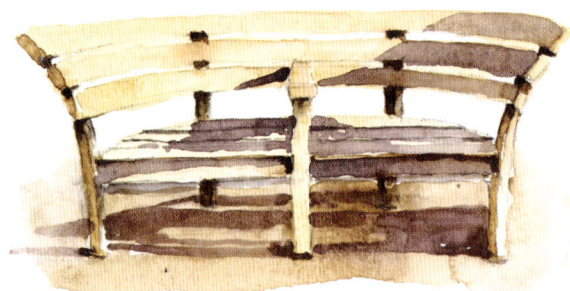

Benches with slats for seats create thin shadows on the ground. Check the position of the light to ensure that they are going in the right direction.

I chose this subject for the effect created by the sunlight shining through the slats of the cage. The cast shadow was made by mixing a touch of dioxazine purple with yellow ocher and raw sienna, painted onto a dry surface.

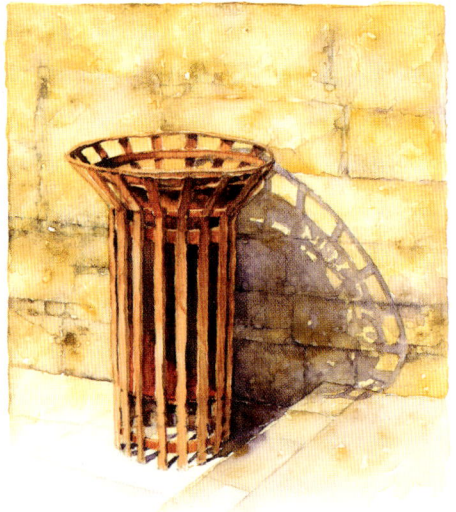

EXAMPLE: PARK BENCH

STEP ONE

Wash raw sienna across all wood—tree and bench—as well as the paving stones.

STEP TWO

Paint the slats of the bench with a watery mix of burnt umber and ultramarine blue. When this is dry, apply a stronger mix to the tree.

STEP THREE

Finally, darken the ultramarine blue mix by adding more burnt umber, and paint the shading on the seat slats to create a sense of form.

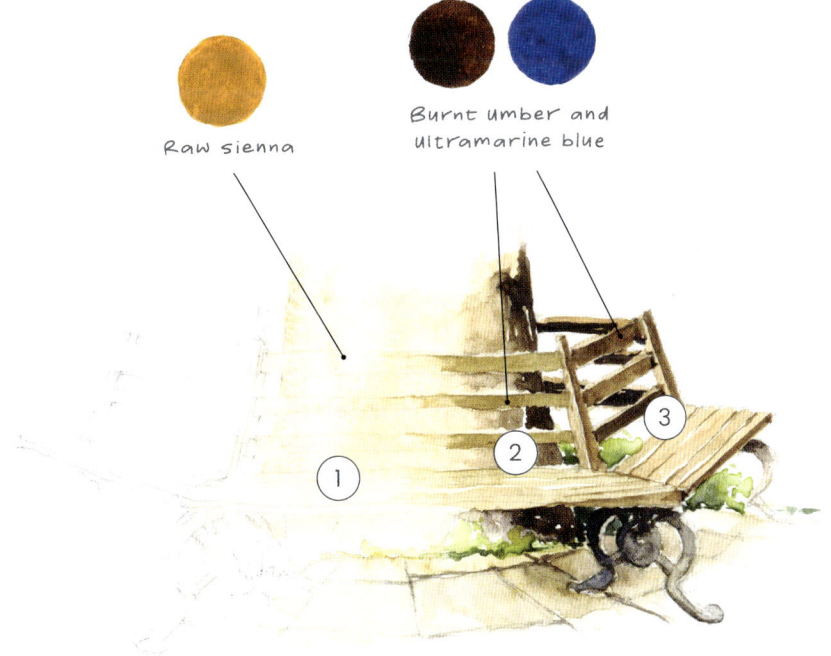

Raw sienna

Burnt umber and
ultramarine blue

Park Gates

Although park gates mark the boundaries of these public areas, it is sometimes the gateposts that offer visual interest. It is also worth looking for some smaller details within these—chains and padlocks, for example, can provide some worthwhile sketchbook studies.

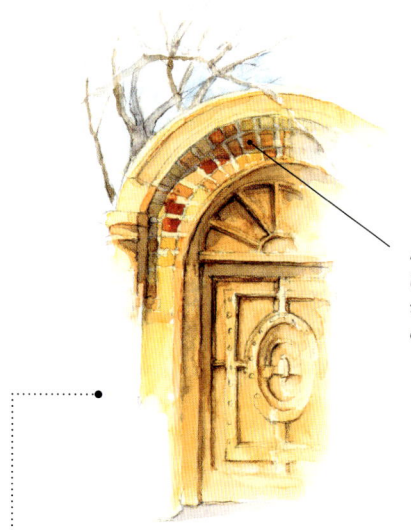

Always check the lines of shadows— some will be curved, others straight.

Once inside a park, other doorways can often be found. The idea of a door to a "secret garden" is appealing.

Rusty chains and locks on park gates are worth studying. Look for shadows on the chain links; these help a study to come alive on the page. Burnt sienna was the main color used here.

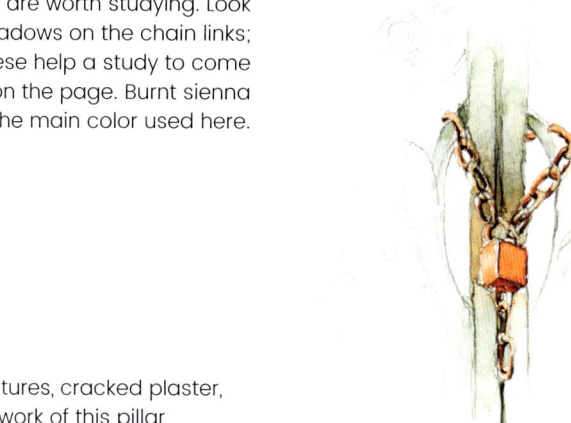

The decorative features, cracked plaster, and exposed brickwork of this pillar made it ideal for a study. The years of weathering evident on the stone were painted using a lot of water and a few washes of palette mud.

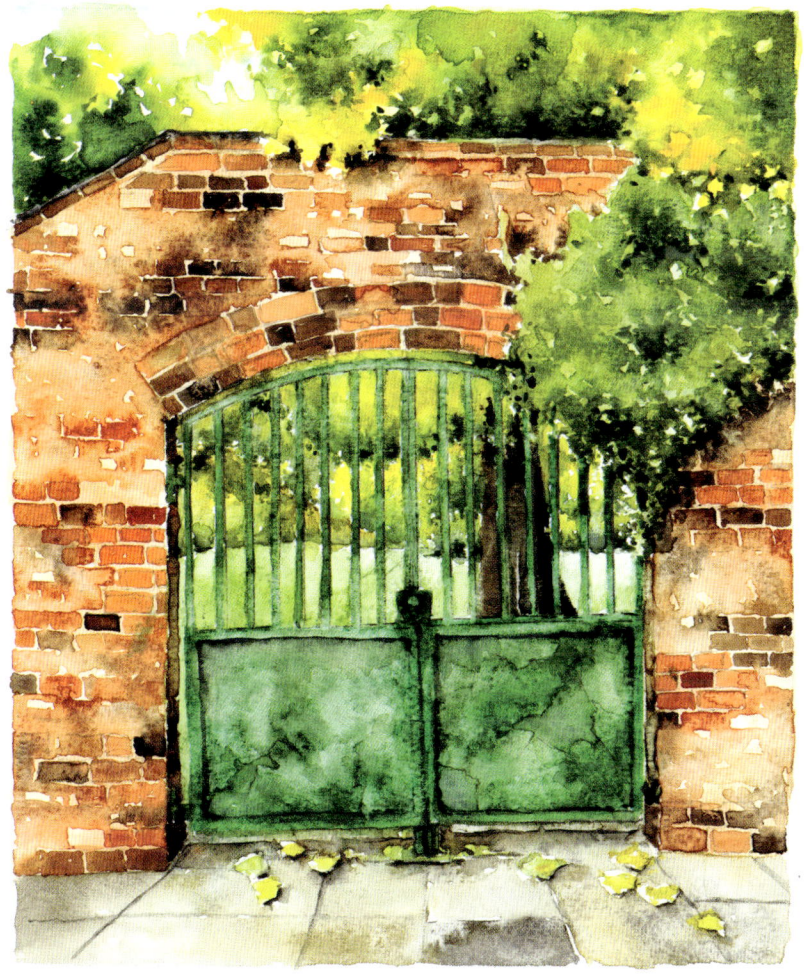

This park gate has been painted over so many times that the metal panels take on a near three-dimensional appearance. This effect is recreated by applying uneven washes to damp paper and not interfering in the drying process. The paint dries unevenly, creating patches of light and dark around a few watermarks.

Formal Gardens

The beauty of a formal garden layout often lies in the geometry and symmetry. Recording these can require a little attention to perspective—especially ensuring that parallel lines of bushes and decorative hedges appear to converge slightly as they move away from your viewpoint.

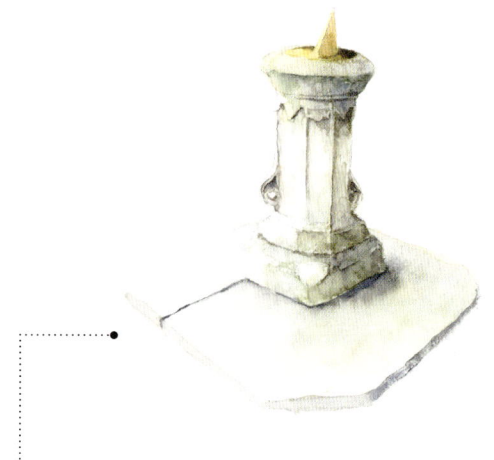

This sundial was created using varying dilutions of burnt umber and ultramarine blue. The green mold was achieved by dabbing on sap green while the gray paint was drying.

This sketch uses only one green (sap green) but two blues. Ultramarine blue was added to the bush, while cobalt blue was added to the planter.

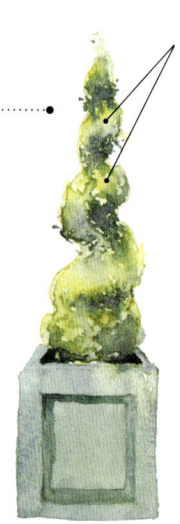

Highlights created by dropping water onto damp paint. This spreads, pushing the paint outward.

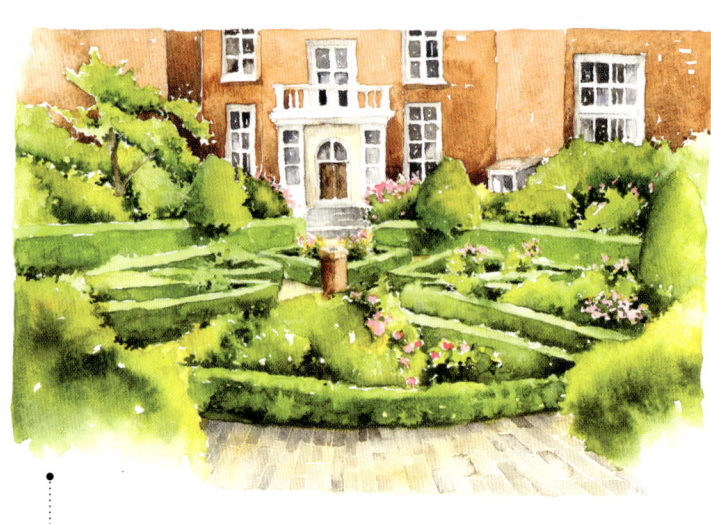

Formal gardens are based around simple geometry. The bushes and shrubs are "ordered," resulting in much harder shapes and shadows than you usually find in gardens. When so much green is required, it is important to seek out any flashes of color that can be found. These help to break up the solidity of the greenery.

EXAMPLE: GARDEN FEATURE

STEP ONE

Apply a watery wash of sap green across the entire study.

STEP TWO

Add a touch of burnt umber and cadmium yellow to sap green for the main tone of the clipped hedge.

STEP THREE

Add ultramarine blue to the hedge mix and use it to create the darker areas, including the near corner of the triangle.

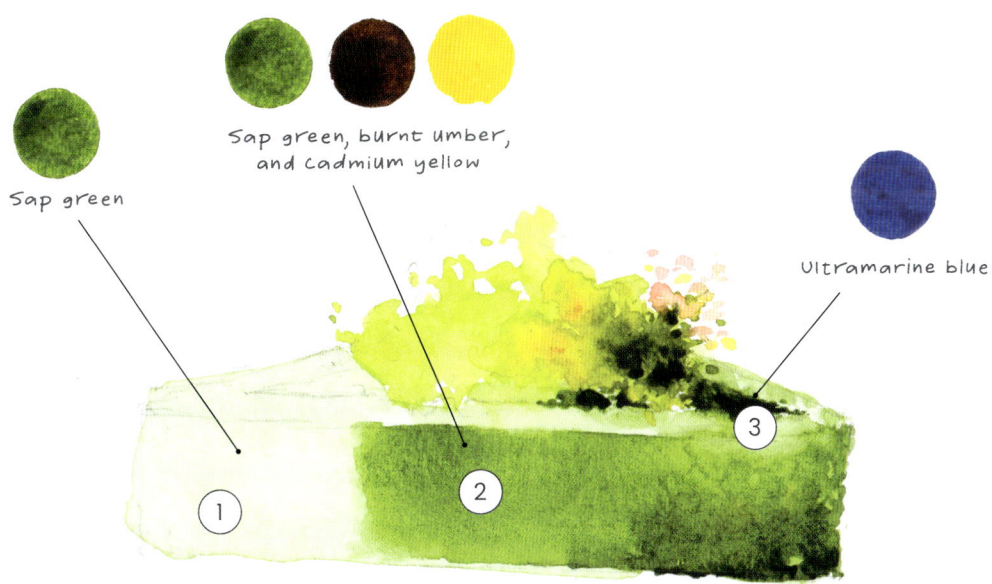

Sap green

Sap green, burnt umber, and cadmium yellow

Ultramarine blue

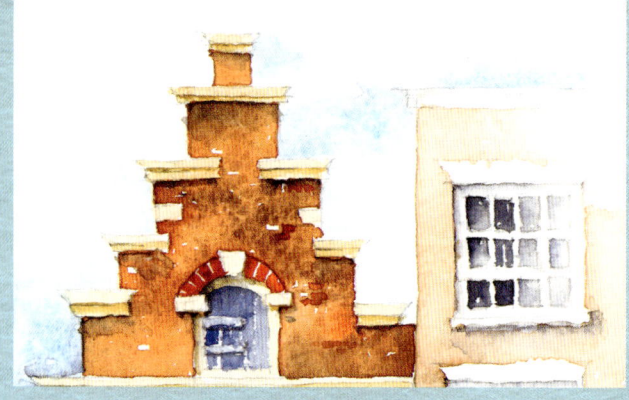

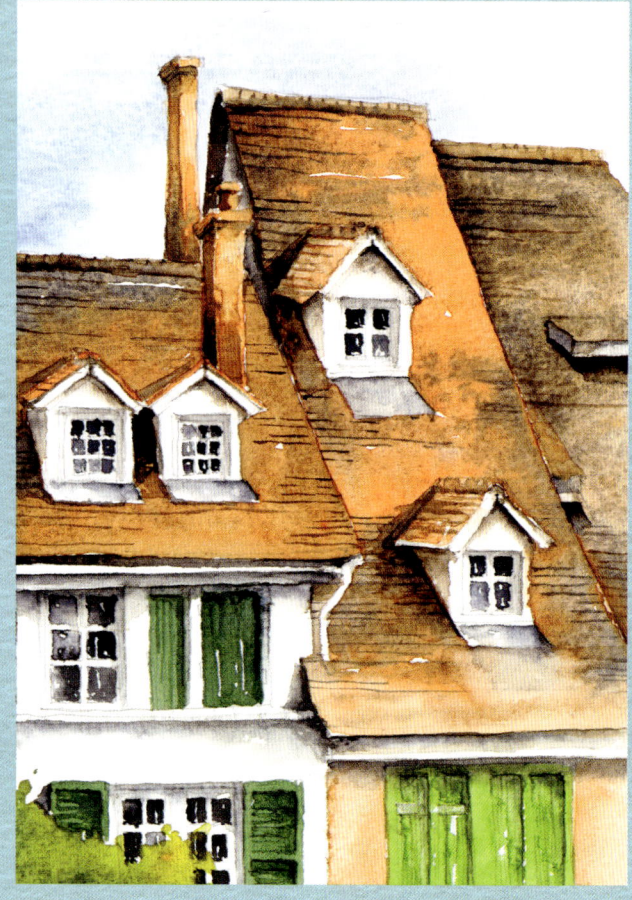

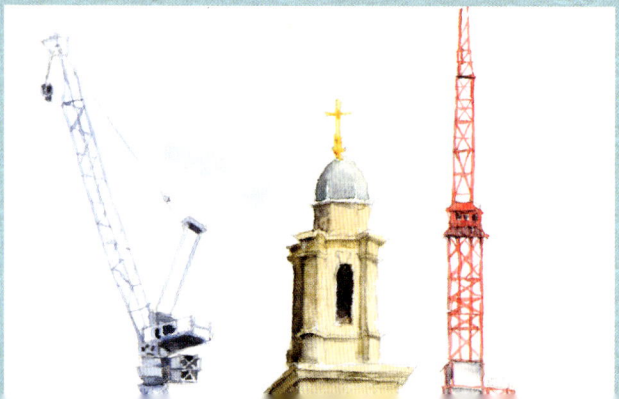

CHAPTER FIVE:
Skylines

So far, we have explored looking down and looking ahead. This chapter aims to encourage you to look up at urban structures to enable you to gain a whole new perspective on buildings. Chimneys and flues are usually the first elements that we look for above our natural eyeline, but many other elements are worth exploring.

Flags and banners will often be seen hanging from the upper stories of buildings, breaking up the natural line of sight and providing much color and many shapes, whereas cranes and scaffolding will often be viewed above the rooftops, providing a much more rigid and organized set of images than the soft unpredictability of flags caught in a breeze.

Rooftops need careful observation—it is neither possible nor desirable to attempt to paint individual tiles in rows. They need to be "suggested" in exactly the same way as bricks in walls.

Flags and Banners

Flags and banners move in a breeze, and wrap themselves around each other. Pay close attention to any initial drawing, watching how the designs or patterns in a flag cross over each other and how they cast shadows on other areas. This can add a whole new dimension to their appearance.

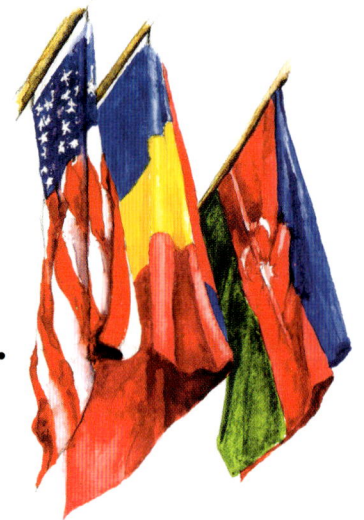

Flags flown from buildings with some level of official status are often well kept and maintain the sharpness and clarity of their colors.

Don't be afraid to let your colors bleed when painting weather-worn flags. This aids the aging effect.

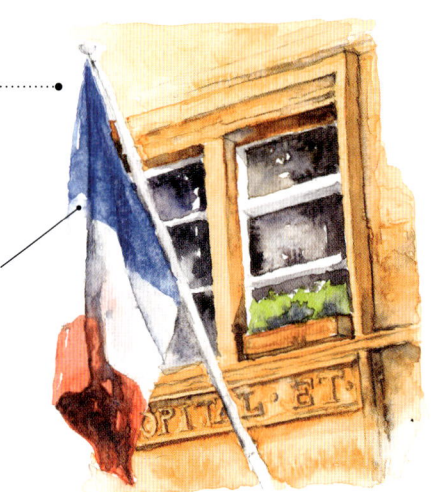

Color bleeds can offer the impression of material left out in all weathers.

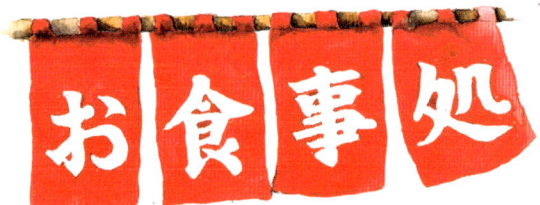

Try to observe movement to create a more realistic study.

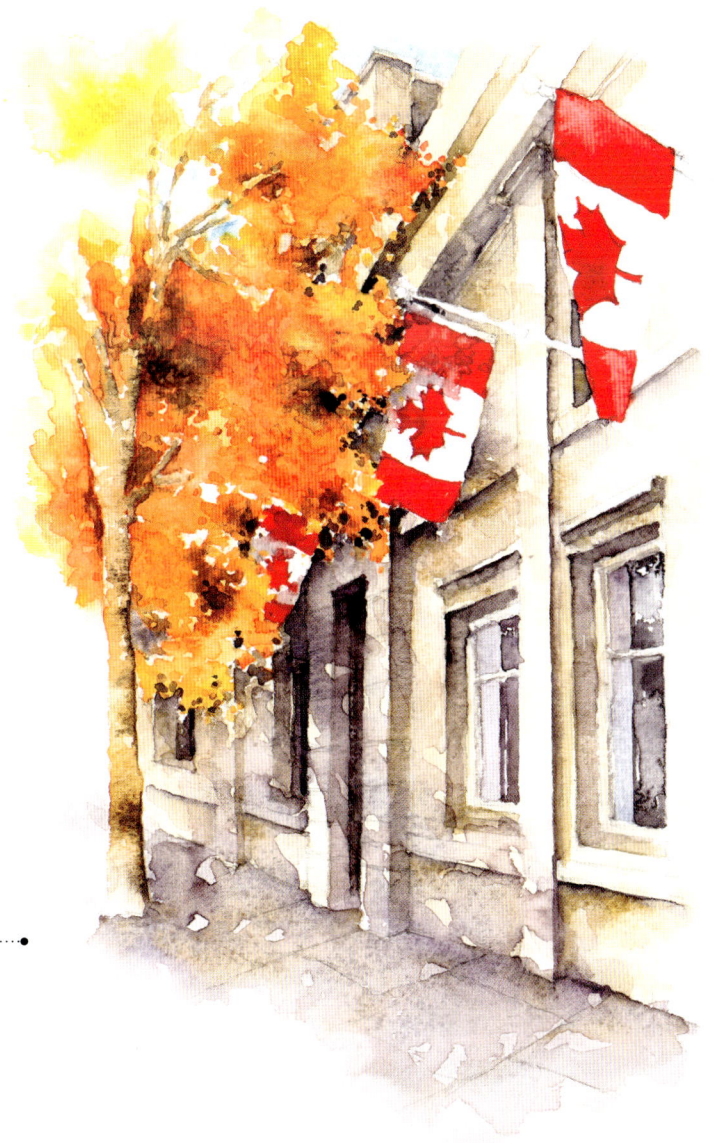

I used a little bit of artistic trickery in this composition by slightly overemphasizing the perspective lines. This can have the effect of drawing the viewer's eye to the flags flying from the top half of the building as they appear to retreat a little more sharply into the distance than might actually have been the case.

Dormer Windows

Dormer windows are set high up in the roofs of buildings, and they come in a real array of shapes and sizes. As with balconies, these are best recorded from a relatively high vantage point— a window or balcony—as this allows you to see the interesting tiles or ridges of the tops of these windows.

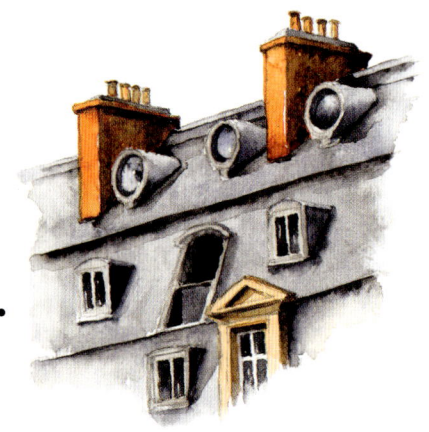

These circular dormer windows are painted in the way that cone shapes would normally be.

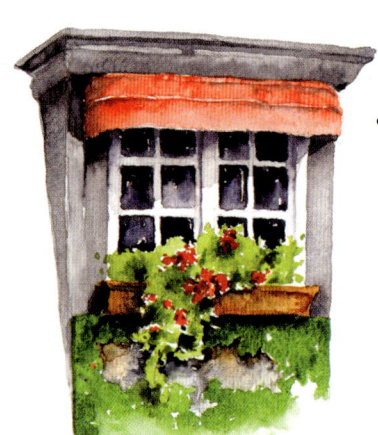

This narrow dormer window is set into a surround of gray concrete, painted using a mix of burnt umber and ultramarine blue, which was applied in various levels of dilution.

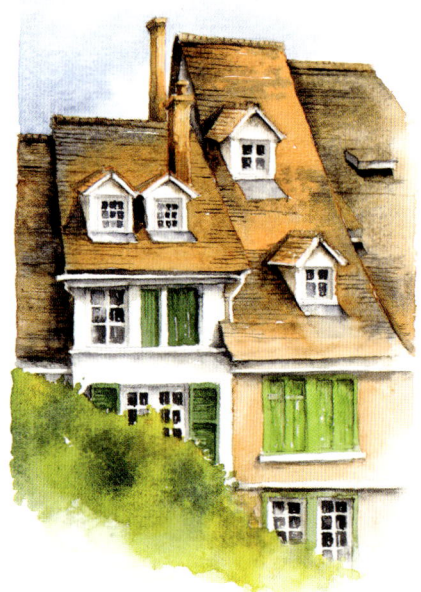

This scene of dormer windows set into very steeply pitched roofs relies heavily on the shadows cast from both the dormers and the tiled roofs. These angular shadows are necessary to make the dormers stand out from the roof, aiding the three-dimensional effect.

EXAMPLE: DORMER WINDOWS

STEP ONE

Use a watery mix of raw sienna and burnt sienna to establish the base tones of the roof and allow to dry fully.

STEP TWO

Paint shadows depending upon the strength of the daylight.

STEP THREE

Work onto the base tone, painting darker burnt sienna and leaving gaps to represent light catching the lines of tiles. Sharpen the lines of the shadow using a darker mix than that used in Step 2.

Raw sienna and
burnt sienna

Ultramarine blue and
dioxazine purple

Burnt sienna

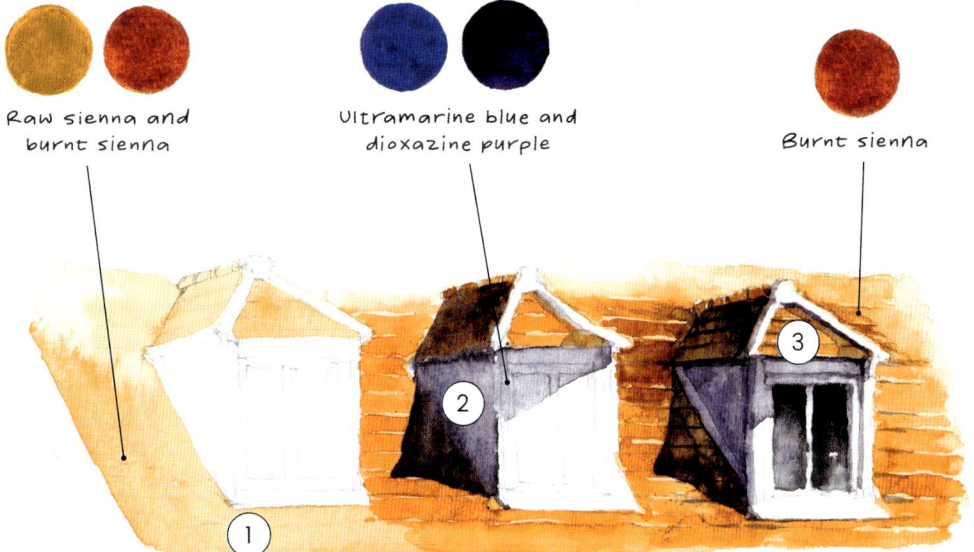

Chimneys and Flues

Chimneys and flues tend to have limited building materials—mainly brick or cement. Given their purpose, they are rarely clean, often being covered in soot or grime from their smoky heights over a period of years. I mix some burnt umber with ultramarine blue, and pick up any other colors used in the palette to paint these.

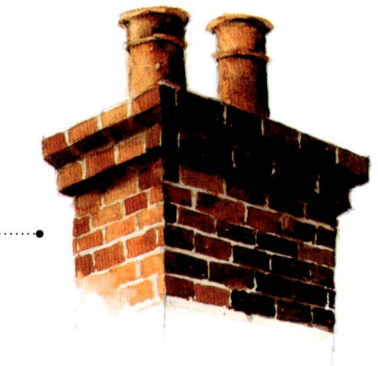

Observe the angle of a chimney stack. Use a more diluted mix for one side, and darker colors for the other, giving you a hard edge between the two.

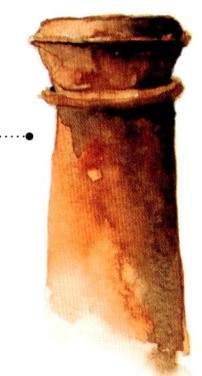

To create the curve on a chimney pot, dampen the pot with a watery mix of the lightest color. As it starts to dry, apply a less diluted mix to the shaded part and allow the paint to bleed "around" the pot.

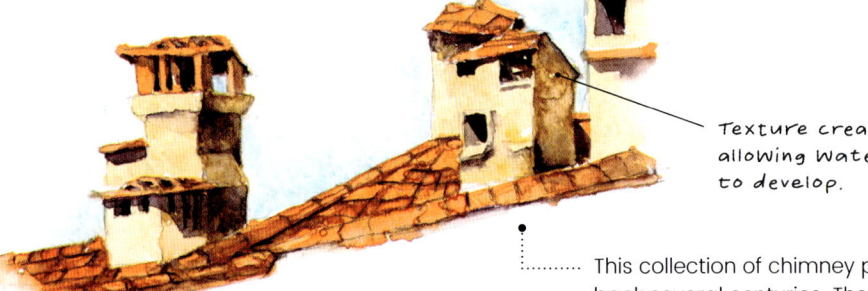

Texture created by allowing watermarks to develop.

This collection of chimney pots appears to date back several centuries. They need the blue sky wash behind them to make them really stand out.

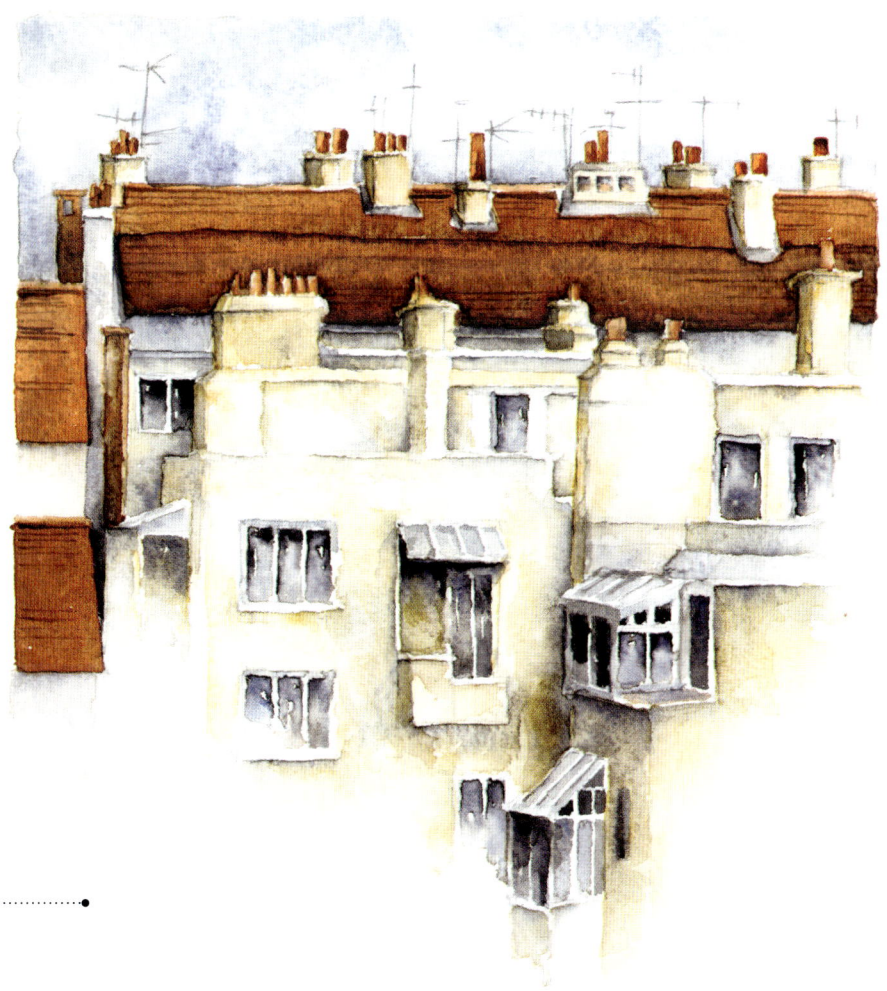

This composition contains a profusion of chimney pots. Some simply sit on a rooftop with the supporting flue hidden within the building. Others have their supporting structure clearly in view. Sometimes it can be both the covered up and the exposed that really make a good picture.

TIP

Even on dull days you will see shadows—ensure that they are always on the same side and of a similar tone.

Tiles and Slates

It is really neither practical, nor even desirable, to record every tile or slate observed on roofs. Suggestion, therefore, is the key to success. This can be achieved by selecting a few "positive" shapes of tiles to paint on to an underwash, or leaving a few "negative" tile shapes—or, ideally a combination of the two. But not too many—less is more in this case!

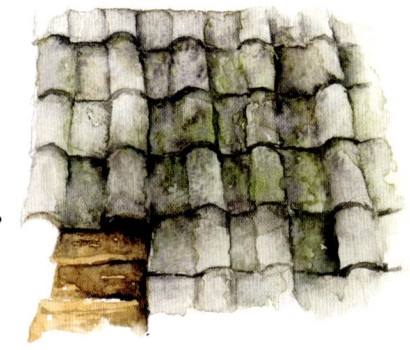

Urban decay and neglect can cause structural problems that can be a delight for the artist. The appeal in this study is the green patina on the tiles.

Very few tiles are painted individually. Dark and light colors are dropped onto the paper and allowed to dry freely, creating shapes that suggest tiles.

The shapes are created by allowing different paints to dry freely.

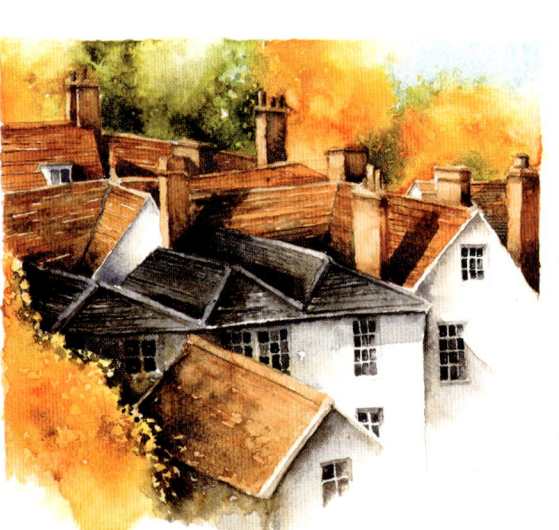

It is not possible to paint individual roof tiles in a scene like this, so the technique of suggestion needs to be employed.

EXAMPLE: ROOF TILES

STEP ONE

Establish the base tone for the set of tiles, using the lightest color you can see—this will remain the lightest color.

STEP TWO

Run a line of the main color seen in the tiles along the shaded side—make sure you use enough paint to be able to pull it across the vertical line of tiles using a wet brush.

STEP THREE

Next use a small brush to "draw" the shadow color underneath each tile.

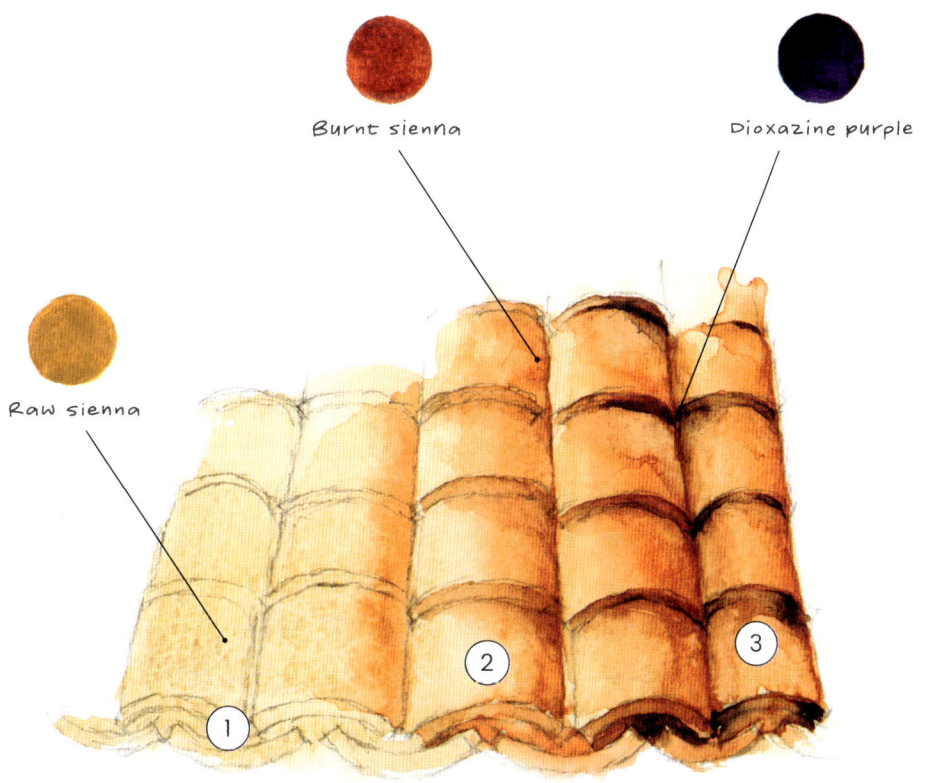

Burnt sienna

Dioxazine purple

Raw sienna

Scaffolding and Cranes

The "mechanics" of industrial scale building dominate the skylines of so many cities, and can provide a fascinating and complex series of vertical shapes as they puncture the horizon and rise high above our eyeline set at ground level. The construction element of the urban landscape is as valuable as the historic and the picturesque.

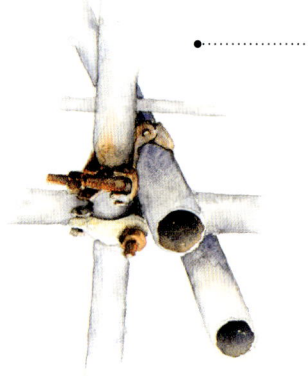

A study of a small section of scaffolding can give you all the information you need regarding color, shape, and structure.

Observation of shadows helps to define these rigid structures.

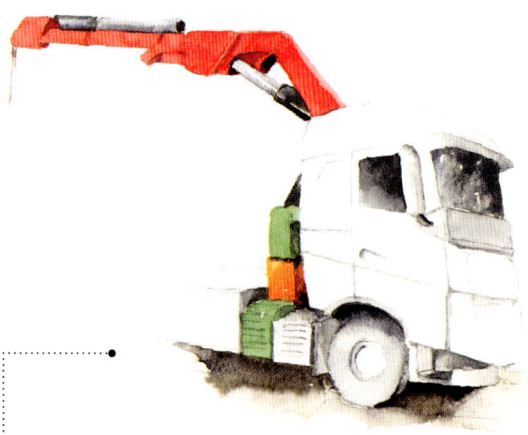

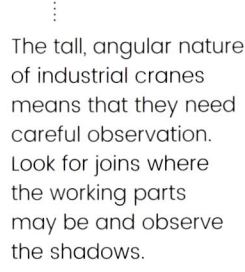

The tall, angular nature of industrial cranes means that they need careful observation. Look for joins where the working parts may be and observe the shadows.

A sketch provides you with information about your subject. Here, I was looking at the physical and visual balance between the truck and the crane. Too much detail behind the cab would have been a distraction.

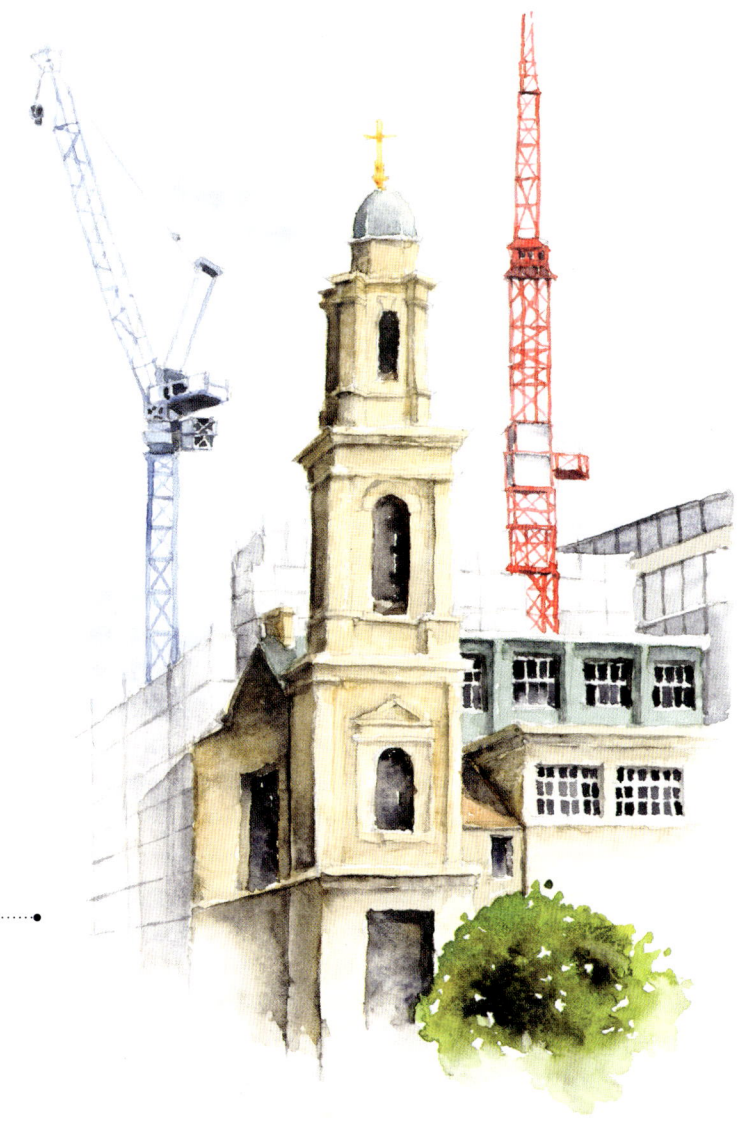

The skylines of towns and cities are often punctured by high-rise cranes thrusting into the skies and creating a whole new vista. They can become the focal point of a composition. Having made sure that the rest of the painting is dry, I usually "draw" these structures using a fine brush and limited amounts of paint as the very last action.

Towers and Turrets

Towers and turrets can be an integral part of some urban buildings, yet many can appear as stand-alone structures. Even though these structures may not be fully curved or round, they will usually require some level of graduated shading to prevent them from looking flat.

It would be difficult to record the impact of this white tower without the inclusion of the sky. It forms a backdrop for the tower to be viewed against.

This array of towers and turrets required close attention to the varying levels of light and shade.

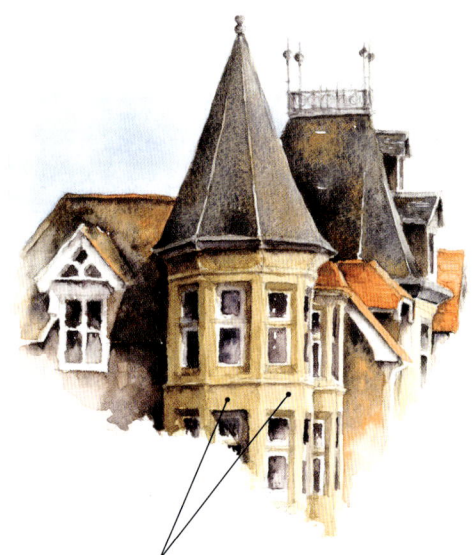

These colors involved much mixing. Raw sienna, light red, Naples yellow, and yellow ocher were all deployed to record this old structure.

Graduated tones aid the impression of solidity and three dimensions on a flat surface.

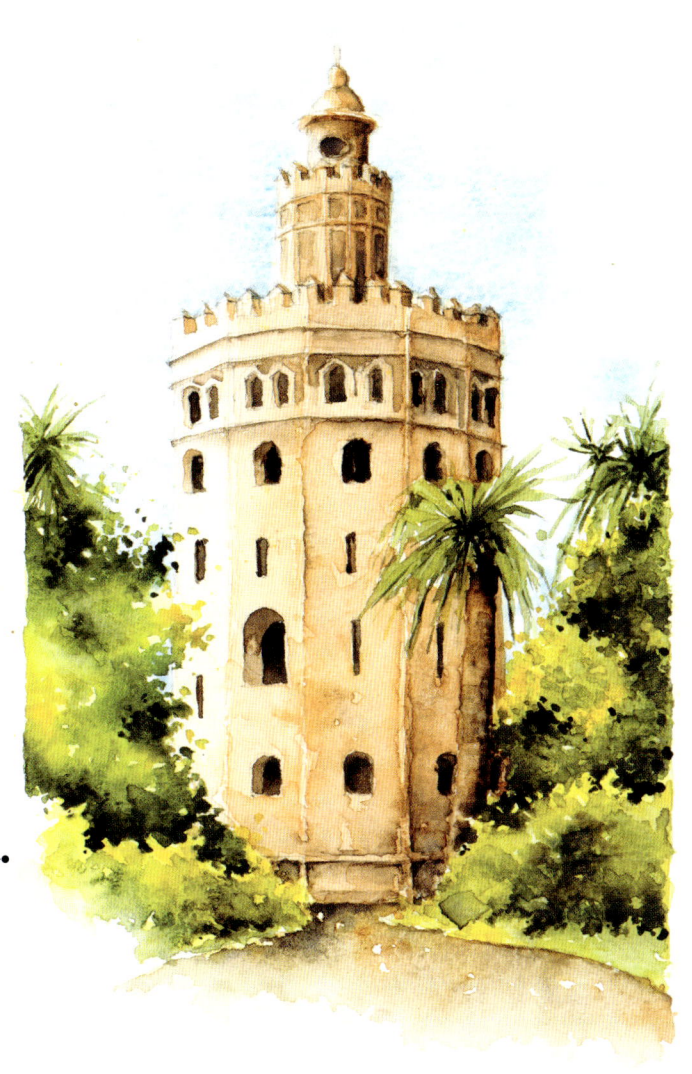

The complex perspective of this multifaceted tower required a lot of initial drawing, but I was determined not to lose sight of the fact that I intended to make a painting. A few perspective lines that might go astray are readily sacrificed for the tones, colors, and textures of a painting.

Gables

Gables are architectural features that are frequently seen in the lowlands of northern Europe. They often form an A-shape above the main walls of buildings and stand proudly against the sky, punctuating the skyline.

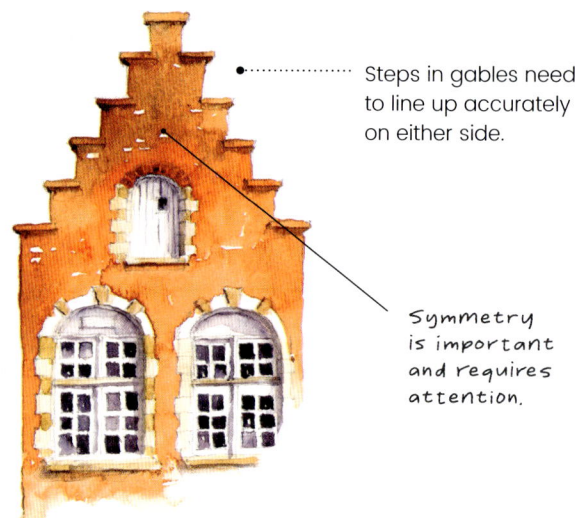

Steps in gables need to line up accurately on either side.

Symmetry is important and requires attention.

In this study, the brick window surrounds help to give definition to the windows set into the building.

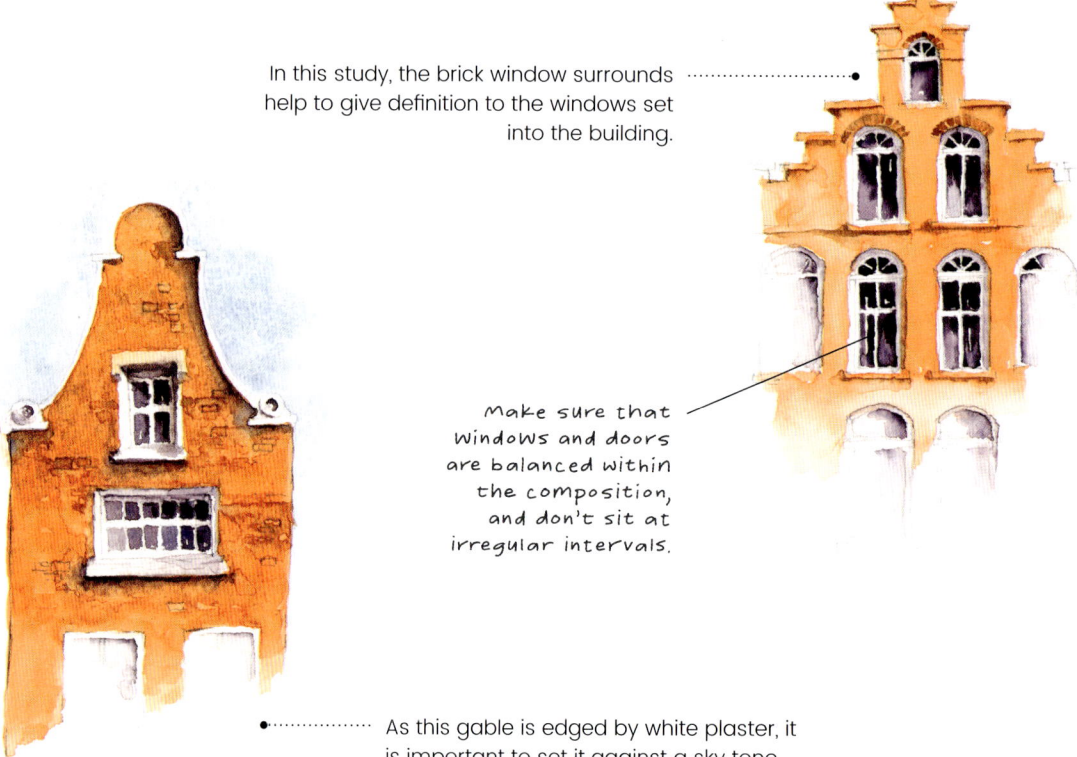

Make sure that windows and doors are balanced within the composition, and don't sit at irregular intervals.

As this gable is edged by white plaster, it is important to set it against a sky tone.

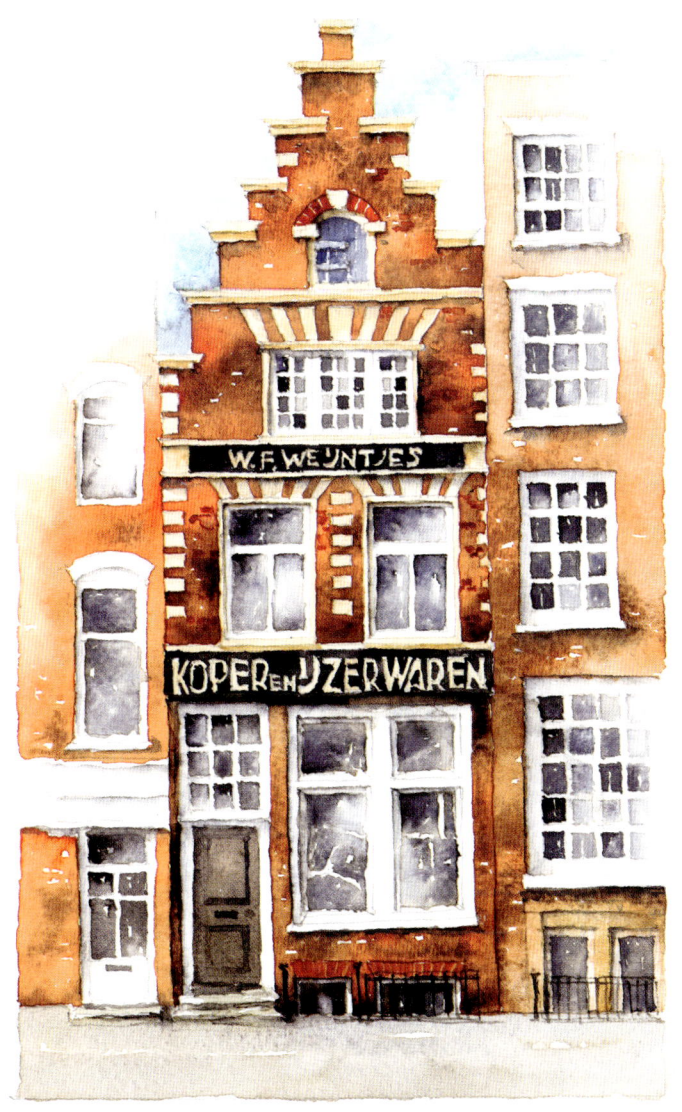

The highly distinctive gable on this building gives it its identity. The geometry of a building like this is important when you first start to establish the basic shapes, but don't be a slave to structural accuracy.

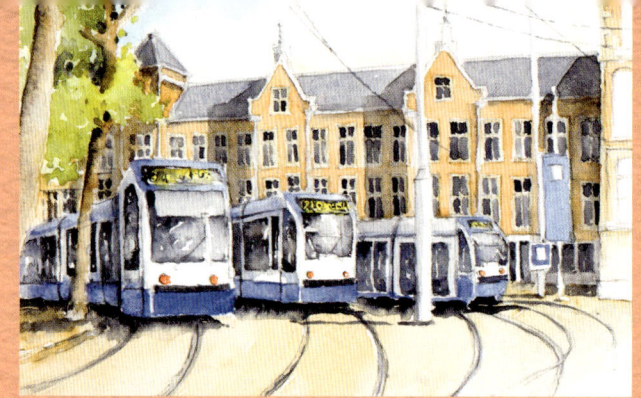

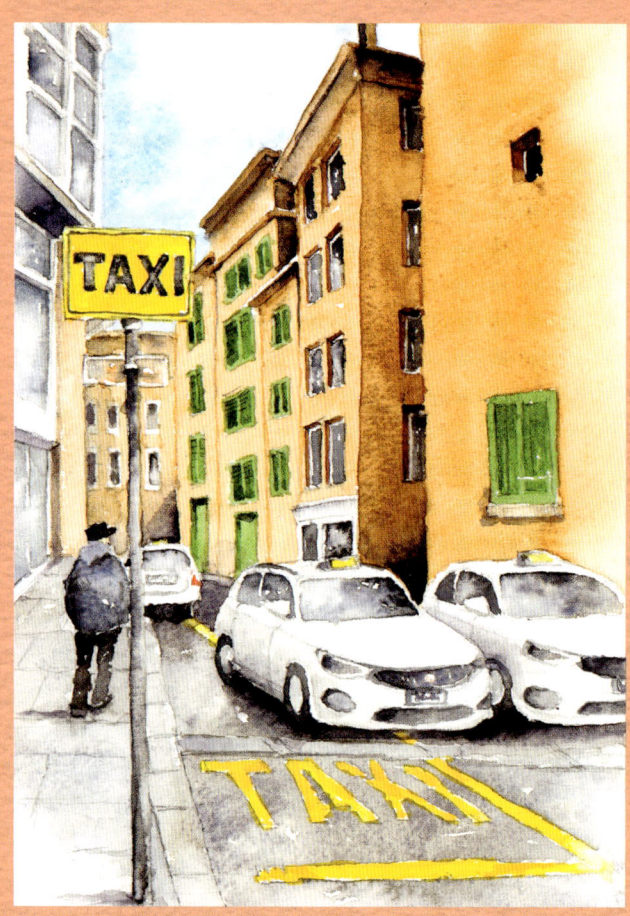

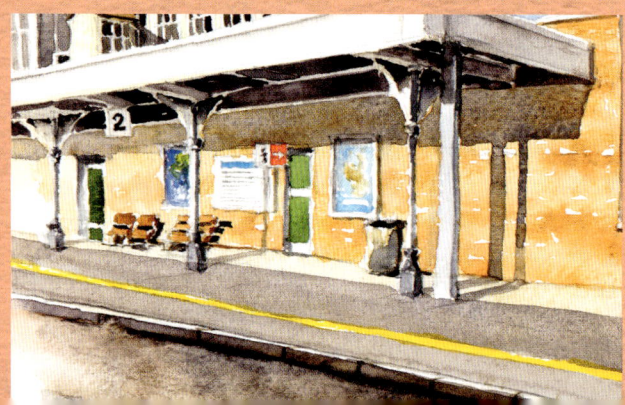

CHAPTER SIX:
Transportation

Transportation is a key aspect of urban life—be it public transportation such as buses, taxis, trams, and trains, or the type of transportation that keeps a city running. These can range from the trucks that keep businesses and industries alive, to the emergency vehicles that help to maintain order and respond to life-threatening situations.

You will also find rivers, canals, and estuaries leading into urban centers, allowing access to river transportation, barges, and ferries. The very nature of transportation is that it moves, making it particularly difficult to record. My suggestion is to seek out sites where vehicles are at rest for a while—taxi ranks, docks, bus and train stations. Here, you will have a few minutes to make sketches and studies.

Color is a major feature of transportation—red buses, yellow taxis, and sky and sea blue tones so often used for ferries.

Trains and Stations

Stations are busy, transitory places full of speed, bustle, and a general sense of urgency. Finding somewhere out of the way to sit and record some of the many subjects can be tricky, but there are usually seats available. Smaller stations are probably better if you wish to record a wider scene, leaving the larger terminuses for sketching only.

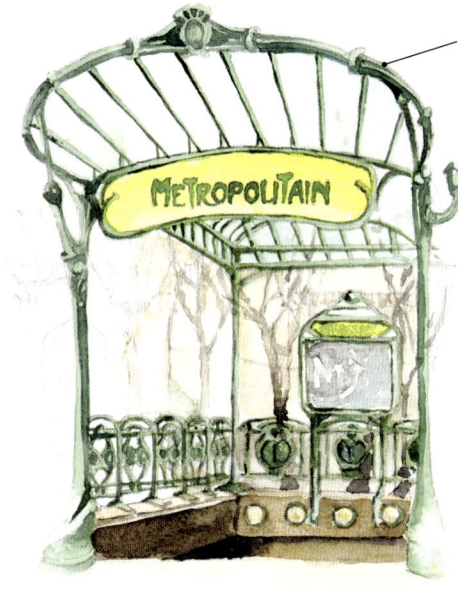

Shadows push the lighter structures forward.

This wrought-iron station structure would appear flat without using a darker green to push the lighter greens forward.

Break up reflections in large glass features by painting around white paper—this suggests light.

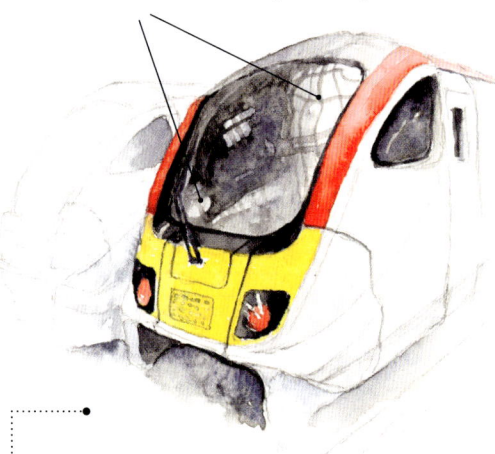

Modern trains are built with a lot of glass. The curvature often allows the structure of the railway station to be reflected.

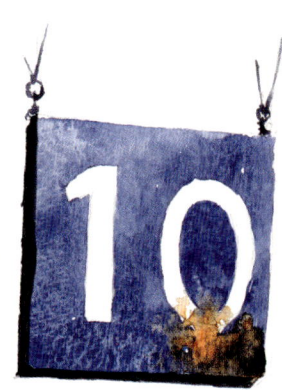

The main color of this rusting platform sign is ultramarine blue, with just a touch of burnt sienna for the rust.

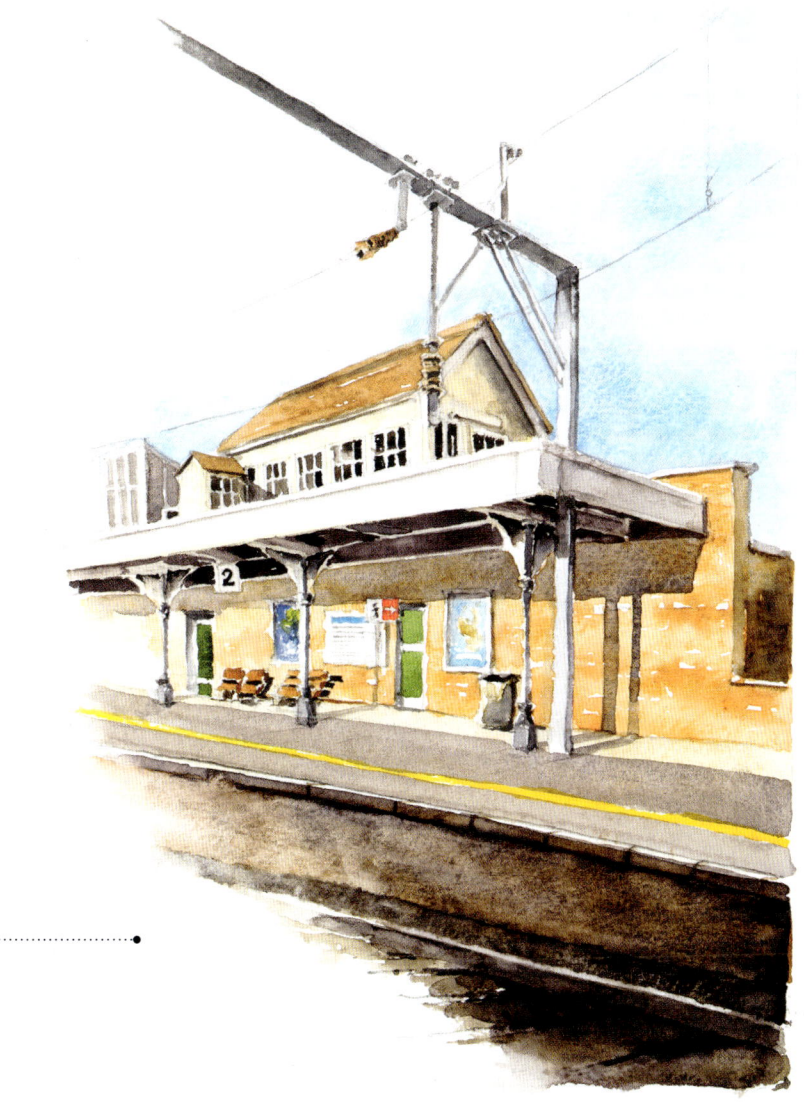

One of the trickiest decisions to make when planning a composition of any transport hub is what to leave out. Railway stations are complex places with a wealth of infrastructure. Here, I chose to sandwich the platform between the overhead lines and the rail tracks—but only just. The tracks are suggested rather than featured.

Taxis and Carriages

Taxi ranks and stations have much in common—they are busy places with people in a hurry passing through them. Seek out the places where the drivers rest, and be prepared to work quickly as they will soon be off again.

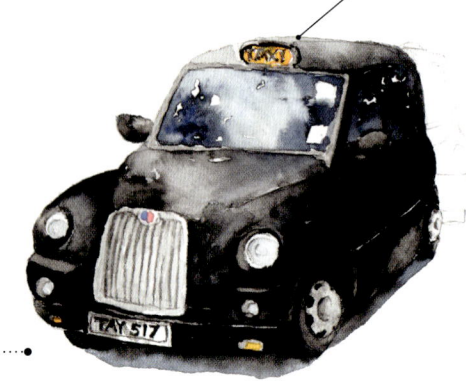

Reflected light achieved by dropping water onto a Payne's gray wash as it began to dry.

This sketch used black paint to record a London taxi effectively. Payne's gray brought a little visual relief to the intensity of the black paint.

Yellow taxis are subject to shadows and reflected light. The cabs in this study use more orange than yellow to create the curvature on the sides and front.

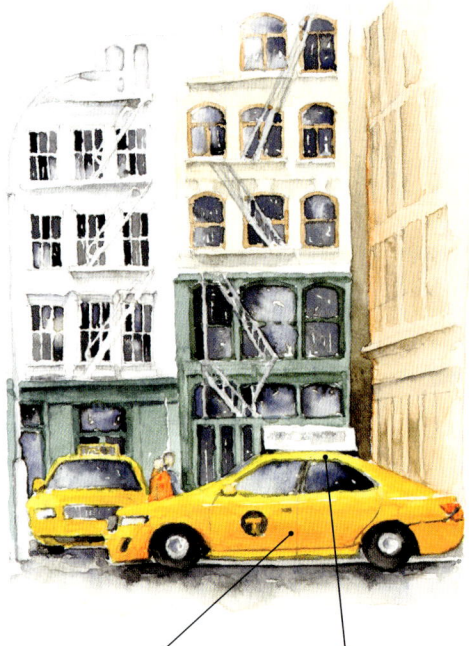

Darkest tones created by adding a touch of orange.

Lightest tone created by diluting yellow.

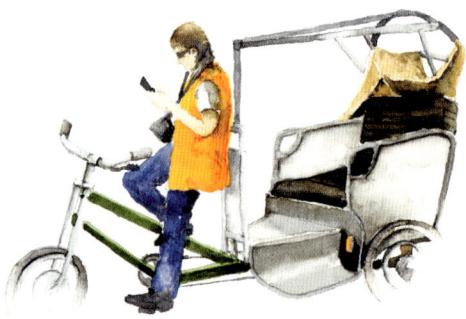

Modern rickshaws are usually solid metal. It is the human element that makes them worth a study.

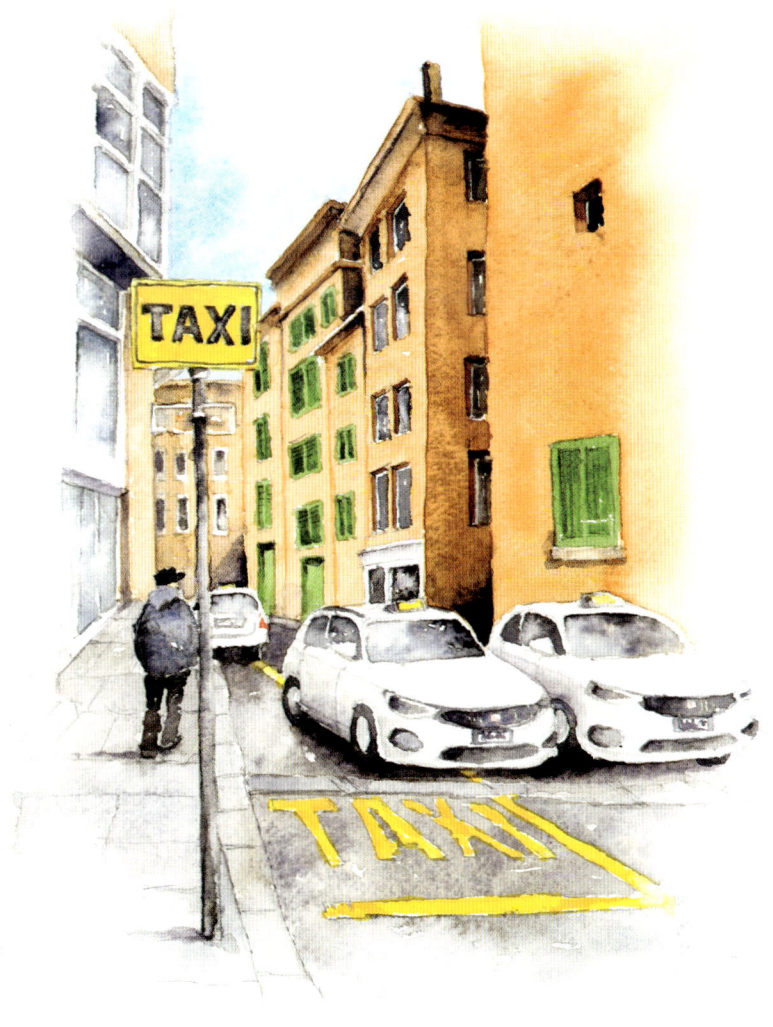

In this painting, the foreground is dictated by the relationship between the gray of the tarmac and the shading on the white cars—this requires a delicate balance, making sure that one gray isn't allowed to overwhelm another.

Buses and Trams

The means of moving the residents, workers, and visitors through the streets has become a major part of a city's identity, making these vehicles all the more interesting. They are, however, moving objects and therefore tricky to record. I suggest positioning yourself at a bus or tram station where they will always stop for a while.

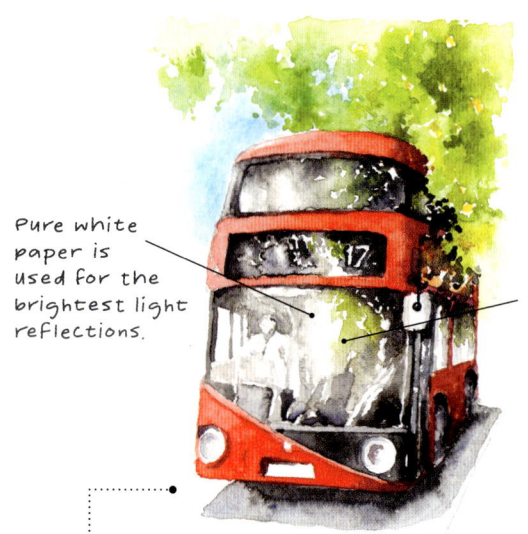

Pure white paper is used for the brightest light reflections.

Tree tones dropped onto window colors while wet.

Where so much glass is involved, including the environmental colors in the reflections is key.

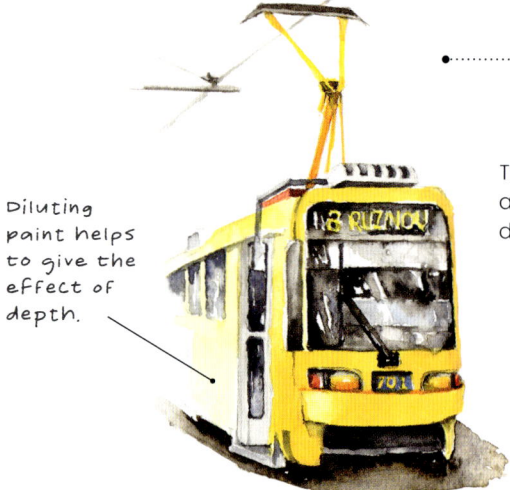

Diluting paint helps to give the effect of depth.

The wheels on trams are not always obvious. To anchor them to the ground often means using very dark shadow tones. Don't be afraid of "going dark."

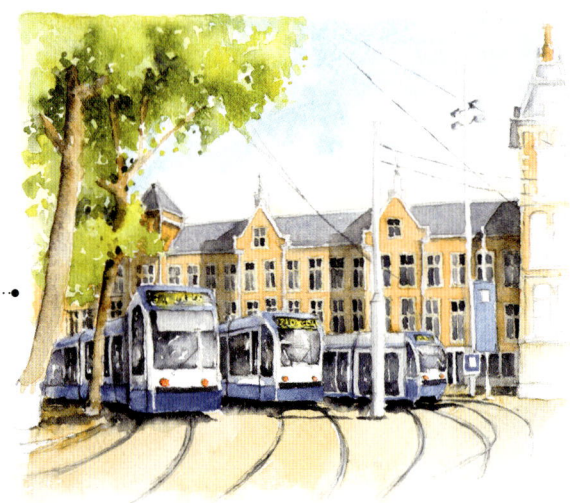

You can unify a busy painting by ensuring the right balance of light and shade. The sky tone is important in this process as this is where the light is coming from. The cerulean blue was washed onto damp paper, avoiding cloud areas, before any other paint was added.

EXAMPLE: BUS DETAILS

STEP ONE

Apply a wash of cadmium red to the drawing and allow it to dry. This color can be disappointing and not like the wet paint you washed on.

STEP TWO

If this is the case, add alizarin crimson to cadmium red and use this to pick out the key features.

STEP THREE

Add a touch of ultramarine blue to create the shadows and darkest sections.

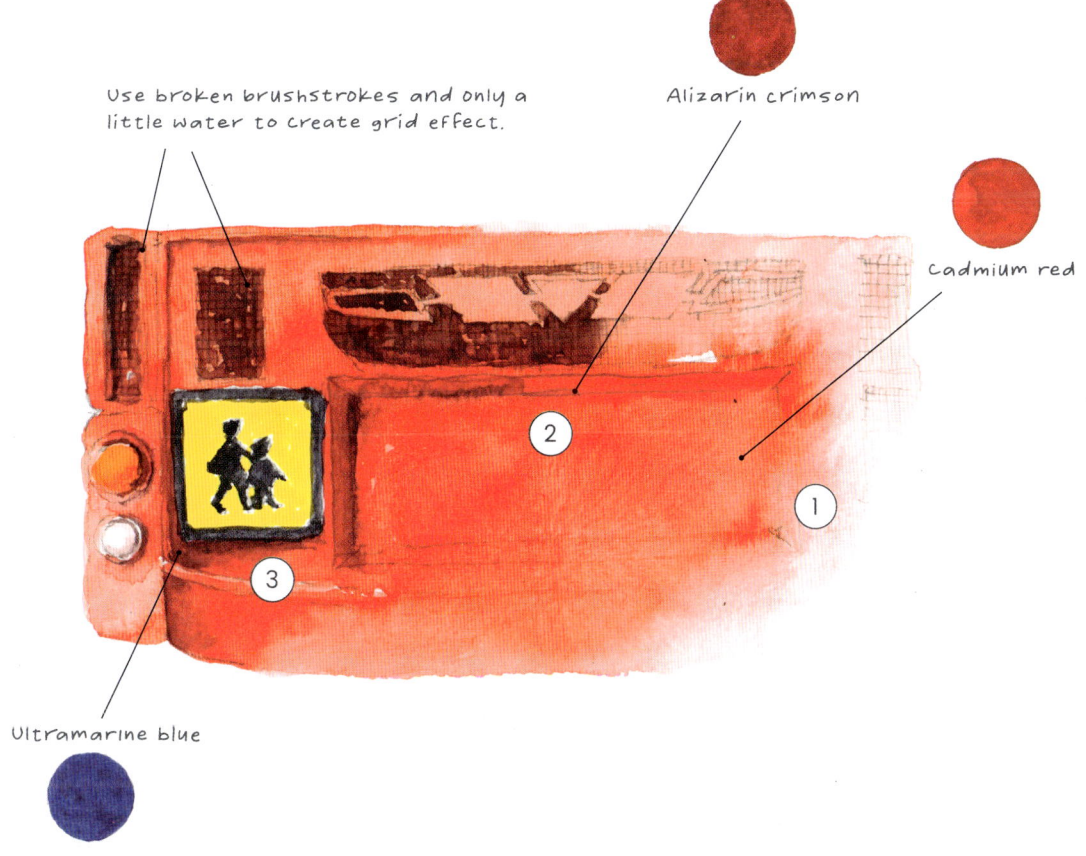

Use broken brushstrokes and only a little water to create grid effect.

Alizarin crimson

Cadmium red

Ultramarine blue

Trucks

The "mechanics" of trucks are probably best avoided. It is the nonmoving parts that are much more accessible to us and are worthy of either color or tonal studies. A basic gray of ultramarine and burnt umber will be particularly useful to you when it comes to distinguishing parts of the bodywork.

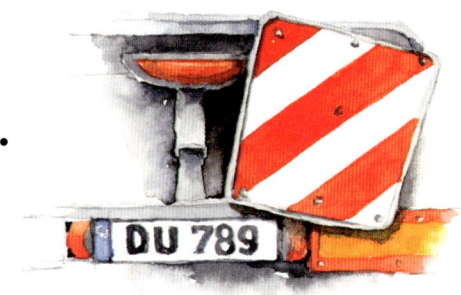

Reds and oranges provide a real visual impact against the dull gray of the mechanical parts.

Highlights act as reflections.

Paint around dry white paper to create flashes of reflection.

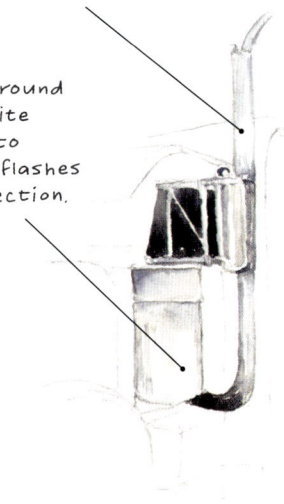

Most commercial trucks are white—especially the cabs. You need to mix your gray tones to create a sense of form.

Lightest gray helps to define detail.

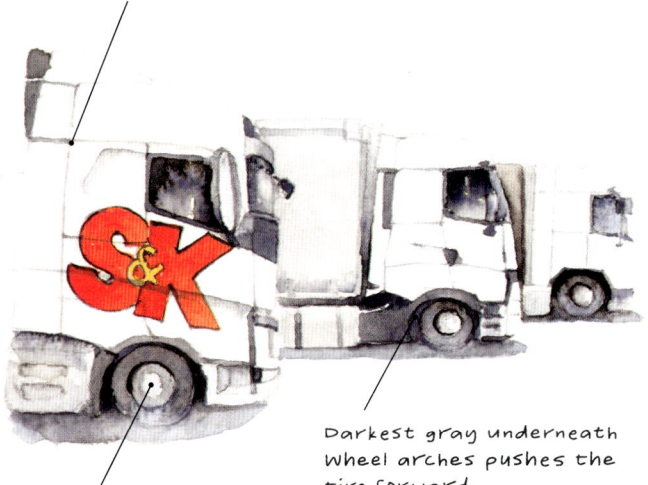

The exhaust pipe of this truck is highly reflective—an effect that is best achieved by painting onto dry paper and leaving lines of white showing through.

Darkest gray underneath wheel arches pushes the tire forward.

Mid-gray pushes light tones forward.

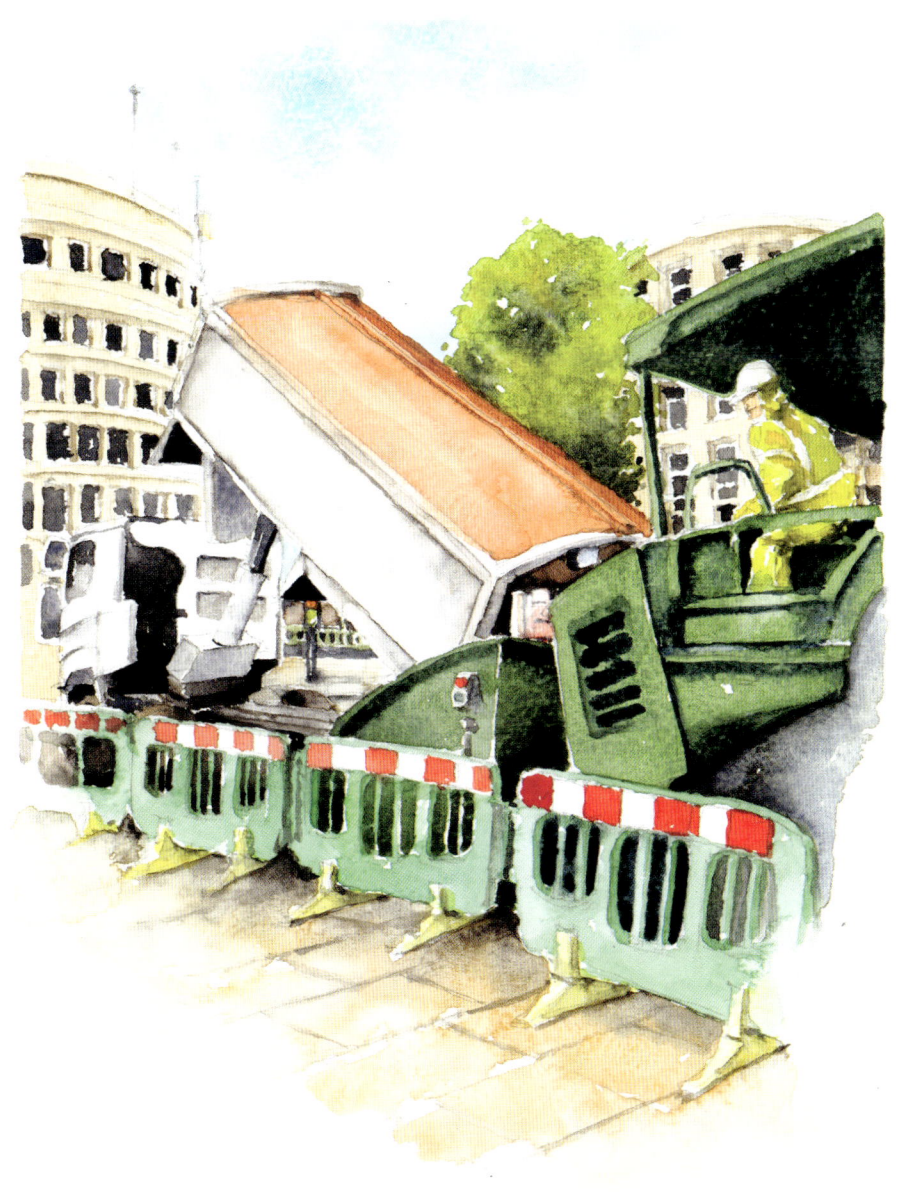

This construction scene requires an unexpected number of green tones. The middle-ground trees and truck being operated both used sap green as their base. The plastic safety barriers in the foreground, however, required a mixture of Hooker's green to properly emphasize the differences between the assorted green elements in the painting.

Docks and Ferries

The industrial nature of a dock always fills the artist with awe and excitement—so much to see and to record that it is hard to know where to start. I find it easier to move away from the main dock area and find some quiet spot in the hinterlands—this also avoids the attention of overly zealous security guards!

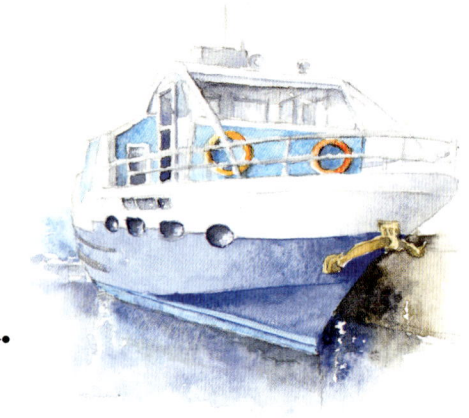

This boat is adorned with a variety of blues—cerulean blue for the superstructure, cobalt blue for the hull, and ultramarine blue added for shadows.

The grid surrounding this buoy utilizes push-pull effects—light and dark colors working to enhance each other.

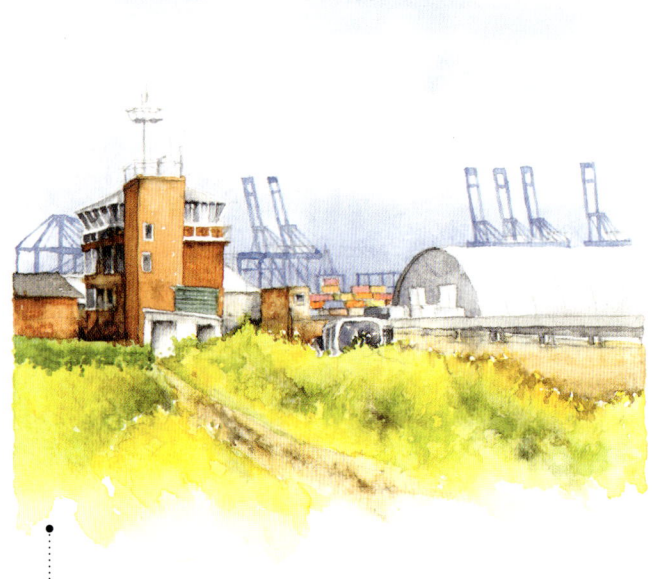

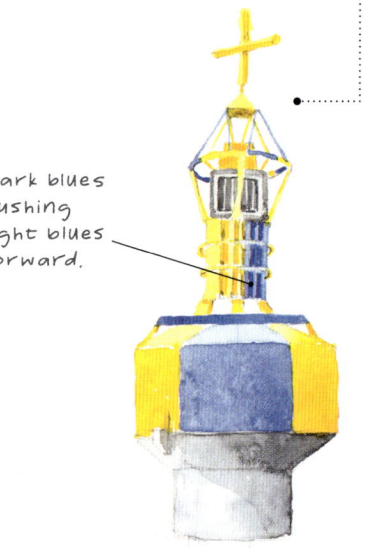

Dark blues pushing light blues forward.

Sometimes you need to step back a little for a composition to fall into place. I chose to walk a little way from the dock to find a position in the hinterland with a wider view.

EXAMPLE: DOCKSIDE CHAIN

STEP ONE

Apply an initial wash of raw sienna across the collection of industrial-sized chain links.

STEP TWO

Create the basic color of the chain with an application of burnt sienna. Blot the highlights out using a paper towel.

STEP THREE

Complete the "push-pull" effect by adding ultramarine blue and burnt umber to the other colors and painting between the links. Darker tones push the lighter tones forward.

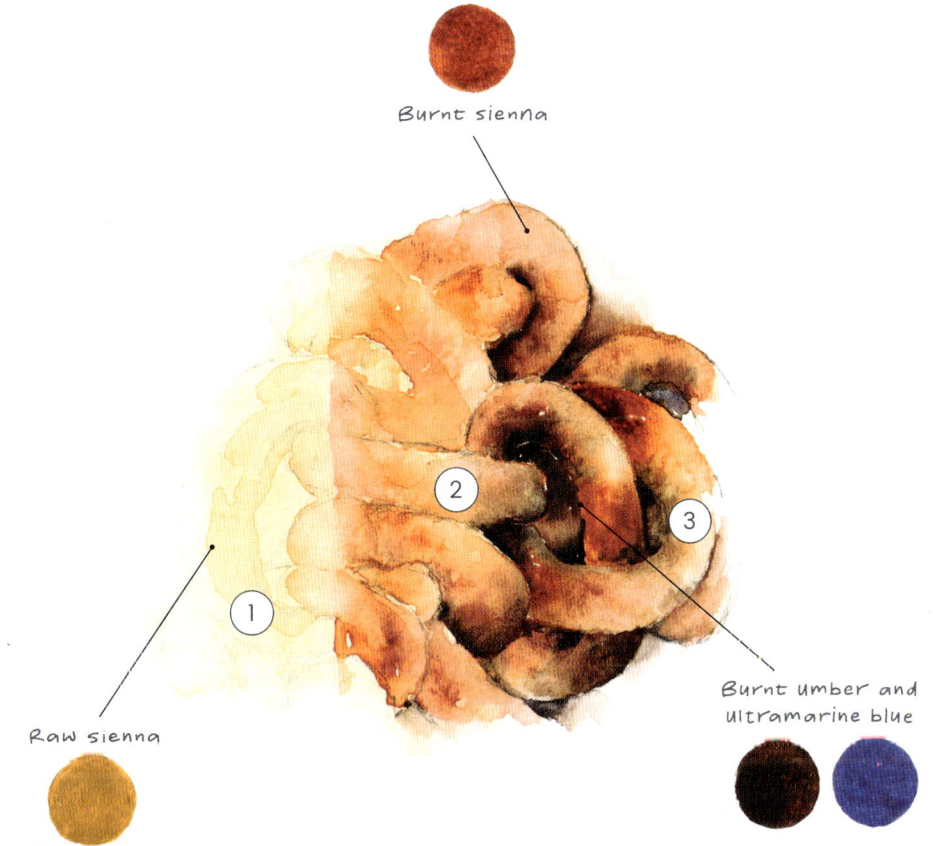

Burnt sienna

Raw sienna

Burnt umber and ultramarine blue

Emergency Vehicles

Bright, unmistakable colors are always a major feature of emergency vehicles—they need to be seen easily. This makes them great painting subjects. There are ethical issues regarding sketching at the scene of an accident, but emergency vehicles have bases that they return to—and the doors are often left open.

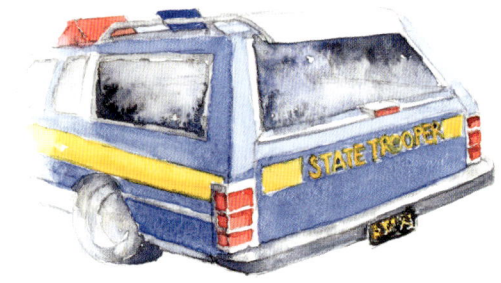

Emergency vehicles need to be easily noticed and tend to use color to achieve this. Bright reds and yellows are common.

Lighter blue on top adds three-dimensional effect.

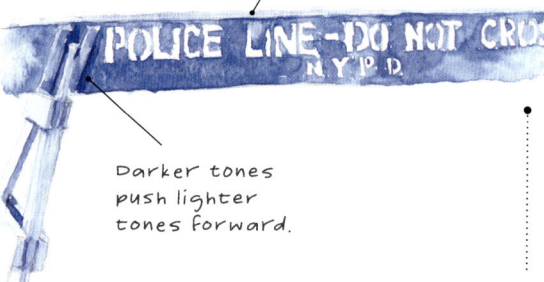

Darker tones push lighter tones forward.

This study uses one color only—ultramarine blue. The different tones were created by different levels of dilution.

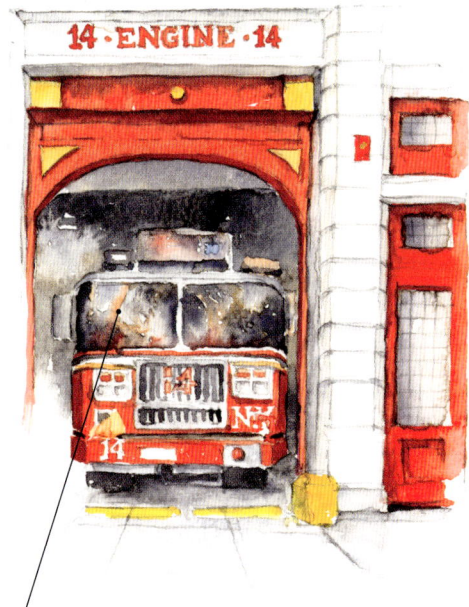

Environmental colors reflected.

Sometimes much detail has to be suggested to capture colors successfully. The reds are mixed using cadmium red, alizarin crimson, and ultramarine blue.

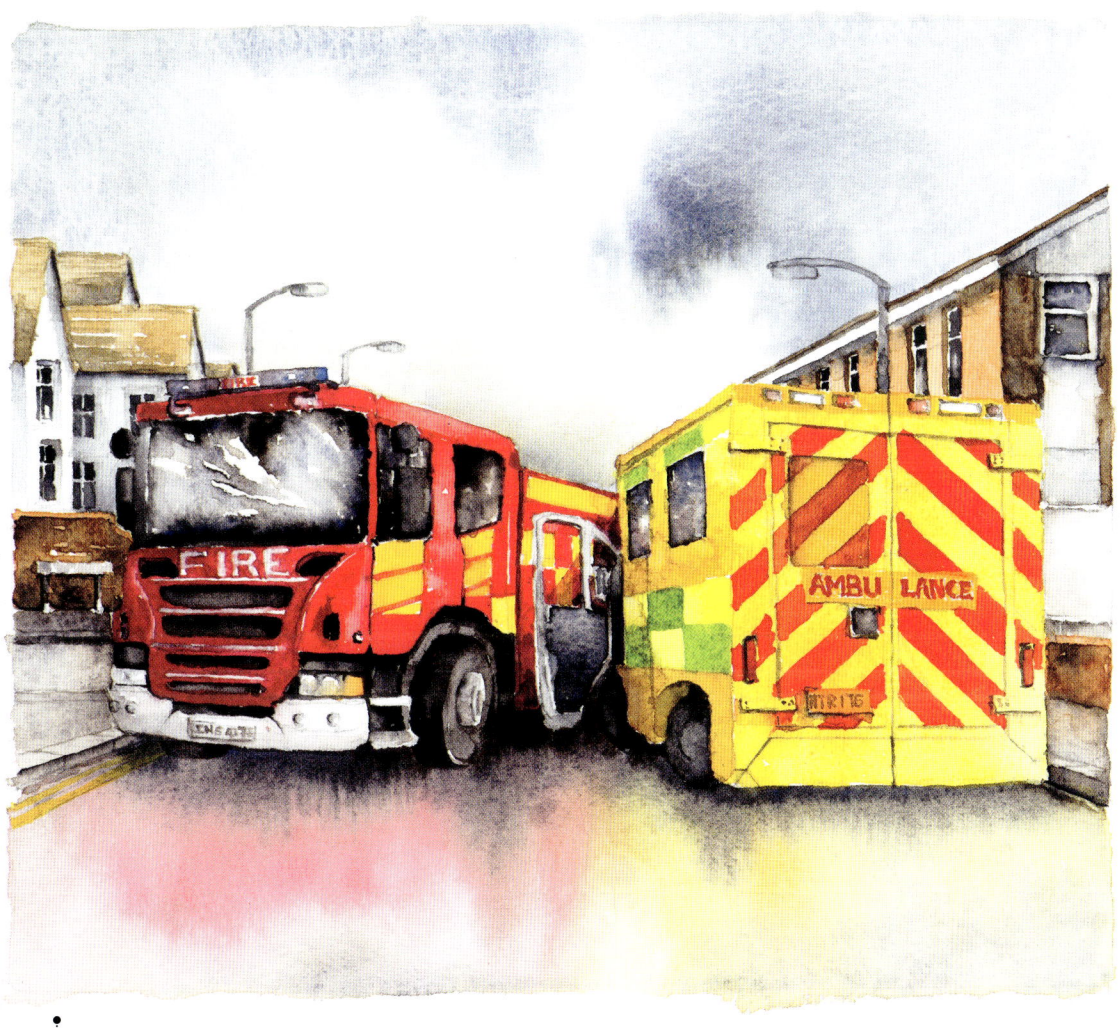

These two vehicles were called out as a misunderstanding: no one had been hurt and no one was in distress, so it seemed acceptable to stop and record the scene.

A passing shower had left the road wet, so I pulled the reflections from the brightly colored vehicles downward onto very wet paper.

I chose colors carefully in order to harmonize the scene. The key mix for the fire truck is cadmium red, with the addition of some alizarin crimson. Cadmium yellow with a touch of dioxazine purple (to darken the yellow) make the base color for the ambulance.

River Traffic

Rivers and canals often flow through the industrial parts of the urban environment. While many areas have been gentrified, others still hold onto the grime of their previous identity. Sometimes you will find both side-by-side. The old and the new often sit well together without contradiction—it's just progress.

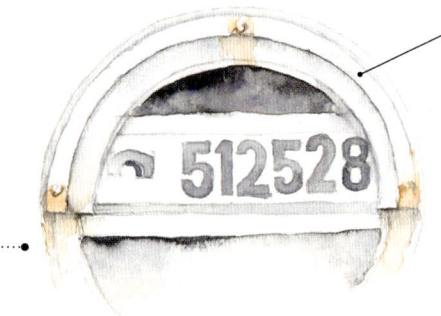

Inner rim sandwiched between two gray metal circles.

This type of detail is worth a study. The way the glass sits in the porthole will always be of value.

Bikes are often seen on river barges. The way they hang matters more than details such as the spokes on the wheels.

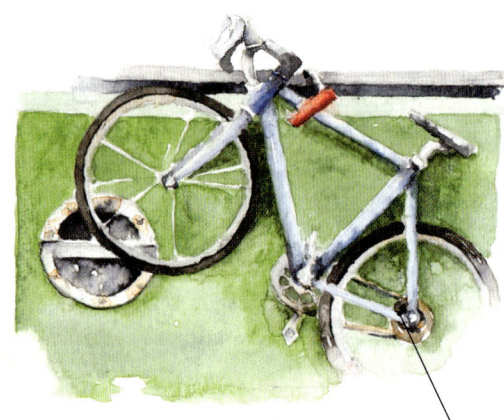

More visual weight created by darker paints, aiding the way in which the bike hangs.

Shadows created by adding a touch of the roof color to the blue.

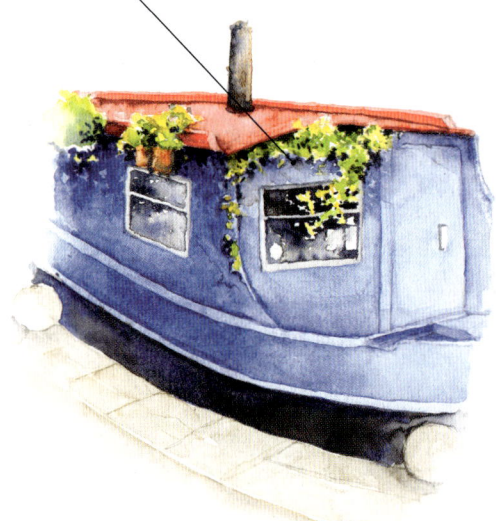

To vary the tones on a boat's curved hull, load a brush with paint and pull it along the line of the curve. As the paint runs out, the tone will lighten.

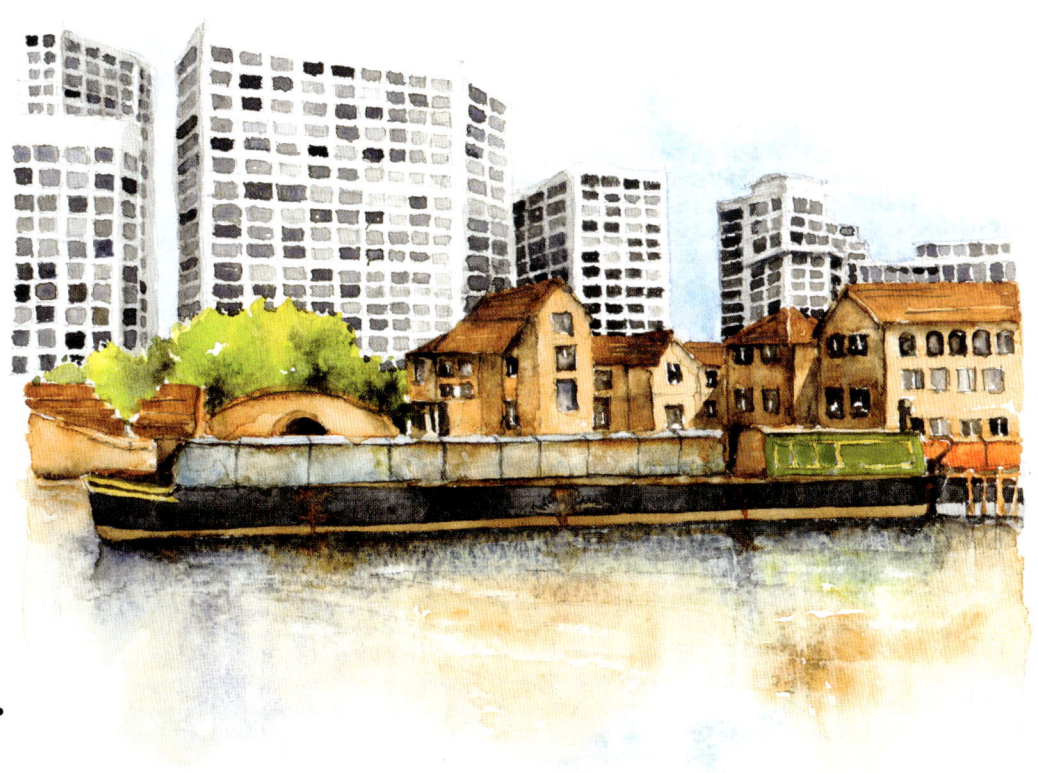

This is an incongruous scene, with the grime of the industrial barge set against the backdrop of modern buildings. Also, the sharp lines of the background buildings sit in marked contrast to the soft, still waters of the canal. This juxtaposition made the scene irresistible to paint.

TIP

To create reflections in water, pull a diluted version of the subject's colors down onto the water tone, but only when the paper is damp.

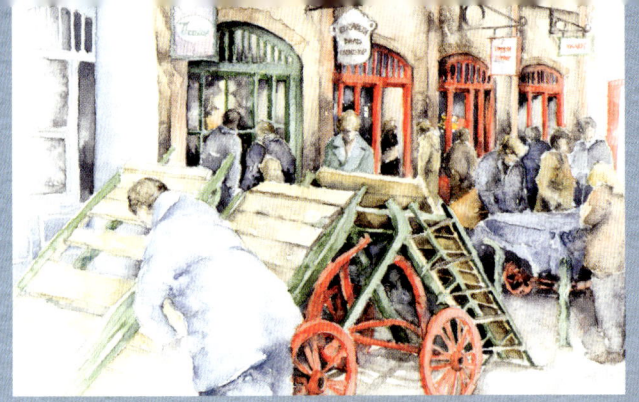

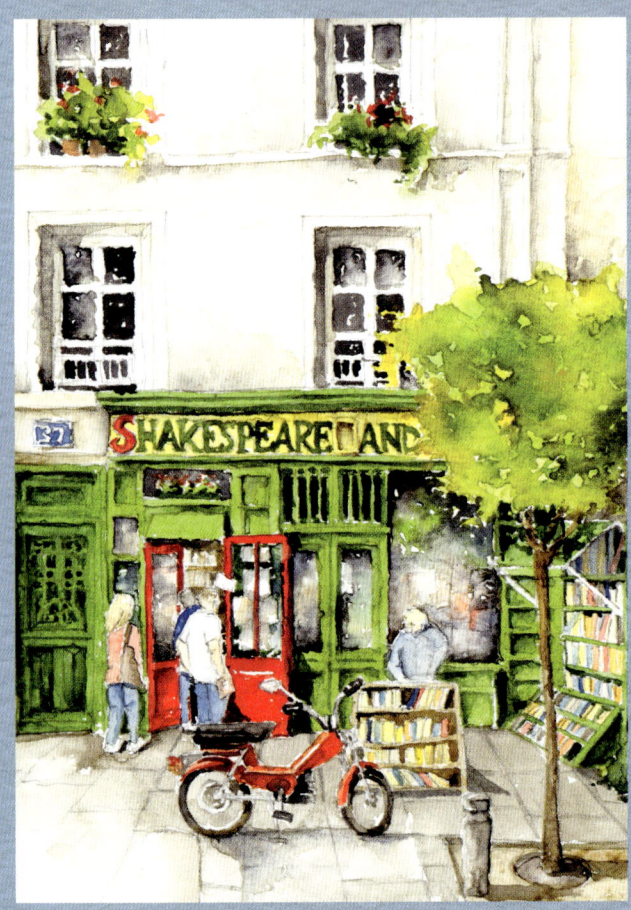

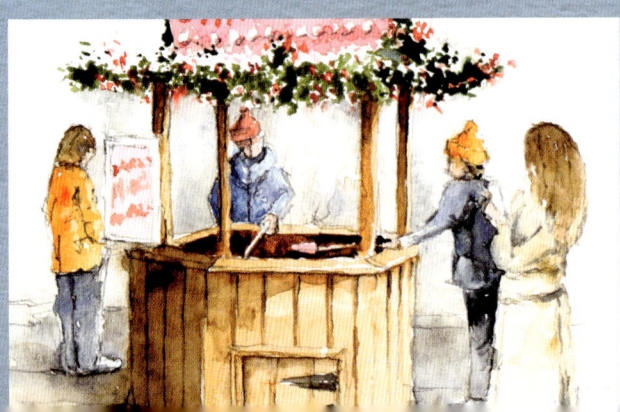

CHAPTER SEVEN:
Commerce

Main streets, back streets, shopping malls, and station forecourts inevitably contain a variety of stores and vending outlets. Then there are market stalls, street food outlets, and outside diners, all of which offer a remarkable array of subjects of all shapes and colors.

Most, if not all, storefronts will have some form of lettering—either on signs or the windows. This can require careful observation and sometimes "lining up" to ensure that all the letters remain the same size—or ensuring that they all fall in with the correct set of perspective lines. But these sites will never exist without visitors, clients, and customers. People sitting at bars, café tables, and diners can, understandably, be very sensitive about being observed, noted, and sketched. My advice is always to engage with any individual or groups of people you wish to record—explain what you want to do, and just be prepared to accept that "no" does mean "no."

Coffee and Cafés

In Europe, in the early 1900s, it was the tradition for artists to sit at café tables and sketch their surroundings. YIf you wish to do this, you will have to work quickly to record the movement of the waiters, and don't try to be secretive about what you are doing, Openness and honesty will nearly always be the key to sketching people successfully.

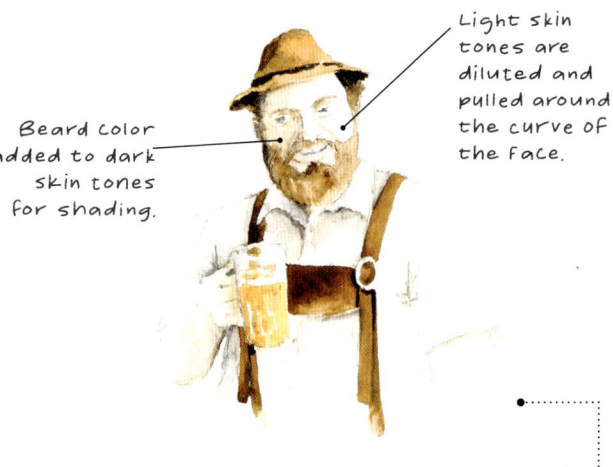

Café windows, doors, tables, and chairs tend to stay put for long periods of time. Customers, however, come and go. Establish the surroundings first and add the figures to your studies after the structures are in place.

This small study of a couple of young people was made all the easier for their willingness to engage.

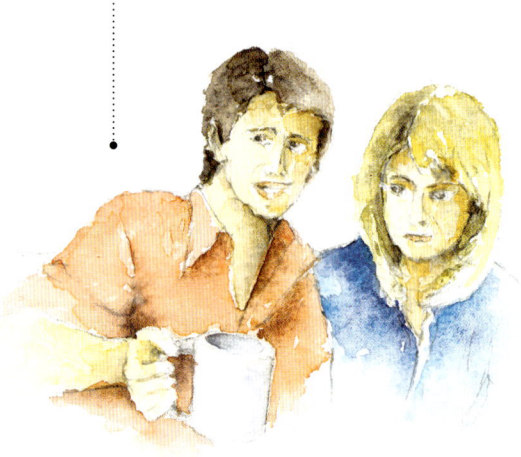

Beard color added to dark skin tones for shading.

Light skin tones are diluted and pulled around the curve of the face.

Some figures require personal engagement. Talk to your subjects, explain what you want to do, and take it from there.

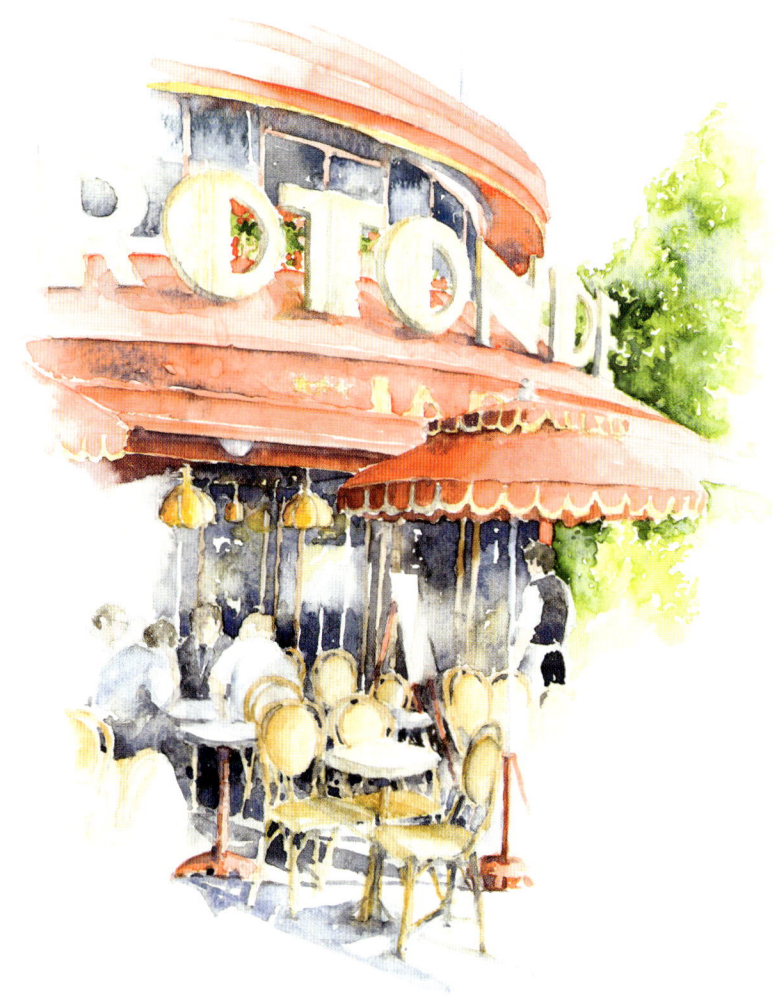

Street cafés are often iconic places and many hold a history unique to their part of the world. I found the foreground clutter attractive here—the chairs casting strong, early morning shadows and the groups of figures viewed against the dark tones ot the window were the key features for me.

TIP

The tangle of chair legs requires close observation, and the application of some dark tones in between to create negative shapes.

Markets

I love to rummage around behind the stalls in markets to seek out color in some unusual situations—packaging, pallets, machinery, and so on. This is as much a part of the market environment as the stalls and the vendors themselves.

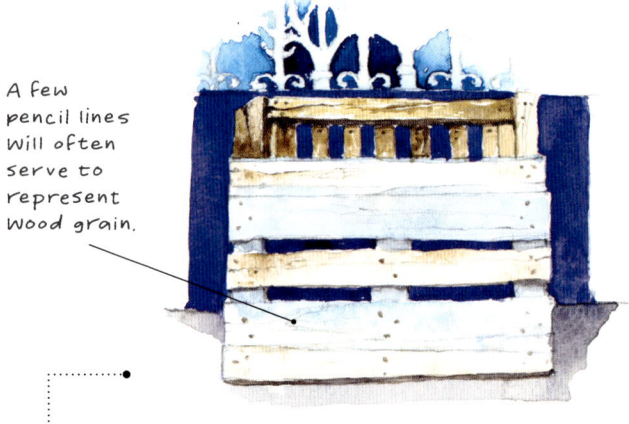

A few pencil lines will often serve to represent wood grain.

I was attracted to this abandoned pallet left against a wall, due to the range of blues I noticed. Always be on the lookout and search beyond the obvious.

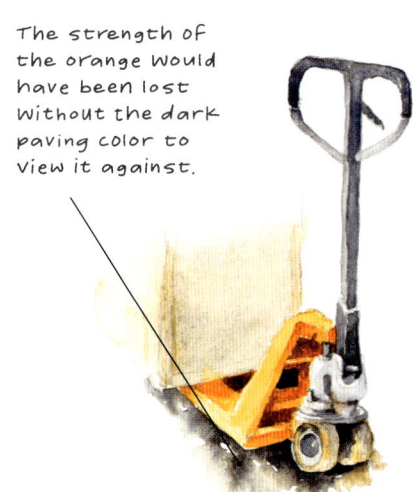

The strength of the orange would have been lost without the dark paving color to view it against.

This mechanical lifting machine is so much a part of the market environment that it warrants a study.

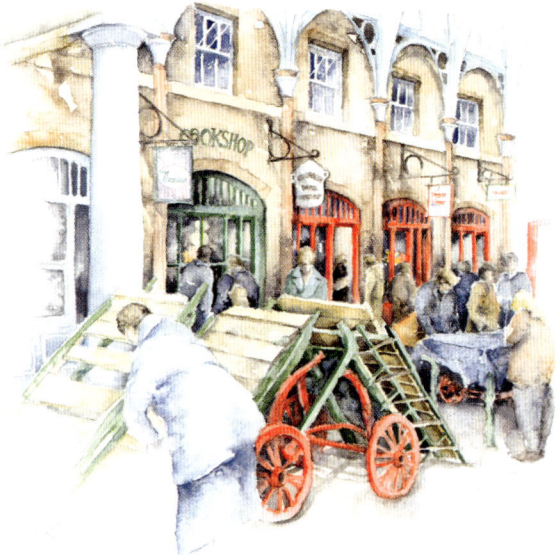

Markets are busy places. If you look behind the human element, a wealth of opportunities exist for the artist.

EXAMPLE: MARKET STALL

STEP ONE

Apply a wash of cadmium yellow to the entire contents of this market stall. This will influence the colors that follow.

STEP TWO

Once the yellow underwash has dried, use cadmium orange to establish the color of the fruits. The yellow underwash helps to create a more substantial orange color.

STEP THREE

Just before the orange application has dried, add a touch of dioxazine purple to the shaded areas. As the paper is still damp, this application will bleed gently, enhancing the roundness of the oranges.

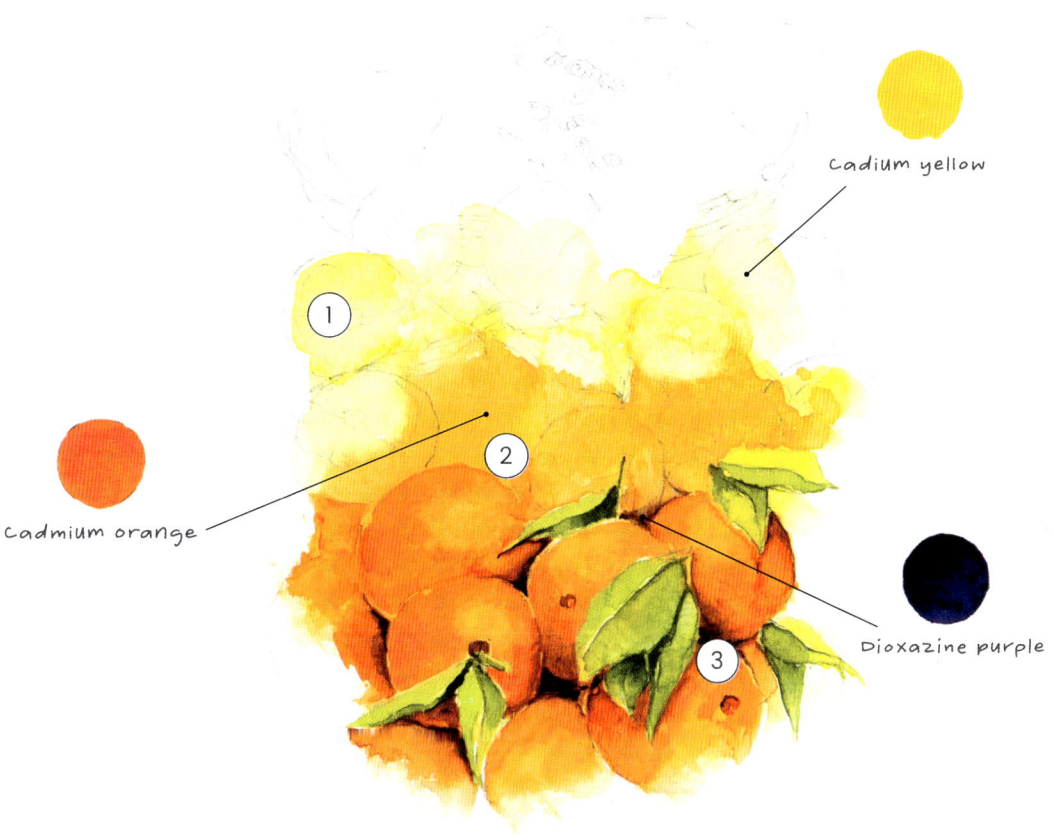

Cadium yellow

Cadmium orange

Dioxazine purple

Storefronts and Windows

The principles for painting glass are described earlier (see Windows and Glass). The difference here is scale. Storefront windows can be huge, and aim to display a variety of goods for sale—paint these a slightly lighter tone to the ones that you see, in order to create the impression of diffusion.

Reflected light effect created by painting around the strip of light.

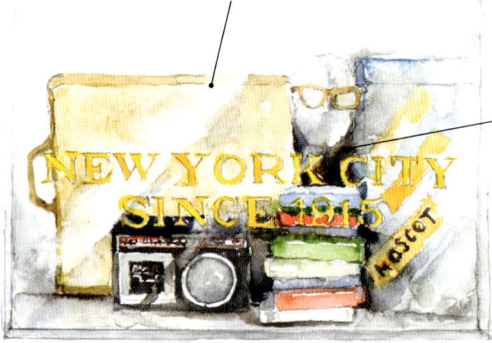

Dark tones help the light lettering stand out.

The flash of light running diagonally across this window study represents the reflected light of the day and is a particularly important feature.

This useful study shows how everyday store signs fit into the windows.

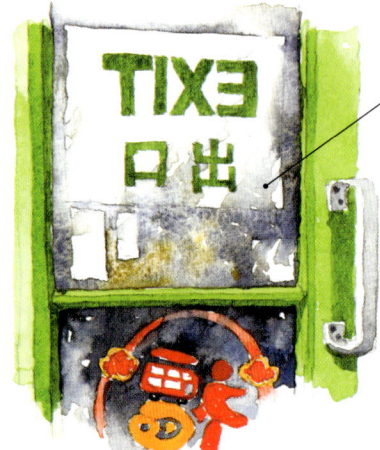

Background mixture washed across the shop sign show it's on the inside of the glass.

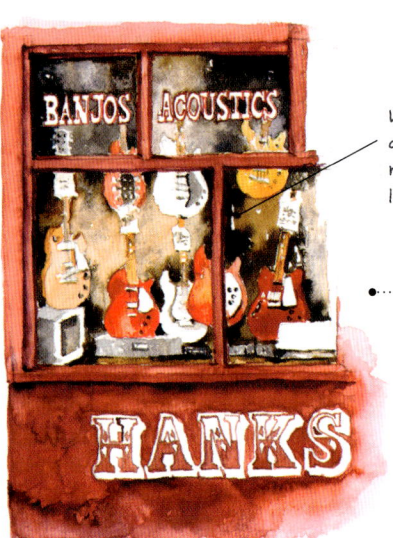

White paper acts as reflected light.

Much of this window display was painted using broken brushstrokes to allow for flecks of plain white paper to suggest reflected light.

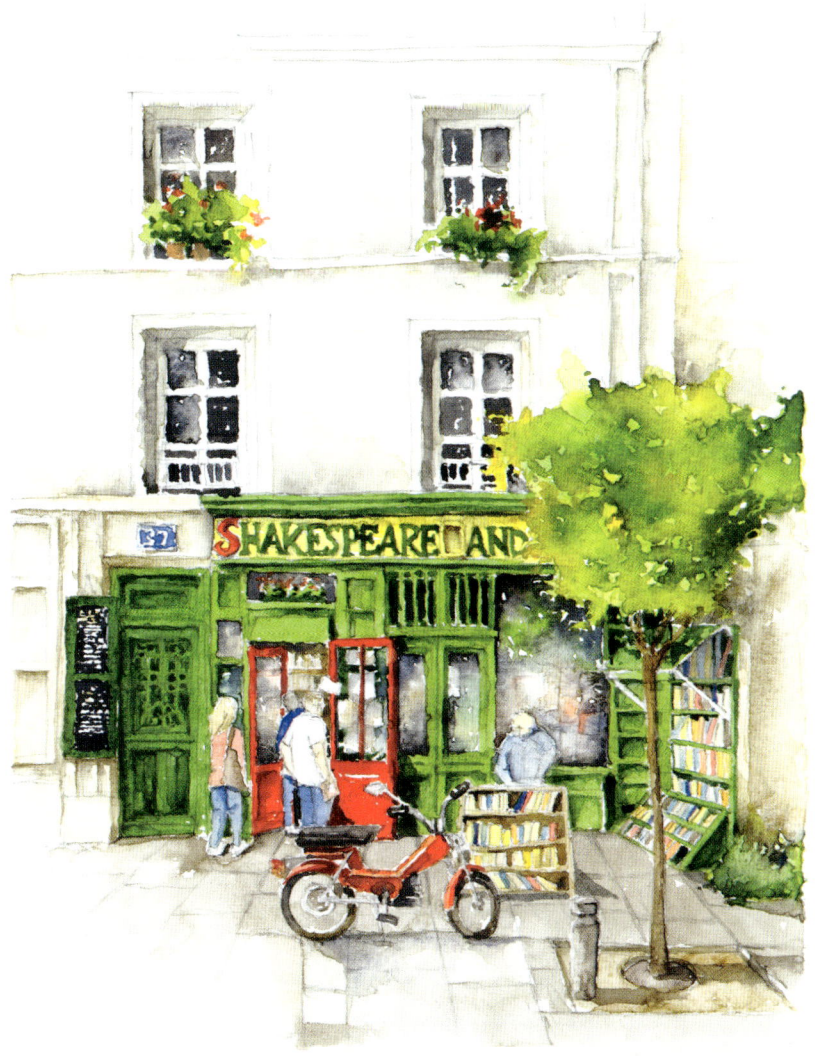

This bookstore spills out onto the street, creating a multifaceted scene. My eye was immediately drawn to the color clash of the red and green doors and door surrounds. This was surrounded by some subtle tonal blends from the window reflections and the books in the display stands. It would have been easy to leave the moped out of the composition but this gives the scene some human context.

Diners

Road vehicles that have been converted to food outlets are great fun to paint. They usually hold a lot of color to attract clients, but are usually on a fairly small scale, making them easy to record. Remember, perspective doesn't just apply to buildings.

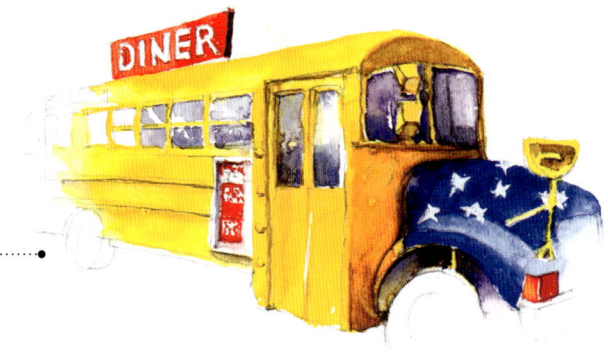

The color of this American school bus diner was recorded using cadmium yellow. The shadows were painted using a thin wash of dioxazine purple.

The angular nature of this van requires careful observation. Two-point perspective is important, especially as so many shapes in the interior of the van are visible.

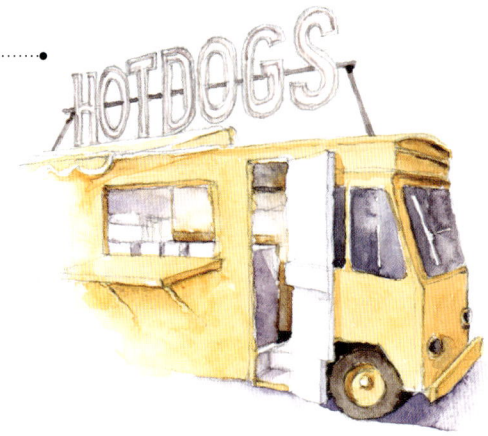

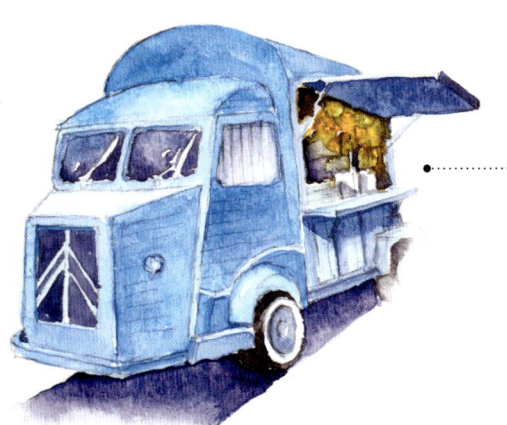

This diner van needed three types of blue to record the tones. Cerulean blue for the highlights, with cobalt blue added for the main color and ultramarine added for the shadows.

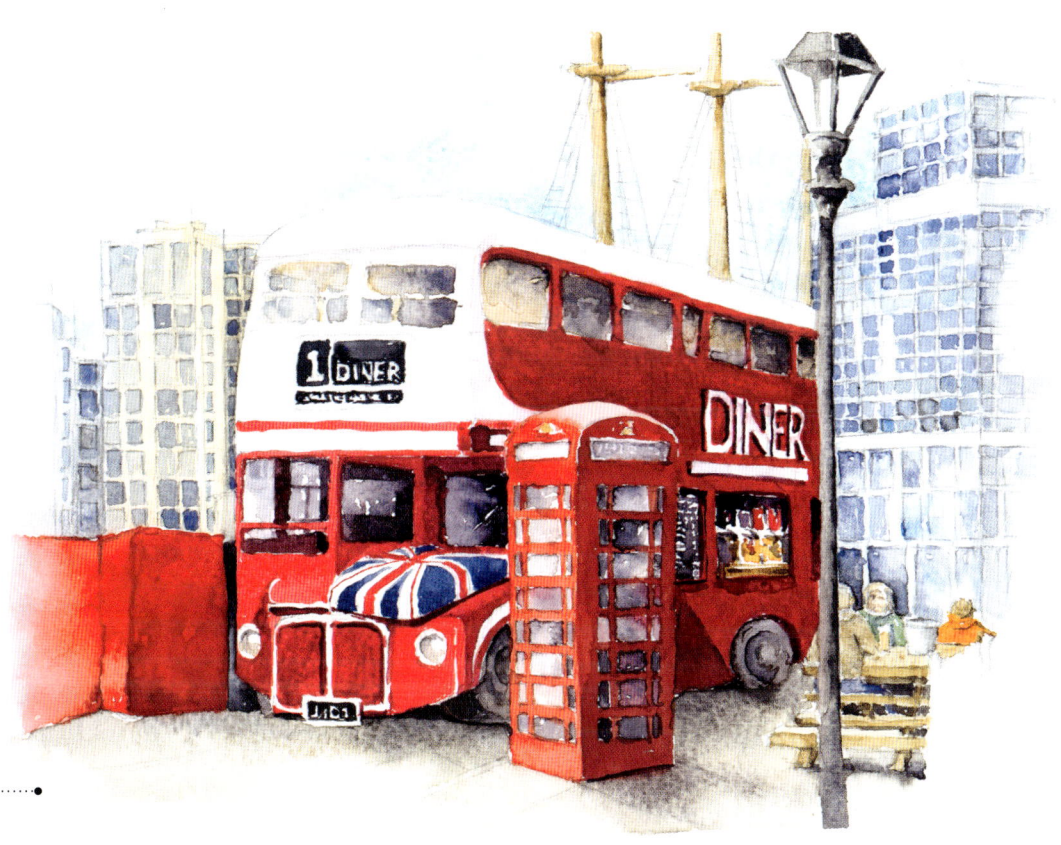

This iconic red bus has been taken from its natural environment and converted into a street diner. There is both a cultural and tonal clash between the background and foreground. The new high-rise buildings behind the bus are a mark of the future, while the bus and telephone box are very much part of the past. The flashes of color that dominate the foreground need to be carefully balanced so that both parts of the composition work together and not as two separate units.

TIP

Darken reds with alizarin crimson and just a touch of dioxazine purple to create shadows.

Street Food

The popularity of street food has soared over the past few years and you will find few towns and cities that don't have street food districts. It will, in reality, be the food vendors that you will be recording as the food itself, however colorful, will be on quite a small scale.

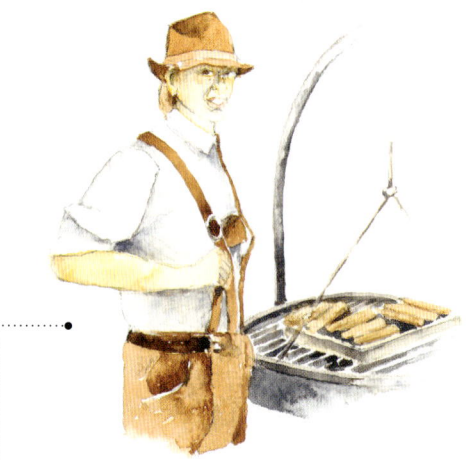

Street food vendors can be as interesting as the food itself. They will usually be working and won't stand still for long, so engage with them.

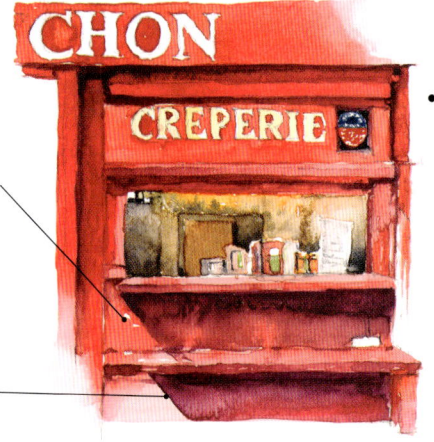

Chipped paint represented by painting around sections of white paper.

Angled shadows add interest to the study.

I painted the faded red of this crêperie using watery cadmium red. The darker areas are a mix of alizarin crimson with cadmium red. I added dioxazine purple to this mix for the shadows.

The separation of cheese and tomato was achieved by dropping clear water onto the paint before it had fully dried.

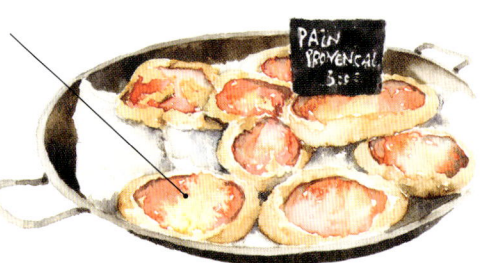

This pan of street food was sketched quickly, using water to create the bread topping where the ingredients appear to separate.

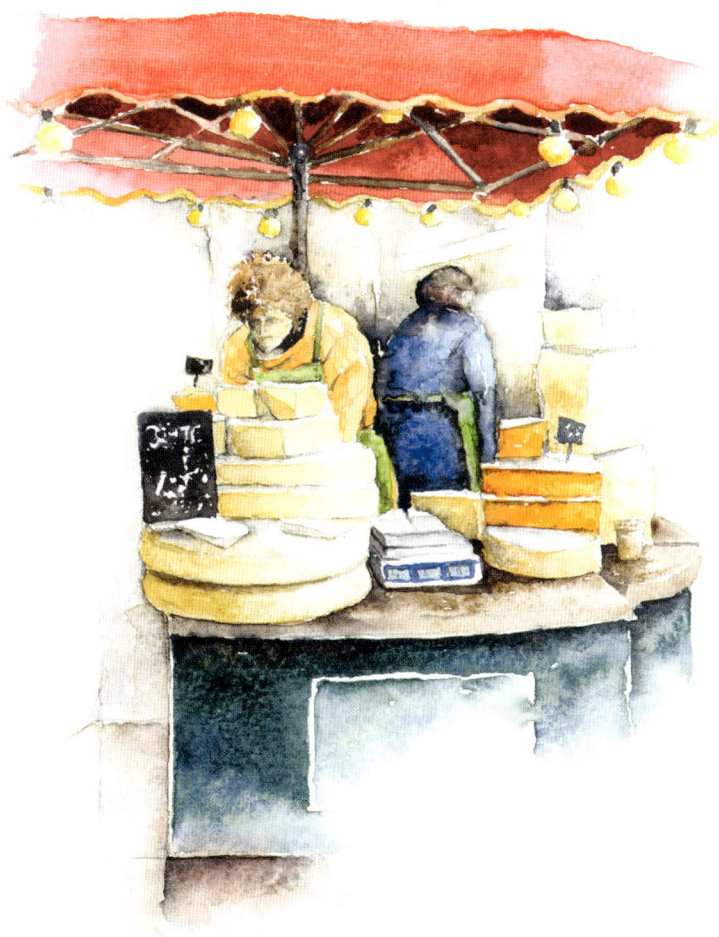

Artisan food sellers tend to pop up around towns and cities. Their goods are not always awash with color, but frequently have some individual qualities. The cheeses on this stall require tonal observation rather than concentrating on the separation of strong, bright colors. The color is found in the vendors and their stalls.

TIP

Don't try to fit too much information behind your main subject. Reduce what you can see to a couple of neutral washes

Festive Markets

Festive markets are usually filled with different kinds of activities to the more regular markets. They will often have more food and drink, and a lot more decorative products on sale at the stalls. You can purchase these and take them home for a more leisurely study.

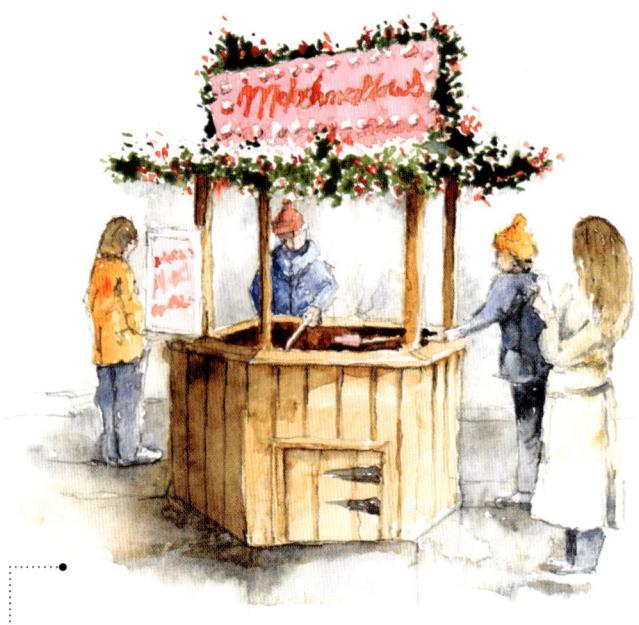

Eating hot marshmallows is a popular festive pastime in many parts of the world. People are often dressed up against the cold, so look for their bulky, padded clothing.

Festive market stalls are usually full of gingerbread and chocolate cookies. The decoration here is piped on, so needs shading to give it a sense of depth.

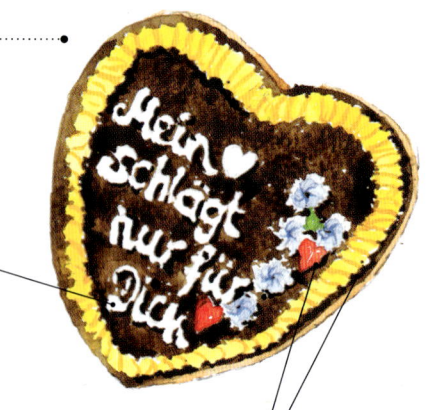

Plain white paper used for icing.

Decoration is darker on one side, suggesting a small shadow cast from the piped decoration.

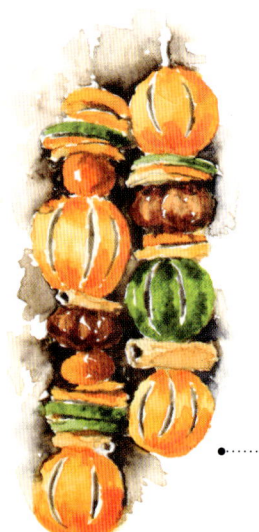

One market stall that I visited was full of aromatic dried fruits, suspended on a single string. The seasonal colors are particularly attractive.

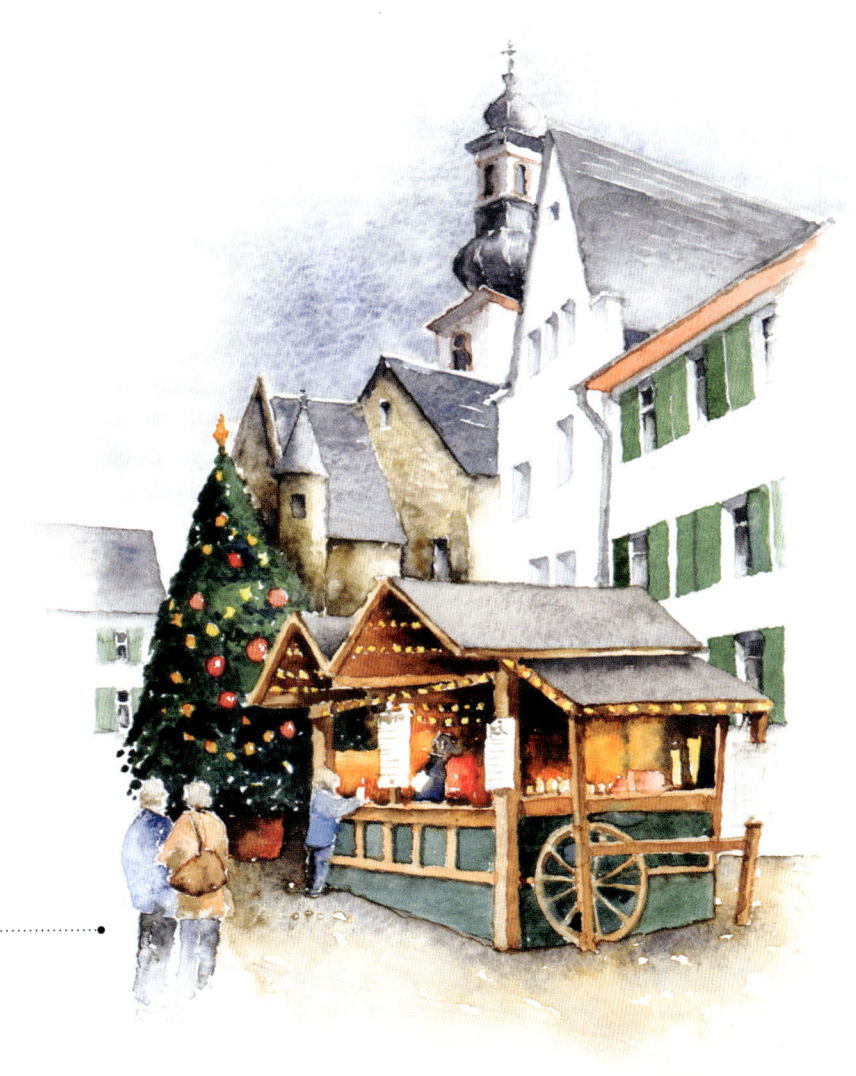

This festive market scene is muted a little by the dying daylight, allowing a warm glow from the food stall. This is achieved by dropping oranges, reds, and yellows onto damp paper—much stronger than might usually be mixed, but this strength diminishes with dilution as the colors sit on the paper.

Flower Stalls

Flower stalls are, by their very nature, awash with color. I found that this is enhanced even more by going out on a wet day to record the reflections of the wet paving between showers. I find the cadmium range of reds, oranges, and yellows well suited to painting the colors found on flower stalls.

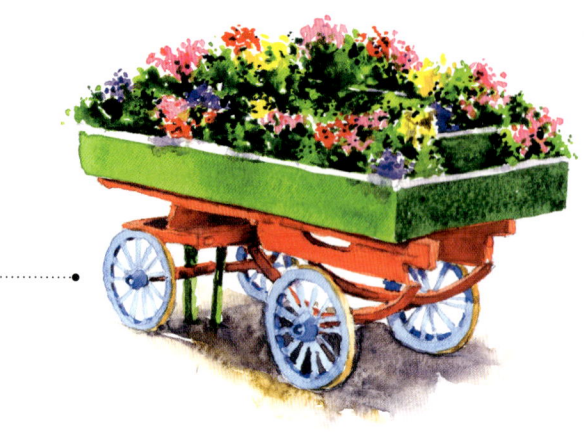

The greenery on this flower cart is its key feature. The three levels of greens—light, mid-tones, and dark—were mixed by applying sap green on top of cadmium yellow, with ultramarine blue for shadows.

When painting flowers, I paint the colors of the flower heads first and always wait until they have fully dried before adding the greens—this avoids bleeds, which diffuse the brightness of the blooms.

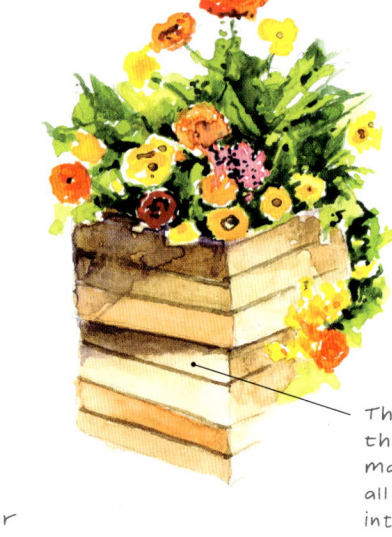

The angles of these boxes made the study all the more interesting.

Light leaves created by painting darker foliage behind.

Sunflowers are big and bright. They are ideal for exploring positive and negative shapes.

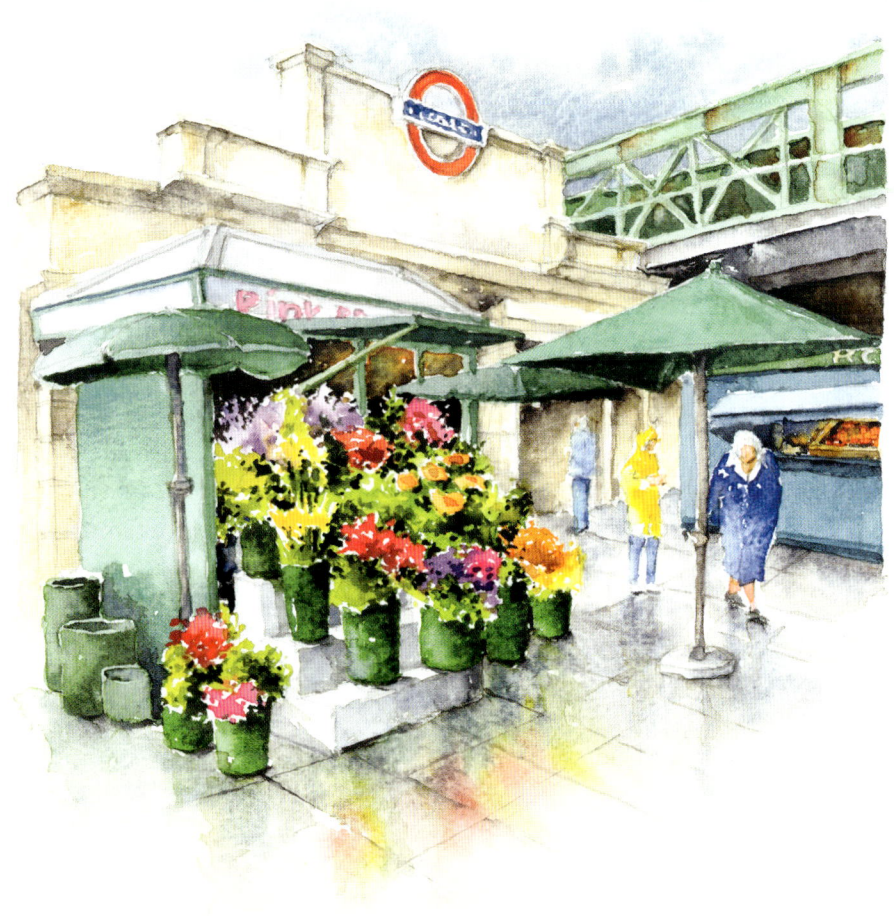

Flower stalls are usually a riot of color—enhanced considerably on this rainy day by the flower colors being reflected from the wet sidewalk. Pulling the colors used for the flowers down onto the damp, gray paper is the technique used to create this effect.

TIP

Look for the spaces in between flowers and containers. These are best painted with very dark greens and blues.

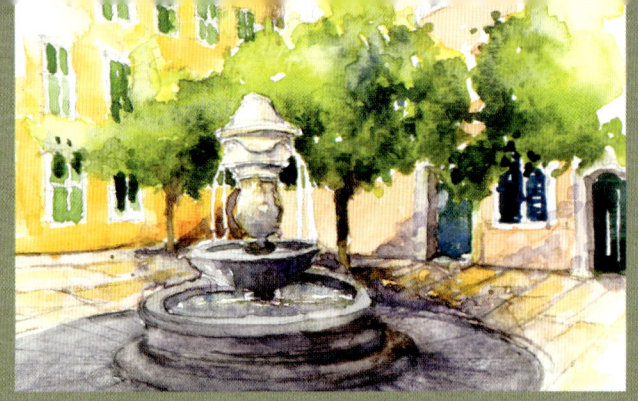

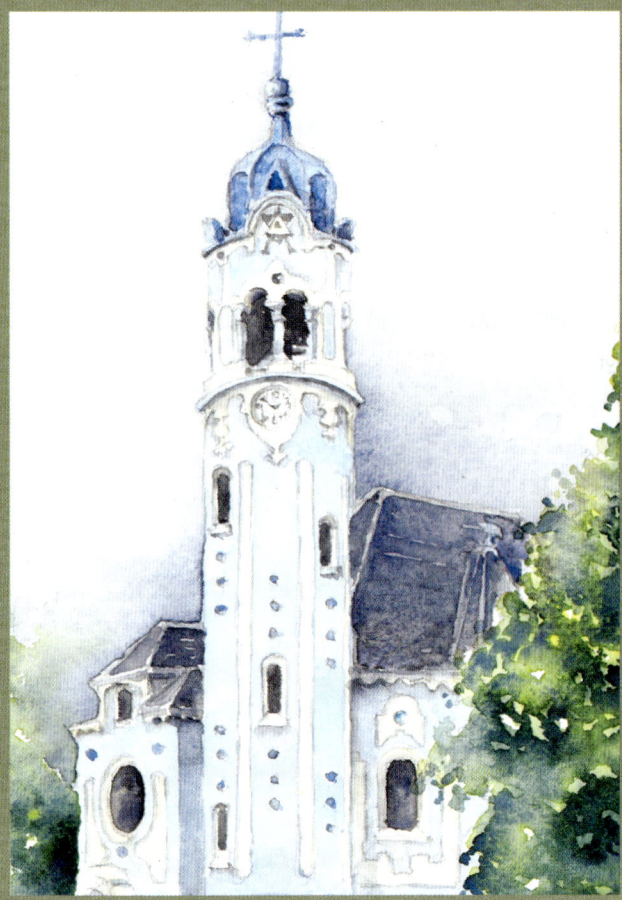

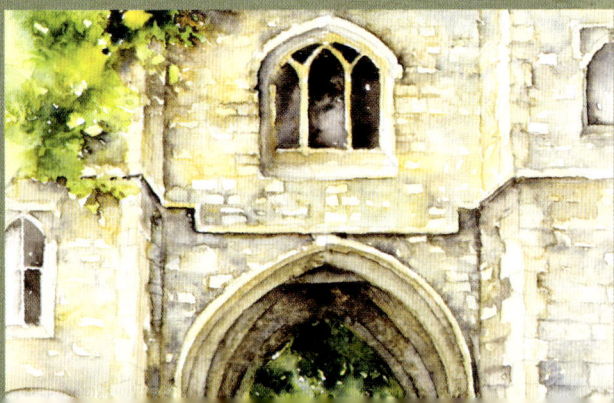

CHAPTER EIGHT

Heritage

Towns and cities are made up of a vast range of building types with many functions. This chapter deals with buildings and sites that have cultural functions. Galleries and museums come under this category, and are often identified not so much for the actual buildings themselves, but for the artifacts that you might see on their forecourts.

Other forms can be working or industrial sites that have sometimes been restored and sometimes simply left to show visitors what it would have been like to have lived or worked at the sites centuries ago. I have included "places of entertainment"—cinemas, theaters, and cabarets—in this chapter as these can be as much a part of the heritage of many towns and cities as historic ruins.

Castles

Many towns and cities grew around castles and forts, so it is no surprise to find them often in the center of the urban environment. The stone construction of these historic buildings makes them particularly interesting to paint. I use a limited set of colors—ochers and umbers —and will often concentrate the darkest colors on the gaps in between the stones.

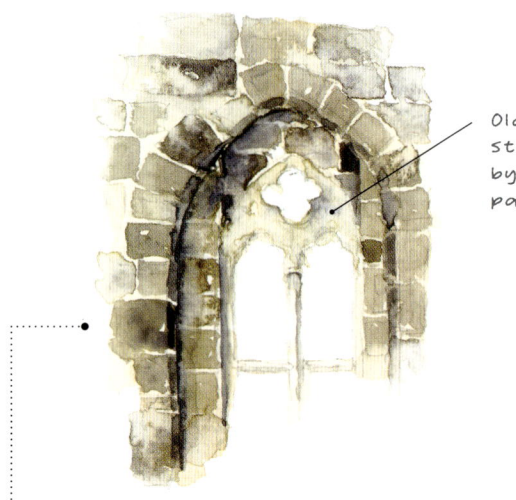

Old decaying stone recorded by allowing paint to bleed.

Castle ruins are common and, by definition, are often in a state of disrepair. This can be of benefit to the artist as blots and bleeds can be employed to full effect.

Some forts have contemporary functions and, as such, are well maintained. The stonework in this study is the result of such care.

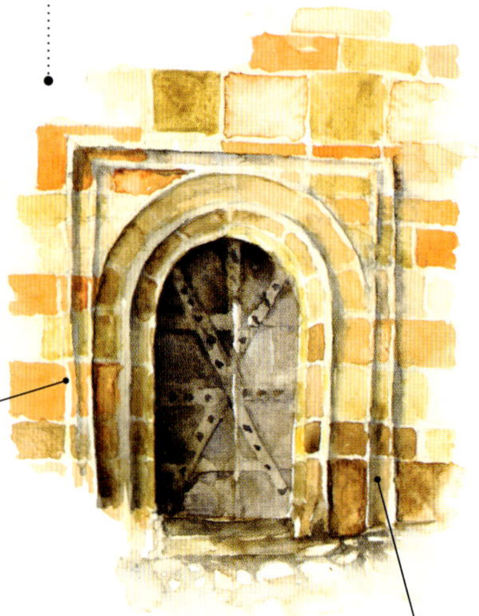

Light decorative ridges were created by painting either side of them.

Shadows help to "push" the ridges forward.

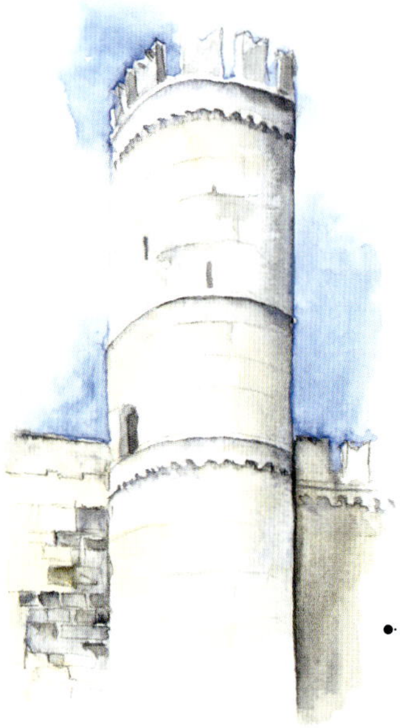

This faded white tower stands out against the cobalt blue sky, defining the quality of the day— cool, sharp, and cold.

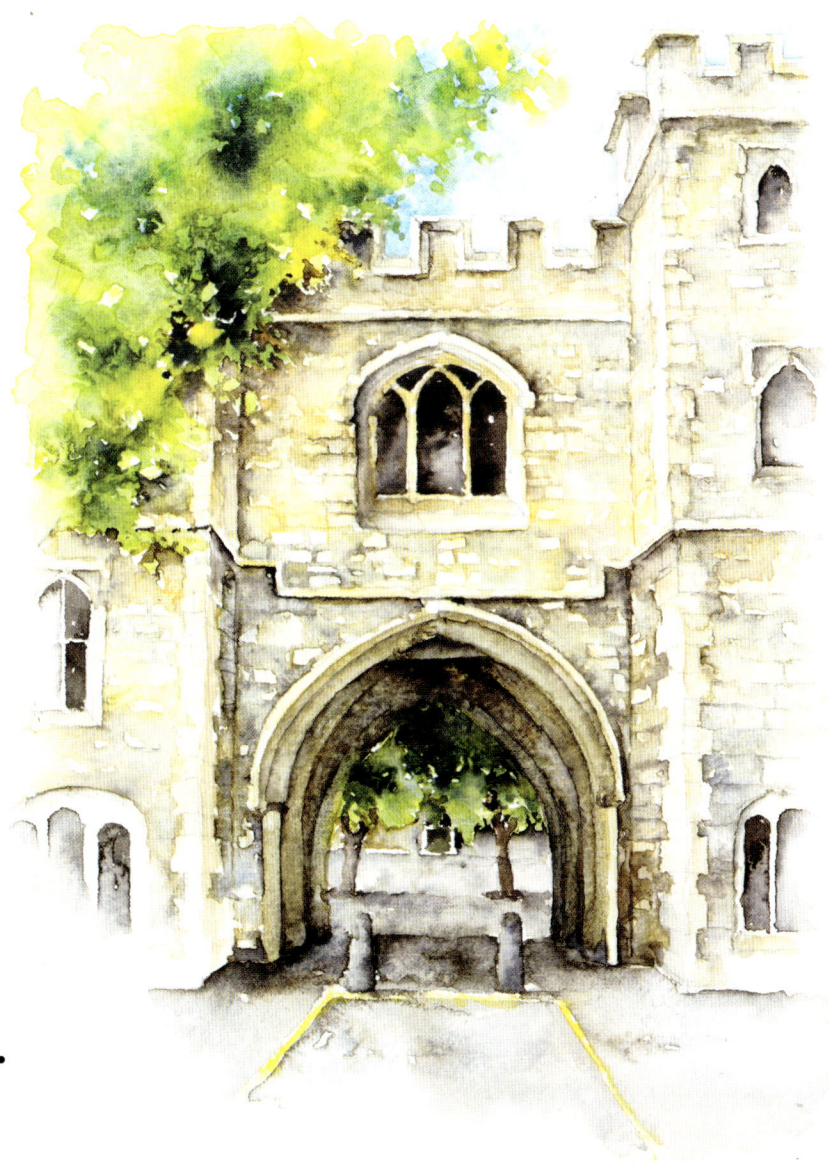

This fort-style frontage embraces both the old and new. A statement entrance, irregular stone construction, and a set of yellow "no parking" lines helped this old building to fit into a modern urban environment.

With a wall this size, suggestion is essential to avoid over-working the composition, so both positive and negative stones appear side by side.

Places of Worship

Many of the places at which people around the globe choose to worship are distinguished buildings and display their own identity outwardly. The structure, the architectural decoration, and the materials used all contribute to this identity. Respectful painting is required at these sites.

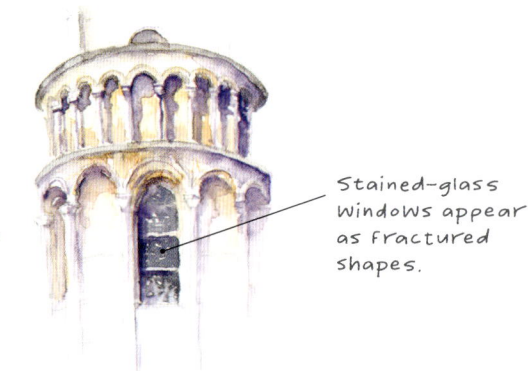

Stained-glass windows appear as fractured shapes.

The bright sunlight falling onto this church section creates a wealth of clearly shaped shadows. Always work onto dry paper to achieve this—it stops the paint from bleeding.

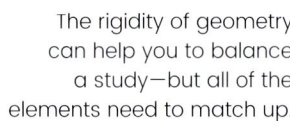

The rigidity of geometry can help you to balance a study—but all of the elements need to match up.

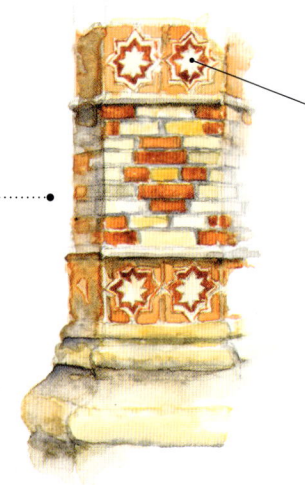

Line up geometric shapes to avoid irregular images.

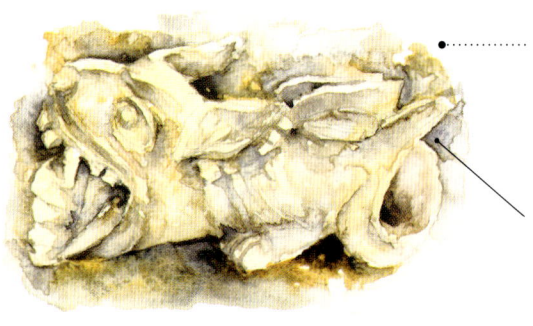

This unusual church stone carving benefited from many watery washes as it holds little color but a lot of tones.

Textures created by allowing wet paint to dry unevenly—mixing different dilutions together helps this.

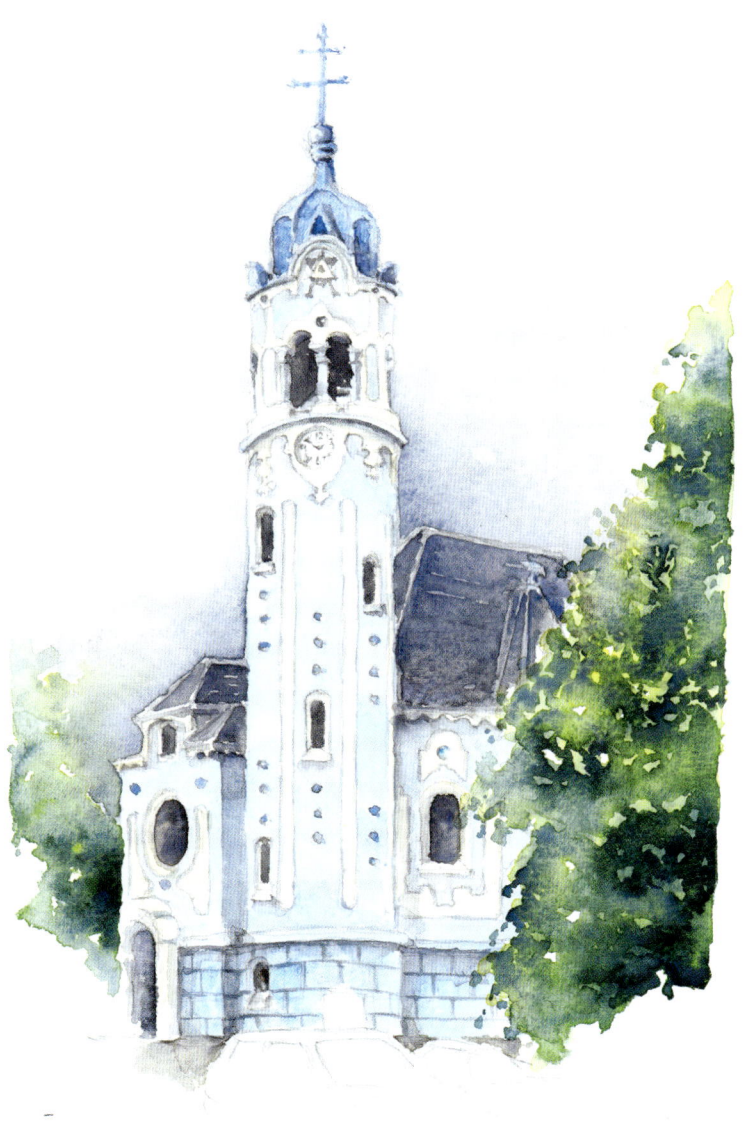

This painting demonstrates the dynamic of color and tone above linear structure. The atmospheric conditions on any day can make a real difference to the ways that we observe buildings. The threatening dark gray sky really makes the unusual blue (a mix of cerulean and cobalt blues) appear to glow.

Places of Entertainment

The nighttime economy, so crucial to the existence of many town and city centers, does not necessarily need to be recorded at night. Cinemas, theaters, and clubs are less likely to be busy during the day —especially in the morning, which is always my favorite time of the day for painting.

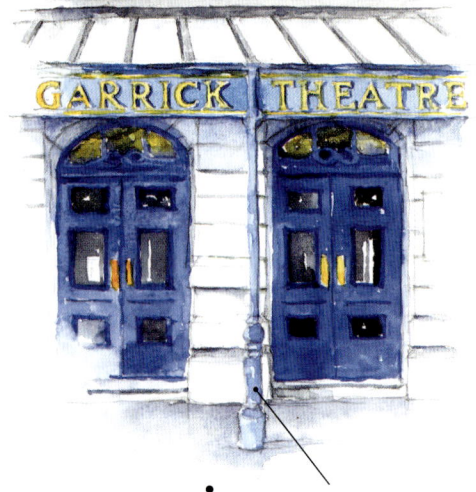

Distance between the post and the wall should match the depth of the awning.

Theater awnings are popular features as audiences can gather under these before or after a show, avoiding any rain.

Don't try to put too much detail into visual features.

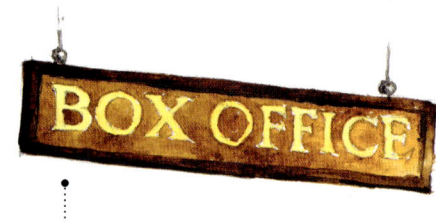

Entrance and exit signs are often in keeping with the architectural genre of a building.

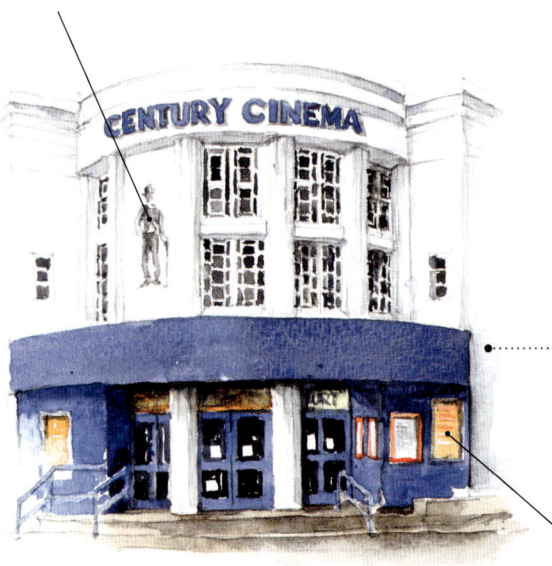

Solidity and a wealth of features allow this movie theater to stand alone without the need for a painted sky to push it out of the flat paper surface.

Apply an overall color of a poster—don't try to recreate it.

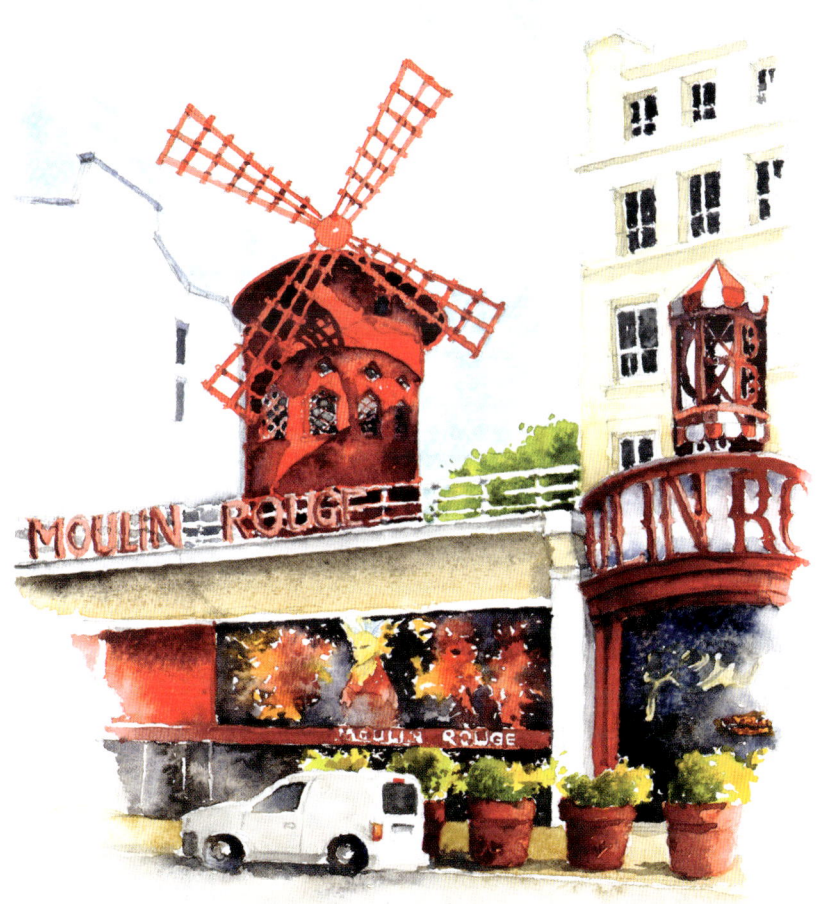

The strong colors of this iconic windmill dominate the scene, which means that it requires very careful handling. Cadmium red and alizarin crimson combinations needed to be balanced carefully to avoid either losing the windmill against the sky, or making it so dark that the additions of shadows would be ineffective.

TIP

With subjects such as windmill sails and scaffolding seen against the sky, paint the sky color across them as an underwash, then apply the main color. Don't try to paint around the shape.

Galleries and Museums

Modern, old, large, or small, most galleries and museums will have a major point of display—what it is and what you can expect to find inside. Seek these out, whether they are lettering, samples of art, or colors, as they are the crucial elements that make them different from the surrounding buildings.

Reflections captured using as much environmental color as possible.

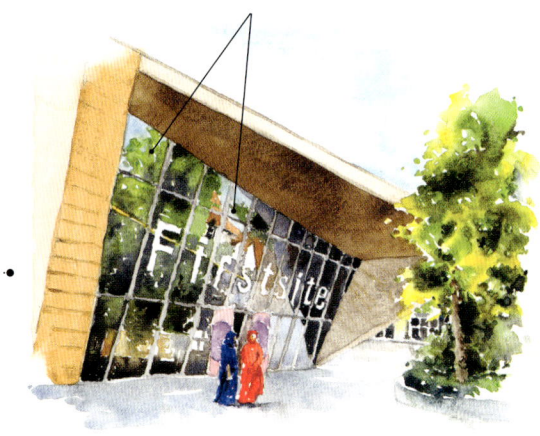

The glass in this modern gallery reflects the surroundings, almost creating a piece of artwork in itself.

Light edge gives the awning a feeling of depth.

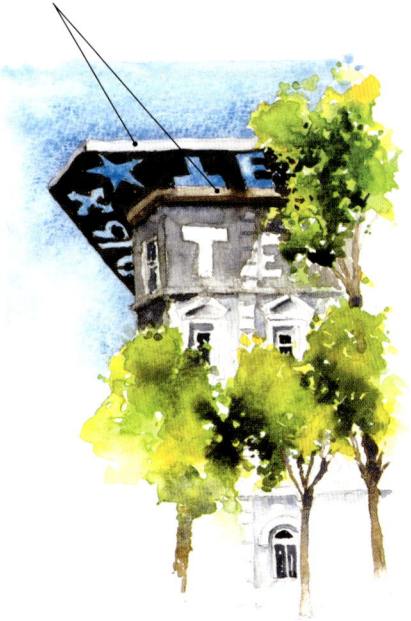

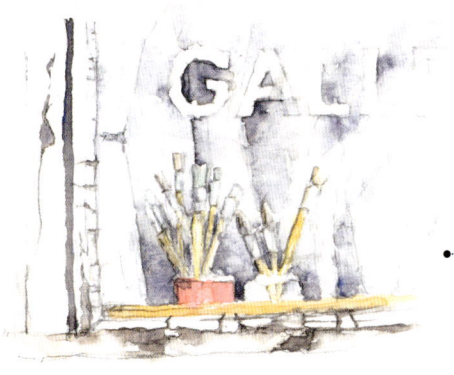

This studio doubles as a gallery for the resident artist, the tools of their trade displayed in the window frame. It makes a good sketchbook subject.

The lettering created by light falling through the cut-out letters on the awning creates a fascinating feature in this unusual museum.

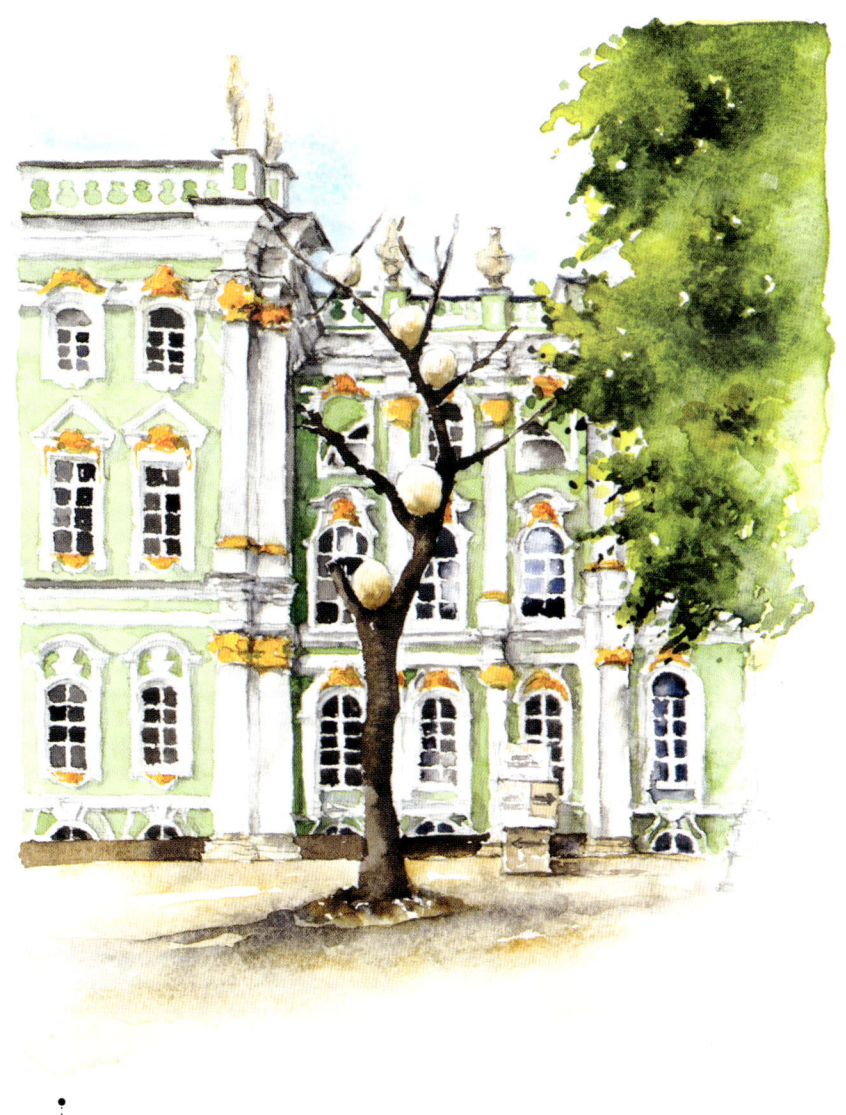

Some galleries and museums are recognizable at first glance only by the artworks that they display on their forecourts or external walls. In this composition, it is the unusual tree with balanced boulders that gives away the identity of this grand building.

Squares and Piazzas

The idea of a town square as a meeting place has existed since ancient civilizations realized their importance. These places often have central features such as fountains or statues, while others are surrounded by bars and restaurants. Either way, you can expect to record a lot of people.

This study features two figures contemplating the milling crowds. Skin tone matters here, and is a combination of soft Naples yellow, with just a touch of cadmium orange.

The lack of sharpness on much of this fountain is created with a succession of watery washes.

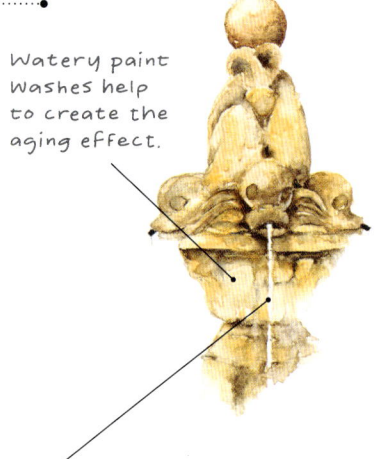

Watery paint washes help to create the aging effect.

Make sure that lines of falling water are absolutely vertical and straight.

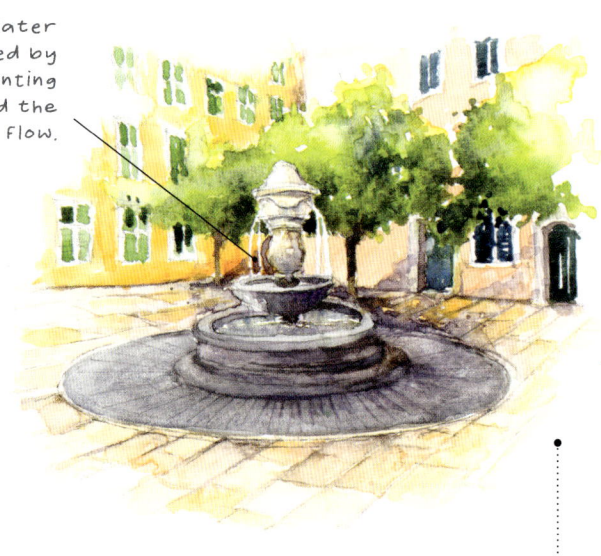

Water created by painting around the line of flow.

This small town square was worthy of a quick sketch. As the fountain is in the center of the square, it gains much visual importance.

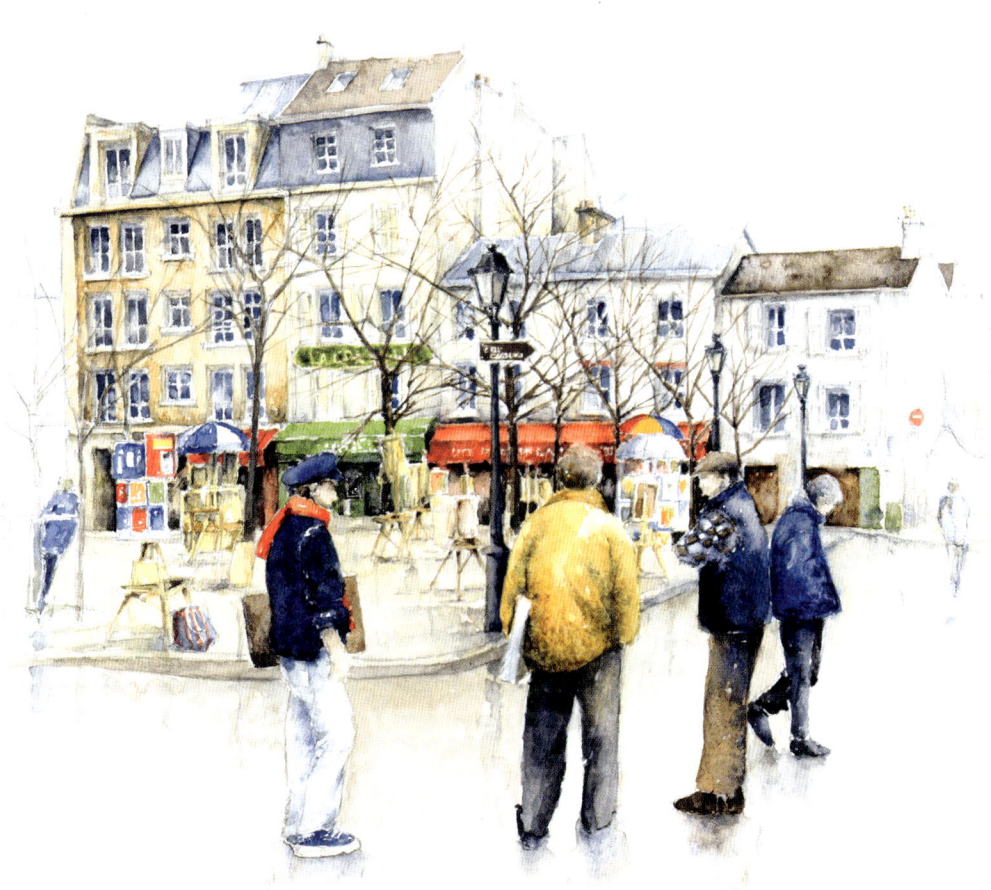

Squares and piazzas around the globe often become focal points for artists. These sites are best painted early in the morning before the crowds arrive. This small group of artists is manageable—many more would be difficult.

TIP

Be selective when painting groups of people. Three is a good uneven number, allowing you to play with the dynamics of the composition. It's OK to leave some figures out.

Colleges and Cloisters

I have always found the filtered light in cloisters fascinating, especially the shadows created as it falls on flagstones. The old and hallowed nature of the academic environment is enhanced by this light. In these places you will find somewhere to sit in peace and enjoy the silence that reflection and contemplation can bring.

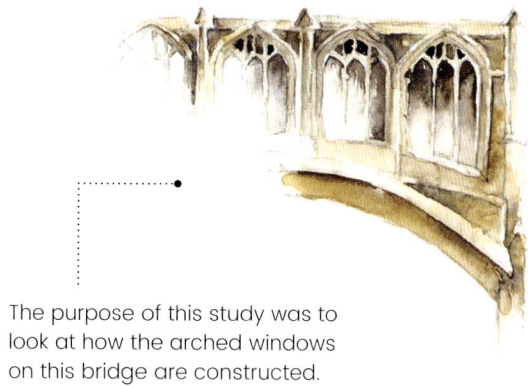

The purpose of this study was to look at how the arched windows on this bridge are constructed.

The brickwork of this arched support is a little deceptive. Many bricks have been painted, but many are also the result of washes and negative shapes.

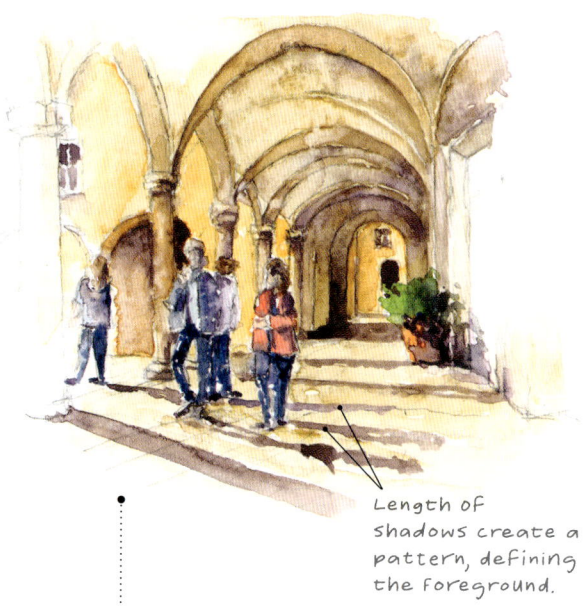

Length of shadows create a pattern, defining the foreground.

The elongated shadows cast across this cloistered walkway indicate the late hour of the day.

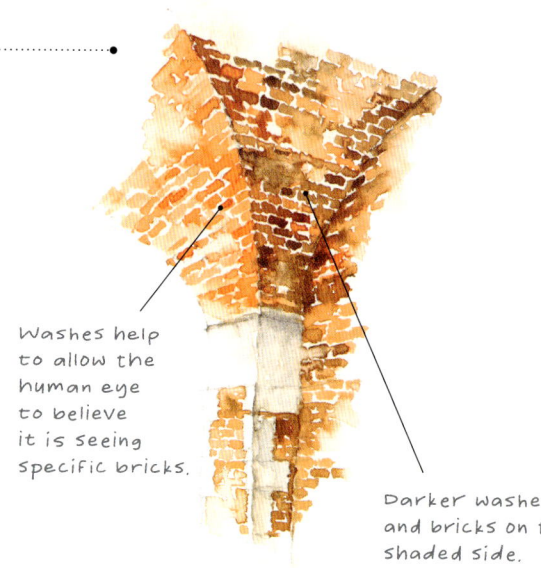

Washes help to allow the human eye to believe it is seeing specific bricks.

Darker washes and bricks on the shaded side.

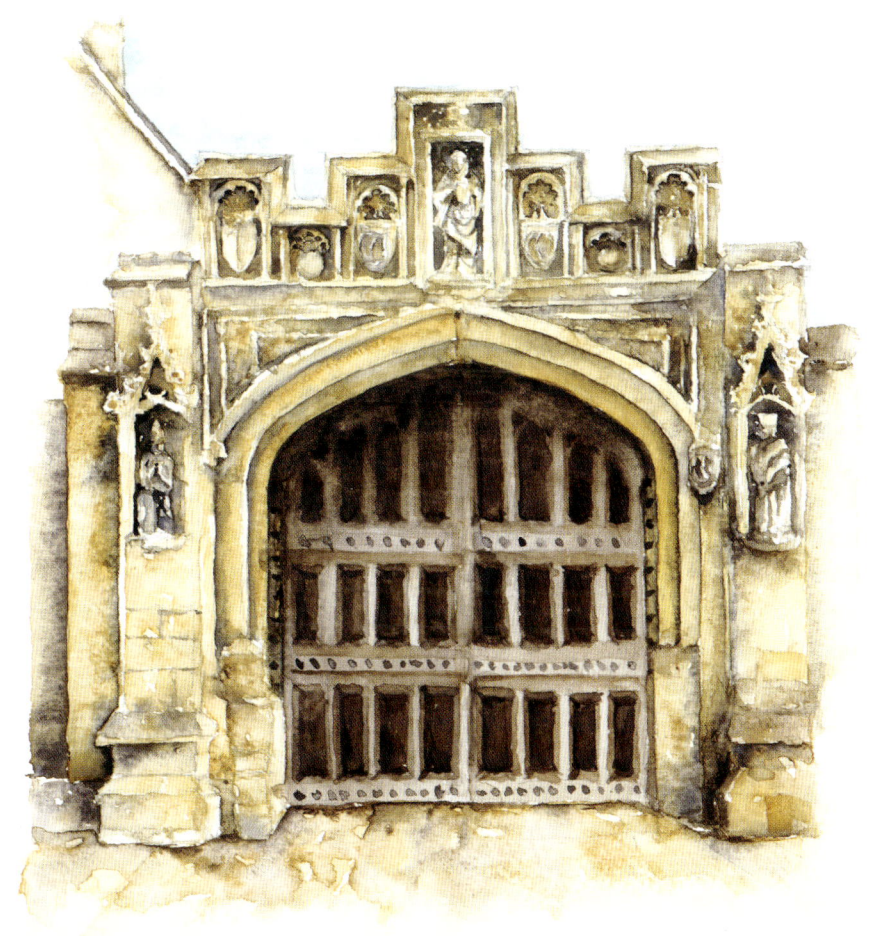

This painting of a historic university gate is a result of a succession of washes—initial washes to establish tone and colors, washes to create texture, and washes to secure the structure onto the foreground paving.

Heritage Buildings

These heritage buildings once had a function, but are now more decorative features of the urban landscape. They do, however, offer a view of the region's past.

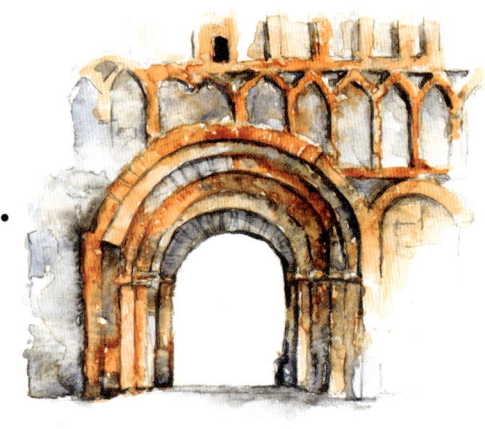

The arches in this ancient gateway require careful use of shadows, ensuring that none are lost.

The sheer number of bricks used in the collection of buildings in this old industrial site make it a challenge to distinguish one building from another. Shadows are required to achieve this.

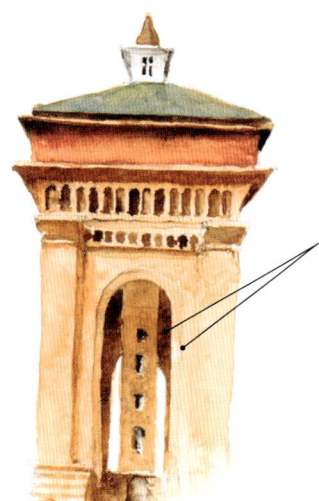

Dark and light tones help to give a sense of height to this study. They draw the eye upward.

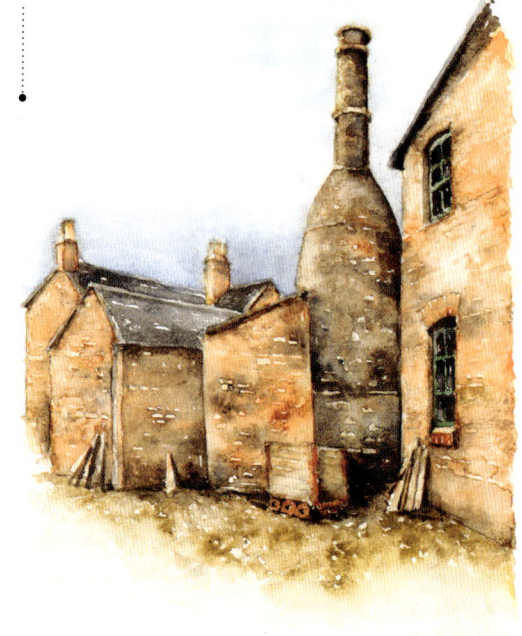

This disused water tower is very tall and needs a focal point to emphasize its height. The tones around the narrow central tower help this.

EXAMPLE: FOLLY

STEP ONE

Add light, watery washes of burnt sienna to the walls and allow to dry.

STEP TWO

Add burnt umber to burnt sienna and paint around cracks in the fabric.

STEP THREE

Add shadows using a touch of ultramarine blue, and paint underneath prominent features. Mix ultramarine with a touch of burnt umber for the roof.

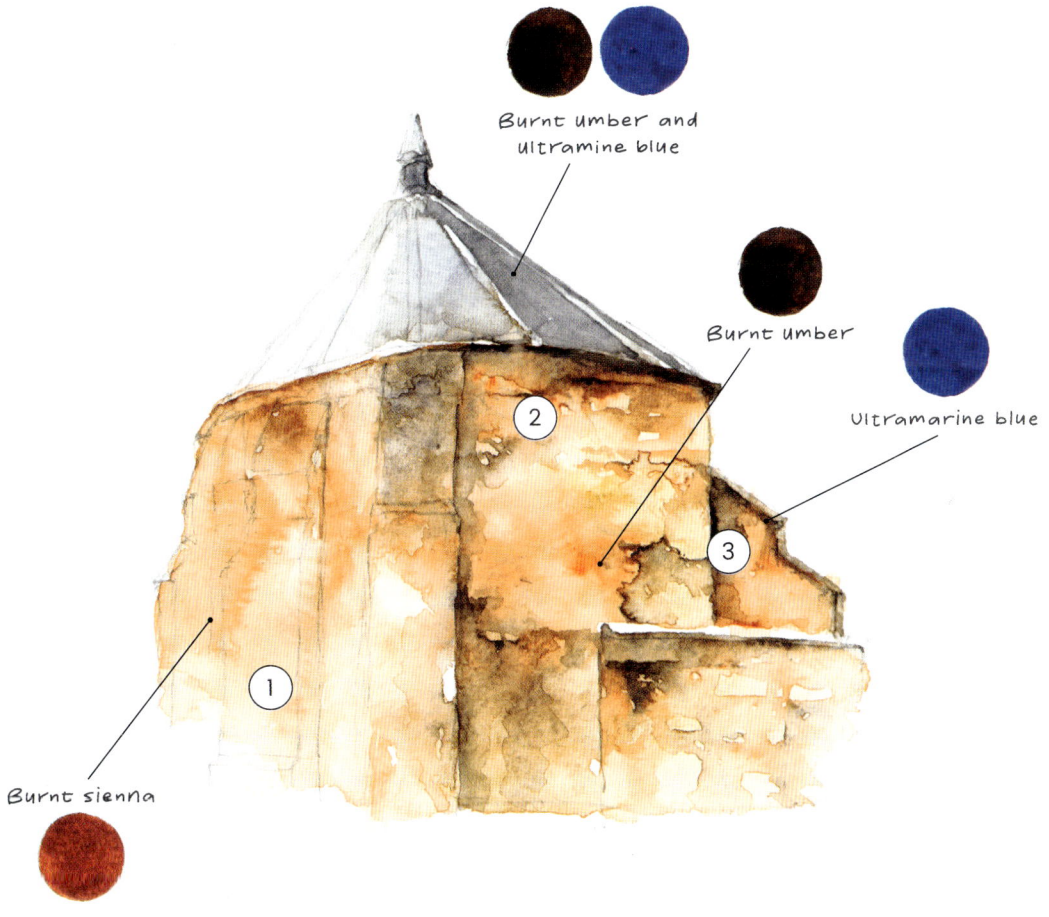

Burnt umber and ultramine blue

Burnt umber

Ultramarine blue

Burnt sienna

About the Author

Richard Taylor holds the rare distinction of being both a recognized artist and an art educator. He is an art teacher qualified to Advanced Skills Teacher level and holds a first degree in Art History and a Masters degree in Fine Art Authorship. Richard is also an elected member of the Society of Architectural Illustrators.

During his long career, Richard has run courses in almost every type of school and educational institute imaginable, including teaching a watercolor summer school at The Heatherley School of Fine Art, Chelsea, and a period training teachers as an associate university lecturer. He has also worked as an art teaching advisor to a County Education Authority, visiting schools and colleges to help establish specialist courses and develop art teachers' skills. Richard has written articles for an assortment of instructional art publications and worked as consultant to *The Art Course* magazine.

For the past twenty years Richard has taught specialist watercolor courses at the Watershed Studio in the small village of St. Osyth, Essex near his home on the coast as well as running workshops for art groups and societies.

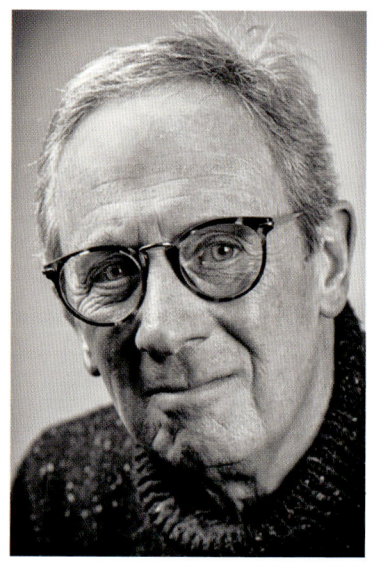

Acknowledgments

I must, as always, acknowledge the help and support given by my wife Debbie throughout the preparation, production, and post-production of this book. She makes everything possible.

Index

Names of manufacturers and product ranges are provided for the information of readers, with no intention to infringe copyright or trademarks.

A catalogue record for this book is available from the British Library.

ISBN-13: 9781446316160 paperback
ISBN-13: 9781446316184 EPUB

This book has been printed on paper from approved suppliers and made from pulp from sustainable sources.

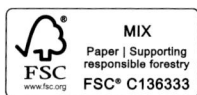

Printed in China by Asia Pacific Offset for: David and Charles, Ltd , Suite A, Tourism House, Pynes Hill, Exeter, EX2 5WS

10 9 8 7 6 5 4 3 2 1

Publishing Director: Ame Verso
Senior Commissioning Editor: Nigel Browning
Publishing Manager: Jeni Chown
Editor: Jessica Cropper
Copy Editor: Anna Southgate
Lead Designer: Sam Staddon
Designer: Nikki Ellis
Pre-press Designer: Susan Reansbury
Artwork: Richard Taylor
Photography: Tom Hargreaves
Production Manager: Beverley Richardson

David and Charles publishes high-quality books on a wide range of subjects. For more information visit www.davidandcharles.com.

Share your art with us on social media using #dandcbooks and follow us on Facebook and Instagram by searching for @dandcbooks.

Layout of the digital edition of this book may vary depending on reader hardware and display settings.